JOURNEYS INTO THE MIND OF THE WORLD

JOURNEYS INTO THE MIND OF THE WORLD

A Book of Places

RICHARD TILLINGHAST

KNOXVILLE
The University of Tennessee Press

Copyright © 2017 by The University of Tennessee Press / Knoxville.
All Rights Reserved. Manufactured in the United States of America.
First Edition.

LIBRARY OF CONGRESS CATALOGING-IN-PUBLICATION DATA

Names: Tillinghast, Richard, author.
Title: Journeys into the mind of the world : a book of places /
Richard Tillinghast.
Description: First edition. | Knoxville : University of Tennessee Press, 2017. |
Includes index.
Identifiers: LCCN 2016024719|
ISBN 9781621902812 (hardcover : alk. paper) |
ISBN 9781621902805 (kindle)
Subjects: LCSH: Tillinghast, Richard--Travel.
Classification: LCC PS3570.I38 Z46 2017 | DDC 811/.54 [B] —dc23
LC record available at https://lccn.loc.gov/2016024719

To my grandson
Hamza Akalın

The man who finds his homeland sweet is still a tender beginner;
he to whom every soil is as his native one is already strong;
but he is perfect to whom the entire world is as a foreign land.

—Hugh of St. Victor, thirteenth century

Contents

Acknowledgments

Thanks to the editors of the following periodicals, in whose pages some chapters of *Journeys into the Mind of the World* originally appeared in earlier versions:

Agni, Bear River Review, and *The Cork Literary Review* for varying versions of "Water Music."

Dublin Review of Books for "Pugin and the Gothic Revival."

The Gettysburg Review for "John Betjeman" and "My Mother's Trip to Paris."

The Hudson Review for "Christmas in London" and "Looking at English Art and Architecture."

Irish Pages for "From Venice to Tipperary: Architecture and Empire" and "George MacBeth at Moyne Park."

The Irish Times for "A Village on Galway Bay."

The New Criterion for "Hilo, My Hometown," "Max Beerbohm: Taking the Starch out of Eminent Victorians," "Saving England," and "William Morris: Maker."

New England Review for "Eastward Bound, Across a Storied Landscape" and "From Venice to Tipperary: Architecture and Empire."

Parabola for "Days and Nights in a Sufi Khanqah in Pakistan."

The Sewanee Review for "Nathan Bedford Forrest: Born to Fight" and "Questions of Travel."

South 85 for "The Police Chief of Mustafabad."

Southwest Review for "On Pilgrimage in India" and "Sewanee and the Civil War."

My Mother's Trip to Paris

My life as a traveler began in 1930, ten years before I was born. That was the year my mother made her trip to Paris. Mother's time in the City of Light glowed in her memory like a magic lantern along the journey that made up her young life before she married. She spoke of it often.

A thick scrapbook with "My Trip to Europe" printed on the cover, its browning pages pasted full of souvenirs, crumbling and falling apart when handled, emerged from the attic of the house where I grew up. Along with the scrapbook came a thick but smaller diary, seven inches by four, black leather, the gold letters of the word "Record" faded. I open my mother's diary at random and come across simply phrased, lovely sentences like "I'm riding on a boat on Lake Lucerne and it's about 5:30 in the afternoon and it's raining." It sounds like Hemingway.

As is the case, no doubt, with other driven, exacting, and ambitious sons of driven, exacting, and ambitious mothers, my relationship with my mother was not easy. She formed so many of my tastes and standards, I almost feel I *am* her. And yet my ways are not her ways. I never could, never wanted to, live by the rules of her middleclass propriety. So I disappointed her on many occasions I wince to recall. And I do recall them, vividly. My amatory track record has not been such as to win the approval of a married-for-life, church-going Southern lady like her. It hurts me to think of myself as a bad son. Still, what can I say? I had to be myself. All that hardly seems to matter anymore. Part of me feels the boundary between the living and the dead is permeable and porous, and it's hard not to believe she is somehow right here with me and that all is forgiven.

But back to our story. On June 13, 1930, Mother sailed with a group of friends on the Anchor-Donaldson Line's *Letitia* from Montreal to

Glasgow. *Letitia* was a sleek, twin-screw, one-stack liner, riding hand-somely—on the picture postcard Mama pasted inside the front cover of her diary—over a choppy, aquamarine sea, its bridge, upper cab-ins, and lifeboats gleaming white, its hull sporting a fresh coat of black paint down to the waterline, scarlet below. The night she sailed, "15 minutes after midnight," she wrote in her diary, "I am sitting on the floor of my stateroom, D58, writing by the light out in the hallway. I have on my new pyjamas—the silk sailor ones with swanky glass buttons up the front and bell bottom trousers. I believe I am blissfully happy."

I too love clothes, and I love swank. I relish the vividness of these descriptions of her travel wardrobe. Like me, she adored being at sea, and it is clear she had shipboard romances. She writes of them with a literary flare:

> To stand with almost anybody out in the wind, leaning on the rail of the boat, at night and to hear almost anybody say, "When we are very old I'm going to ask you if you remember our standing out in the wind, watching the waves and feeling the spray, and your hair blowing, and the coolness and breath-takingness of it, and you're go-ing to remember because it's one of those times one does remember" just has to thrill you.

Strange how the idea of my mother having shipboard romances makes me uncomfortable—but then she was not my mother yet, and I was years away from being a person at all. I was among those whom Charles Lamb calls "the numberless ranks of the unborn waiting to be summoned into existence."

On one page of her scrapbook, Mother pasted in two wine lists and the elegant list of cocktails and liqueurs on offer aboard ship: gin fizz, Singapore sling, sidecar, gin rickey, golden fizz, sherry cobbler, morning glory, lemon squash—the intoxicating list goes on. If you wanted to drink champagne, you could buy a bottle of Mumm's Cor-don Rouge, 1923, for $5.48. Beside this catalogue of delights she notes: "And we tried them all."

Sitting out in her deck chair cosseted in a tartan lap robe, drink-ing beef tea as the ship traversed the steely waters of the North Atlantic, Mother must have pinched herself, wondering if this adventure she had saved her pennies for was really happening at last. In the shipboard photo of herself with the *Letitia*'s captain, their arms linked, she couldn't look more pleased with herself or more fashionably turned out. She is wearing a tweed suit cut chic for her slim figure, a Liberty scarf, and two-toned heels—gray suede with navy blue leather toecaps I imagine, though the photograph is sepia.

London, the first stop on her tour of Europe, was still in its prime as a world capital. In Piccadilly she saw "more Rolls-Royces than I dreamed existed" and met a very nice Englishman, who "explained to us—in the usual polite English way—and at our request—why the English don't like Americans—We're too unconventional, too boastful, too mercenary, too uncouth." Some things never change.

While in England she visited Shakespeare's birthplace in Stratford-upon-Avon, drank a glass of English bitter at Ye Olde Cheshire Cheese, and saw the changing of the guard at Buckingham Palace. In London she also bought briar pipes at Dunhill's for friends back home. George V was on the throne, and his son, the Prince of Wales, had not yet caused the scandal of the century by abdicating to marry "the woman I love."

Germany when she saw it was still recovering from its defeat in the Great War—French forces had just been withdrawn from the Rhineland. My mother was witness to the wave of nationalistic fervor that would culminate in the rise of the Nazi party and then the World War that followed. Like many visitors, she was charmed by German fervor, just as she was impressed by German efficiency, little knowing the horrendous measures to which that fervor and efficiency would be put only a few years later:

> The customs officers were so much neater looking, so much quicker, so far superior to the others we've had that it was quite noticeable. When we got off the train we got much more efficient service than we've had anywhere else. I am crazy about Germany and the German people.

With the benefit of hindsight, I want to shake her and demand, "But Mother, don't you see the evils, the ruin of an entire civilization, the tens of millions of deaths, that this patriotic fervor is going to lead to?" But of course she had no way of anticipating that.

At the end of a concert she both notes the German enthusiasm for the Fatherland and says something about herself as a Southerner of her day:

> The audience—an open-air concert it was—stood and sang the German national anthem. My heart beat fast when I heard how they sang it—how they felt it. They seemed to feel the same reverence that the English do when they sing "God Save the King." I wish I could feel that way when they play "The Star-Spangled Banner." I do feel it when I hear "Dixie."

In Rome she saw Pope Pius XI on his balcony at St. Peter's and later she and her friends obtained a private audience with him during the course of which they got rosaries blessed for their Catholic friends back home. She saw the leaning tower of Pisa, the Bay of Naples, Pompeii. In Florence, like the assiduous student she was and never stopped being, she dutifully collected reproductions of paintings by Titian, Giorgione, Botticelli, Fra Lippo Lippi, Raphael, and the rest. There she is in a gondola in Venice, gliding underneath the Bridge of Sighs. In Nice she swam in the Mediterranean; in Monte Carlo, she notes, "We lost our money quickly."

Then came a summer in Paris. "It is not beautiful like quiet Venice, nor as rushing as London, nor as grand as Rome, but it thrills me indescribably," she wrote. She took a room at the Hôtel de l'Avenir on the Rue Madame near the Luxembourg Gardens. Her sense of the direction her life was taking must have found resonance in that name. It means "The Hotel of the Future." She was twenty-eight years old. Two years later she would be married. Six years later her first child, my brother David, was born. Mama would be pleased that he has kept up his French.

The ashtray she got from the Tour d'Argent on the Left Bank overlooking the cathedral of Notre Dame on the Île de la Cité became a fixture in our living room in Memphis. (I like to think of her slipping the ashtray into her handbag on the sly as I would have done, but Mother was too proper for pilferage.) I see that it was broken in two at some point, but someone glued it back together. No curator's assistant in the workrooms at the British Museum ever took more care over a Minoan pottery shard than did the mender of that relic, probably my father.

Walking through the city, seeing the Eiffel Tower, climbing the steep hill up to the Sacré-Cœur in Montmartre, visiting Napoléon's tomb, marveling at the exquisite medieval stained glass in the Sainte-Chapelle, browsing through the booksellers' stalls along the Seine under the plane trees that shade the banks of the river, all the while practicing her French in the restaurants and cafés—and her French must have been better than most, since she taught French and Latin at Miss Hutchison's School in Memphis—these things had great allure for a young woman from Tennessee. Although, like many of us, Mama found she didn't really like the French, she loved sitting in a wicker chair drinking coffee at a little marble-topped table at a sidewalk café along le Boul'mich and writing in her journal, buying perfume at the Parfumerie Fragonard in the Faubourg St. Honoré, having her hair done by Jules, a specialist, his card says, in *"Tout ce qui concerne la coiffure et la beauté féminine."*

She was fortunate that, for someone with dollars to spend, Paris was cheap back then. Always thrifty, she jotted down her expenditures in a tiny notebook she got from the Galerie de Rohan on the Rue de Rivoli. In 1930 one French franc was worth four American cents. Mama got a pair of shoes mended for F 2.50, plus a tip of twenty-five centimes—a total of less than eleven cents. A taxi ride typically cost her four francs, or sixteen cents. A ticket to the opera cost five francs, or twenty cents. An expensive lunch of F 67.50 amounted to $2.70. A week at the Hôtel de l'Avenir, with breakfast and occasional suppers, cost her F 160, or $6.40.

Judging from the stickers pasted into my mother's scrapbook, a big part of Paris's appeal was its nightlife. Here is one from Pigalle's, with its *"plus élégants soupers de Paris-Montmartre,"* the Cabaret du Néant with its macabre furnishings like the *lampadaire funéraire,* a chandelier constructed from human bones, its candles held by skeletal hands, a skull in the center. She writes that her favorite spot was an "inelegant place" called La Boule Noire, "a dirty, dark little hole frequented by the lowest possible class of people, and which we have gone back to three times because it's so much fun." She liked the *apache* dancers in the floor show there and snapped a picture of them.

Mama and her friends spent their last night in Paris at the Moulin Rouge, then rounded off the festivities at three AM in time-honored fashion with the *soupe à l'oignon* they used to serve in the market at Les Halles—the ones that come in stout white crockery bowls and are crusty and cheesy on the top—and drinking red *vin ordinaire* among the late-night crowd of butchers, greengrocers, truckers, and fish-mongers who drive up through the night from the French country-side to bring their goods to market.

The bohemian side of Paris held just as much appeal for me as it had done for my mother thirty-five years earlier. During the winter of 1966–67 that I spent in Paris, I too stayed in the Latin Quarter, in the fifth and sixth arrondissements, and rounded off many an evening at Les Halles. While Mother went there to see Paris, I was there to write. The crowd of expat bohemians and artists I ran with was, of course, more louche than Mama would have approved of. *Autres temps, autres moeurs.*

My days were spent writing poetry in one of the cheap hotels on the Rue Monsieur-le-Prince or the Rue Saint Jacques and the cafés along the boulevards, my nights going to avant-garde films at the Ci-némathèque Française, listening to gypsy jazz, dining on tagine and couscous and drinking strong thé à la menthe in the cheap Algerian restaurants in the quarter, smoking hashish to achieve that dérègle-ment des sens that Rimbaud praised. Lucas Myers and Henry Wolff were writing fiction. Henry and his wife Nancy Hennings were amass-ing the collection of instruments they would use on their 1971 album, Tibetan Bells. Robert Grenier, whom I knew from Robert Lowell's writing classes at Harvard, later a godfather of L=A=N=G=U=A=G=E poetry, was at work on the poems that would go into his first book, Dusk Road Games, in 1967.

Greg Gillespie occasionally visited from Rome, where he had learned to employ meticulous detailing and glazes in his paintings from a careful study of Italian Renaissance masters like Crivelli, Mantegna, and Carpaccio. He used these techniques to create assemblages and mock altarpieces featuring subject matter that was often bizarre, even pornographic, and reminiscent of Hieronymus Bosch. Peter Warshall, whom I knew from Harvard and who was later celebrated as a writer on environmental issues, was in Paris on a Fulbright, taking Claude Lévi-Strauss's seminars at the Sorbonne—his French was that good—while judiciously dealing the occasional lid from his attic room in a Left Bank hotel.

Everyone smokes weed now, or so it seems. Medical marijuana is available in twenty-three states—I have my card, have you?—and it is legal for recreational use in at least eight states, more to follow. The New York Times writes editorials in favor of legalization. Two US presidents have owned up to smoking it, though one "didn't inhale," ha ha. So it is hard to convey what it felt like to be part of a tiny in-crowd in those high and palmy days. It was new back then, at least among people like us. We recognized each other through some sixth sense and were gleeful about being part of an elite fraternity.

My nights might not have met with Mother's approval, but she would, I believe, have been envious of how I spent my days. As I think is clear from the passages I have quoted from her diary, she herself was a natural writer with a romantic soul. The notion of having a poet for a son thrilled her.

Martha Williford from Memphis, Tennessee saw Paris at the same time those other Americans, Ernest Hemingway from Oak Park, Illinois, F. Scott Fitzgerald from Minneapolis, Minnesota, Ezra Pound from Hailey, Idaho, and Oakland's own Gertrude Stein, were making literary history there. The Hôtel de l'Avenir on the Rue Madame was just a stone's throw from Stein's apartment at 27 Rue de Fleurus and within walking distance of where Hemingway lived nearby in the fifth arrondissement. The time Mother spent in Paris came just a few years after the era Hemingway would write about in *The Sun Also Rises* and *A Moveable Feast*.

Whether she read those new American writers, I do not know. Her diary does show that she had lunch at Les Deux Magots, so it must have been a well-known literary café even back then. I can't recall hearing her mention Hemingway, Pound, Stein, or Fitzgerald, ever. Her taste inclined more to French authors. True, I fail to share her enthusiasm for Victor Hugo, but I am glad to have her copy of Marcel Proust's *Swann's Way,* in the Scott Montcrieff translation. On the title page she has inscribed her name in her elegant rounded script with its terminal Greek d's like eighth notes and its wonderful feeling of balance and self-confidence—a tiny act of writing that manages to convey the pleasure she must have felt when she bought this book by one of the most celebrated avant-garde authors of her day.

Though she has been gone for almost thirty years, I miss my mother, and I often imagine conversations we might have had. I miss her more and more the older I get. Because I am so much like her in so many ways, I feel I understand from the inside her tastes, her likes and dislikes, her humor, warmth and snobbery, her combination of sophistication and plainness. Perhaps this closeness was the reason I had to distance myself from her when I was younger. Now that I have no need to protect my own individuality from her strong personality, I can relax in her recollected presence.

In her handwriting on the title page of *Swann's Way* I recognize the imprint of Mama's Parker pen, which I write with now myself. From her I have acquired an enthusiasm for fountain pens, the novels of Proust, and dozens of other things, including what the old song calls "those faraway places with strange-sounding names, far away over the sea." Paris will always top the list of those places for me, because it was there that my life as a traveler began.

BEARINGS

Four Directions

A fox, a house cat, a salmon, and a warbler all have a sense of where they are in the world. Birds know north and south. Salmon find their way back to where they were spawned. Foxes know where their den is; the cat comes back. As for myself, whether I emerge out of the subway into a New York neighborhood I have never seen before, or find myself river miles from the cottage where I am staying while fishing my way upstream along the Au Sable River and it starts to get dark—wherever I am when I need to find my bearings in the world—I stand at the center of my childhood outside our family home in midtown Memphis, facing north between two trees: a magnolia and a water oak, at the midpoint of my four directions.

As I write these words I am facing east. The Irish farmer who built this house a hundred or two hundred years ago trued it, so that the gable ends point precisely north and south. When set on the newel post at the top of the stairs, the needle on my compass darts north. My task is to figure out where I am beyond the bed, beyond the breakfast table, beyond the room where I write.

About the east I know little more than that the sun rises there. A line of tall pines at the edge of a pasture, and a ridge beyond, define that direction of sight. I know that when I walk north I follow a path through gorse and heather and brambles into acres of pine trees planted by the Irish forestry service. The road west leads farther uphill onto the sparsely populated slopes of Sliabh na mBan, "the Mountain of the Women." As you walk up that road you know you are leaving the settled communities behind and entering the abode of the mountainy folk. The road becomes steeper, the trees scarcer, the farms scrappier.

South is the direction by which I connect with the world beyond. Going out is like tunneling. On many of these bowered roads the trees have formed canopies overhead. I know that if I drive down the boreen past the neighbors' houses, none of them close to any other habitation, each of them gradually acquiring in my mind a family's name and a story, down to the town of Ninemilehouse, and if I turn left onto the main road there, I will get to Callan, where there are shops, the ruins of a Franciscan friary, a supermarket, and a post office—and eventually I will reach the ancient city of Kilkenny, site of St. Canice's Cathedral and the Butler castle, ancestral home of the Dukes of Ormonde. Kilkenny is where you board the train to Dublin.

If on the other hand I keep going straight at the crossroads where Willie Walsh's bungalow stands, down underneath the dark beech trees at South Lodge, and turn right onto the main road, I can get to other centers: scruffy little Carrick-on-Suir, which has a beautiful name, a river, and a Chinese restaurant with mediocre food and an entertaining maître d' from London called Sammy. And then Clonmel, a sunny, bustling town where my bank is, which has at least two pretty good places to eat, an internet café, and a good regional library.

>>>>>>>>

The orientation that lives in me, and will never leave until something deeper than my mind deserts me, is centered in that front yard in Memphis, where I stand between a magnolia and a water oak. At some point in my childhood I learned that the city of Memphis is rooted in the far southwestern corner of the long and narrow state of Tennessee—seven hundred and fifty miles from Bristol on the Virginia border—with Mississippi and the Deep South below it.

Across the Mississippi River lies Arkansas, where farms start to be called ranches and where, as a state of mind, the West begins. Some brain cell or inner Global Positioning System must be aware that two busy east-west thoroughfares, Union and Central, run like ribbons before me and behind me as I stand there, carrying the city's traffic like parallel stop-time photographs, from its deteriorating downtown to its affluent eastern suburbs—one of these avenues directly to my north, the other eight blocks to my south.

Our family lived in a residential neighborhood whose respectability and architectural integrity were unraveling as the city's commercial center straggled eastward into the ever-expanding metropolis that sprawled away from the Mississippi River and encroached on the farming country of West Tennessee. In the 1890s there was still a field beside the house—a field where my grandfather grazed his horse, Our Bob, named after Robert Love Taylor, sometime Governor and US Senator from the State of Tennessee and ancestor of the author Peter Taylor. Behind me now, where I stand as a child in the 1940s, South Cox Street unspools, its asphalt surface wavery in the summer heat, undulating past the cindery playground and the brick Gothic Revival school whose construction my grandfather, as local alderman, oversaw.

Then the rows of wooden, Carpenter Gothic houses—unremarkable when they were built, made exquisite by the passage of time—down to where Cox crosses the L&N tracks with their night trains that sent intimations of future journeys rattling through my sleep.

The little street ends its southward tack at Central, dangerous and noisy with automobiles, beyond which lay an alien world of mismatched houses, make-do poverty, misfortunate lives, washing machines on porches, and old Chevrolets with their hoods raised, baseball games playing on radios in the open air pungent with the smoke of barbecue, all the way down to the Mississippi line.

Children observe and understand more about the world they are born into than we give them credit for. I saw a minor traffic accident on South Cox Street when I was a boy. The driver of one car was white, the other was black. I saw the whole thing, and clearly the white driver was at fault. Yet when the police arrived, the white driver was able to convince them that the black man was at fault.

How old I was at that moment I don't recall. But something clicked in my mind and told me that whenever a black man and a white man disagreed, the white man's word would always be believed. I use the terms "black" and "African American," but the word back then, fifty and sixty years ago, was "colored."

The farm near Brownsville, Tennessee, belonging to cousins of mine, was a vast playground for me when I was a child. I went out into the cotton fields with the black tenant farmers. They tolerated my presence, taught me how to pick cotton, let me ride on the mule-drawn cultivator and "work" beside them with a child-sized hoe while they chopped cotton in the West Tennessee sun. I was fascinated by a man named Napoleon. Napoleon had served time in the penitentiary and had a bullet hole in the flesh of one arm. At noon we would sit in the shade, drink cold well water or buttermilk from a mason jar, and eat cold fried chicken and cornbread together.

I think I knew that black people and white people did not usually break bread together, but that did not discourage me from suggesting to Uncle Frank that we should invite the tenant farmer and his wife to supper. His only response to this suggestion was to chuckle. The idea was outlandish; he didn't even try to explain his response. Segregation was so ingrained in his way of thinking that it didn't need explanation.

I also remember that my cousins' strong-minded maid, Margaret Milam, who never felt shy about giving any of us a piece of her mind, was indignant about our use of the word "black" in the 1960s. She was "colored," thank you very much, certainly not "black"! "Don't you never call *me* black, Richard," she told me. My cousins and I liked blues music, and we used to hang out with the Memphis blues singer

Furry Lewis up at his apartment on Beale Street. To Margaret, our idea of "black music" was outrageously oversimplified. "How you can compare a fine, well-brought-up young lady like Carla Thomas to a low-life like that Furry Lewis is beyond me," she would say.

In North Mississippi, just below the state line, the Deep South began. The sky blinked open blue and unimpeded from horizon to horizon as the land extended back perfectly flat from the levee that kept the Father of Waters within his banks to coffee-colored swampy rivers where catfish and water moccasins swam—rivers with creole French, Choctaw, Creek, and Cherokee names like Yazoo and Hatchie and Tallahatchie and Loosahatchie that emanated from the wilderness of mahogany, red gum, pecan, live oak, sassafras, and muscadine that William Faulkner had given voice to in sentences as long as this one and longer. The South where I was raised was a storied land. That is to say, stories were written about it, songs were sung. It was its own world, existing in both the literary and the popular imagination. If Faulkner had defined it in his books, so had the bluesmen, and so had popular lyricists like Johnny Mercer, who defined a world that stretched

> From Natchez to Mobile,
> From Memphis to Saint Joe,
> Wherever the four winds blow . . .

As a boy from Memphis I had relatives in Mississippi. I visited them, slept in their old houses, sometimes in a pallet on the floor, fished in the lakes and rivers and went to Boy Scout camp there. It was on the first page of Faulkner's *Go Down Moses* that I first encountered the word *alluvial*. That was how he described the Delta. The land and the word were coterminous. I had caught crawdads in the creeks and seen wild canaries flit among the tulip poplars and swung on the muscadine vines that hung from the huge old trees in Mississippi. Now I had a word to describe that land.

Mississippi was a place of dirt roads and tarpaper shacks. On decaying plantations Corinthian colonnades rotted and wisteria swarmed over the backstops of tennis courts, and rows of cotton were worked by black men whose blues notes and accents had survived the passage from Africa and entered our own Anglo-Saxon idiom. Some of the old Mississippi families that I knew were eccentric and inbred and sometimes as tragic as they were in books, sometimes possessed of a brilliance and singularity one hardly ever encounters in our more ordinary world.

The South's mysteries lay behind me as I faced north. The city of Memphis itself is a storehouse of myth and associations and sense of place. I will write about Memphis later. But for now I am talking about the city as a starting point for journeys that would lead elsewhere. My life was a racehorse straining into the future, and the South streamed behind me like a windy mane.

>>>>>>>

I stand there as the child I was and fling my left arm westward toward the Mississippi River over the bluffs at the deckled edge of Tennessee, beyond the river's muddy mile of power, beyond the flood plains of Arkansas and some vague sense of Westernness. The West began in West Memphis, an Arkansas river town where among the farmers and tenant farmers, black and white, with their tractors, their overalls, and their straw hats, you would see men sporting cowboy boots and ten-gallon hats. Spurs sometimes, even. Beyond Arkansas, distances began—and rattlesnakes, sand, cactus, dry wells, and tumbleweed.

Only when I reached my fifties, on a vacation with my family, would I drive along State Highway 50 in Nevada, which bills itself as "The Loneliest Road in America." The name itself is a brand of hyperbole one hears only in America. Later, in the 1960s and 1970s, I would live a dozen years in California and my life would be affected by the spirit of that great state against which the Pacific washes. I would then find myself halfway across the big ocean on Hawaii's Big Island. But to the child I was in the 1940s, the West was no less mythical than it was to any boy anywhere in the world playing cowboys and Indians.

I faced north as nervously as the quivering needle of my compass here in Ireland, north toward the pole, the top of the world, whose blue seas and ice caps I touched on the spinning globe of my childhood—like an arrow shooting straight through the east-west stream of cars on Union, up past the park and the college, past the unfamiliar streets of north Memphis, and then, in my mind's eye, up through a part of Tennessee I had never visited.

Beyond that, Kentucky, and above Kentucky the real North: the land of money, progress, triumph, people who talked fast, who took advantage—as far north as Michigan, where even in May the snow-flakes flew, where I would live for twenty years but never quite feel at home except in the woods and on the rivers. My years in Michigan up near the Canadian border confirmed to me that I am by nature a Southerner and an Easterner. To someone of my generation and those older than mine, with the defeat of the Civil War still a freighted memory, the North would remain enemy territory.

<<<<<<<<

Every country has an identity defined by one or another of the four directions. Britain's is east, the direction of empire, a counter-balance to its insularity. The genius and the dilemma of Turkey is that it faces both west toward Europe and east toward the kingdoms of Islam. It hardly knows which way to turn. Ireland's direction is west, turning its back to its conqueror with the hope of rediscovering its essence, as Gabriel Conroy does in James Joyce's story, "The Dead":

> The time had come for him to set out on his journey westwards. Yes, the newspapers were right: snow was general all over Ireland. It was falling on every part of the dark central plain. On the treeless hills, falling softly upon the Bog of Allen and, further westwards, softly falling into the dark mutinous Shannon waves.

The American direction is west, too, in search of its national destiny: "the land vaguely realizing westward," as Robert Frost put it in his poem that begins, "The land was ours before we were the land's." The navigators who sailed from the Old World and discovered our landmass followed their compasses west even as they thought their object was to find a sea route to the Indies. Our pioneers and voyageurs and settlers turned their faces toward the setting sun.

An ancestor of mine sold his farm in coastal North Carolina in 1852 and set off with his family and three slaves to journey by wagon to the newly settled territory of West Tennessee. Property developers had recently bought this part of the state from the Chickasaw and Choctaw chiefs and pushed those people off their land, driving them further west onto the Trail of Tears toward reservations in Oklahoma, then called Indian Territory. Many died along the way from disease and the hardships of the trek.

For those of my generation born in the heartland, with its history of territorial expropriation and settlement of an ever-expanding West, to become educated was to turn back east, to reverse the direction of American history. Though my brother and I as children thought of our father as being from "up North," he himself in speaking of his Massachusetts birthplace always located it "up East," just as the top and bottom of our house were, in his way of speaking, "up attic" and "down cellar."

>>>>>>>>

Highways radiated eastward from Memphis through LaGrange and Ripley and Bolivar and Milan and Jackson: decent little farming towns with their rigid caste systems where blacks and whites lived in a sometimes comfortable and sometimes uneasy equilibrium, with courthouses that looked like Greek temples, summer nights alive with crickets and heat, and town squares where farmers came on Saturdays to sell milk and vegetables and buy seed and sundries—towns with streets of white clapboard houses, jonquils on their lawns at Easter.

East beyond these counties were the sandstone spires of my college and its library that smelled of varnish and mold, a fragrance I can smell even as I write. On the walls of that venerable stone building paneled in dark wood hung portraits of Episcopal bishops and Confederate generals. Paths around the Domain—the official name for Sewanee's campus—meandered through forsythia and old oaks and daffodils planted among limestone outcroppings. The college bore a grandiose antebellum name, the University of the South, but everyone called it Sewanee, after the mountain at the top of which it stands.

In the late 1950s when I became a student there, Sewanee was poised between the past and the future, just as I was. For me the balance point was centered within my own growth from boyhood to young manhood; for the college, the question was where it wanted to live culturally. Adjacent to the library was a perfect little tower modeled inaccurately but gracefully after the pinnacled tower at Magdalen College, Oxford. A suit of armor stood in one corner of the library, and on the ground floor of the tower, a white marble bust called The Cavalier—a man in a floppy hat with plumes, and a frilly linen collar, all filigree and lace, with a roguish smile playing about his lips under a long moustache.

Sewanee's collegiate Gothic architecture declared an allegiance to the Middle Ages; the way it situated itself within Anglican tradition expressed an affiliation with England; its ties to the old Confederacy said something about aristocracy, chivalry, the romanticism of Sir Walter Scott that had tried to flourish in the landed, cotton-and-slave economy of the Old South. The anti-Puritan ethos represented by The Cavalier suggested that the University of the South was also liberal, and its sense of *noblesse oblige* made it progressive on the question of civil rights.

Viewed superficially, my early college education could be seen as conservative and old-fashioned. Viewed from within, it was an awakening to everything new and intoxicating, to beauty and the discovery of aesthetics. The words of poems I read there for the first time are edged, even now, with a glow of early morning sunshine; or else they ring with the charged exhilaration of poetry read aloud late at night when everyone else was asleep, everyone but a few treasured friends.

Four years on Sewanee Mountain were the first step on a journey eastward that would transport me first into books, and then to Boston and Harvard, then to sojourns in London, Paris, and Rome, and ultimately to Istanbul and farther east to Iran, Afghanistan, India, and Nepal. Though I never set out to be a traveler, it looks as though I was destined to become one.

‹‹‹‹‹‹‹‹

If north is the father of all directions—its initial capital letter given pride of place on compasses and maps—east is the mother. East is that end of a church where the mysteries are kept, where the rising sun astonishes the eye with the rose, royal purple, and scarlet of stained glass. It is the lilies and spices and opened sepulcher of Easter. The Neolithic stone chambers of Ireland and Britain were constructed to receive the sun's rays at the winter solstice and to fend off the dying of the light. To the Oglala Sioux, East was "the direction we are always facing." East is where we turn for knowledge and enlightenment, the direction in which we set off on pilgrimages. I see the rising sun bronzing the leaves of the magnolia in that front yard in Memphis. As I write these words, I am facing east.

Water Music

Rain is the most pleasing of sounds. I am remembering one morning years ago when I was still living in rural Ireland I awoke to gusty rain on the skylight and gypsy violin music running through my head. So close is the kinship between wind and rain, and wind and music, that when a gale blew across the mountainside acre on Sliabh na mBan where I lived back then, it caught up under the eaves of the shed's tin roof and blew so tunefully you'd swear someone was playing a flute out there.

Wind and rain, along with the birds, have made music since before human beings achieved it, before music was a word or a concept. Infinitely pleasing, the sound of rain is also infinitely variable. Like music, rain expresses both liquidity and percussiveness. It resembles, to an extent, improvisation in jazz. As I was waking that distant morning I could hear, coming from the kitchen, the unaccustomed sounds of water. Water from our own faucets. First it coughed, then it sputtered, then it gushed and tumbled into the waiting kettle.

We drew our water from a small reservoir further up the slope of the mountain. Four or five families organized their lives around water from this source. Three days earlier our water had dried up, but a hurricane in the Caribbean blew a storm up the Gulf Stream and gave us a good soaking clear over on the far side of the Atlantic.

Since each of the four elements has played a numinous role in the life of our species, I am reluctant to claim that one of the four carries more resonance than the others. Still, among the ancient Greeks and Romans, souls had to pay the ferryman Charon to row them across the River Styx. Water separated the living from the dead.

Christians baptize with water and the spirit. Before they pray, Muslims perform their ablutions at the fountain that stands in the courtyard of the mosque. The ancient Hebrews, another people whose tribal life began in the desert, emphasize in their scriptures and traditions mastery over water more than the use of it as a sacrament. Their God divided the land from the sea to create the world, formed man from earth before breathing life into him. In their migration out of bondage in Egypt, Moses struck the Red Sea with his staff and divided the waters so that the Israelites could cross on dry land to escape their pursuers. Noah gathered two of every living creature into his ark. That craft, a paragon of the shipwright's art, floated upon the waters of the flood that threatened to destroy the world.

Among the Hindus, a more pacific people, purification by water precedes every ritual. The ancient Greeks cherished their holy wells and paid obeisance to the local spirits who presided over them. The pre-Christian Irish had their own holy wells. Even today you can come across a spring with its overhanging whitethorn tree onto whose branches people will have tied bits of cloth and string that symbolize their prayers, hopes, and wishes.

Our reservoir in Tipperary could claim few associations with the sacred. I doubt if many prayers had been uttered there. Christmas afternoon a few weeks before the morning I am writing about, with no better purpose than to walk off the effects of the turkey, we pulled on our wellington boots and heavy coats and walked up to the reservoir across the fields through the horizontal rays of the thin December sunlight. We got there across muddy pasture-ground trodden by the feet of our neighbor's cattle. It was a rough concrete tank, unadorned, roofed with a sheet of corrugated tin. A raw PVC pipe rose out of the ground and poured the contents of an underground spring into the tank, while an equally unprepossessing runoff tube spilled the excess into the surrounding mud. It was nobody's Hippocrene. Still, there it was—an unapologetic example of how water makes life on earth possible.

With the thinning of the earth's ozone layer and the coming of higher temperatures to the northern hemisphere of our planet, Ireland had enjoyed a warmer than usual summer that year. At Trinity College in Dublin, where I spent most of June, July, and August, I sat on a bench in the little rose garden near my digs, took off my shirt as if I were in Italy or Florida, and basked in the rays of unaccustomed sunshine. But that kind of summer meant that the reservoir in Tipperary became depleted.

During the few days we were without running water, we learned what life is like when an abundance of water cannot be taken for granted. A bathtub filled with water became a resource for flushing with a bucket. A rain barrel gave us our drinking water. Drinking that soft elixir, I began to savor water again and I remembered how before modern times people who lived in Istanbul distinguished the taste of water across each of the city's different neighborhoods, each quarter vying with others as to whose was the sweetest. I thought of those who were suffering drought in Africa, and I remembered the jewel-like plots of corn and beans and squash I had seen on the Hopi reservation in New Mexico, how cleverly the Hopis pieced together their fields in descending terraces down hillsides to take advantage of the scarce water available in that arid country.

On the morning I am remembering, three liquid sounds greeted me—rain on the skylight, water flowing from the kitchen taps for the first time in three days, and in my head, a gypsy violin. This awakening triggered several questions: What is jazz? Further than that, what is music, and why does it move us? Why, when the violinist whose name I do not even know rises to the sublime peak of his solo on the band's recorded version of "Summertime," does someone else within range of a microphone cry out ecstatically "Oh" or "Ah" in French or

Romany or Romanian? Filled with ecstasy myself when I awoke that morning, I asked my unanswerable questions.

One might as well ask why we are moved by the sound of rain, or by the sound of flowing river water, or by love. When she wrote her poem "Like rain it sounded till it curved," Emily Dickinson was clearly filled with the same fusion of delight and awe that I felt as I awoke:

> Like rain it sounded till it curved
> And then I knew 'twas Wind—
> It walked as wet as any Wave
> But swept as dry as sand—
> When it had pushed itself away
> To some remotest Plain
> A coming as of Hosts was heard
> That was indeed the Rain—
> It filled the Wells, it pleased the Pools
> It warbled in the Road—
> It pulled the spigot from the Hills
> And let the Floods abroad,—
> It loosened acres, lifted seas
> The sites of Centres stirred
> Then like Elijah rode away
> Upon a Wheel of Cloud.

I have just inserted the CD into my laptop and listened again to that Romanian gypsy who lives in Paris and plays his violin in Bireli Lagrène's jazz group. Imagine Django Reinhardt and Le Jazz Hot transplanted into the present, having retained all of Django's drive and brilliance and *joie de vivre* but having absorbed many new things in jazz and popular music from the 1920s until now.

I was in Istanbul during the jazz festival several summers ago and a friend, the Ottoman historian Caroline Finkel, took me to Babylon, a jazz club on a narrow street in Asmalımescit, a bohemian neighborhood in Beyoğlu—or Pera, to use its Constantinopolitan name. Caroline is a transplanted Scot who lives in Kuzguncuk on the Asian side. Asmalımescit is tucked away in that part of the city where Greek, Jewish, Armenian, European, and Levantine merchants lived during

Ottoman times, in Art Nouveau apartment buildings with elegant ironwork on their balconies. The night we ventured down to Beyoğlu, a powerful thunderstorm had just hit the city, and our taxi plowed through flooded streets as we drove down along the Bosphorus to reach Babylon.

I had not seen a configuration of musicians quite like the one that Bireli Lagrène assembled that evening. There was no drummer. The acoustic bass player stood, shepherding the group rhythmically from the back of the stage. Lagrène, the lead guitarist, sat in front flanked on either side by two rhythm guitar players. Two! They never played anything fancy, they just laid down a solid, strummed rhythmic base for the band's music and served as a kind of Greek chorus for the brilliance of the lead guitarist and my man, the violinist.

The two rhythm guitarists reinforced the chord structure as well as the beat and gave the music a solid bottom both rhythmically and harmonically. On songs with a 4/4 rhythmic structure, they strummed away four to the bar, the way the banjo would play in early New Orleans jazz. The violinist was the oldest man in the group. His physique suggested that he seldom missed a meal, and as he played he sweated profusely.

The band played jazz standards and swing and tunes from the Bebop repertoire. Clearly they had grown up on American music, because they quoted everything from "Old Man River" to the "Rhapsody in Blue" to the opening riffs of "In the Midnight Hour" by Wilson Pickett. They played their own version of Jimi Hendrix's "Purple Haze" as a lead-in to a blistering rendition of Dizzy Gillespie's classic, "Salt Peanuts." Bireli Lagrène then changed the mood, effortlessly executing arpeggios straight out of Segovia. One of the rhythm guitarists sang a love song with syrupy lyrics in French. They played "Laura," which began life as the theme song of an American movie from the 1940s—but I suspect I was the only one in Babylon who knew that.

Toward the end of the long evening the bass player put on his shades and came to the front of the stage to sing, in barely comprehensible English, "Blue Suede Shoes." Whatever they played, from the sublime to the ridiculous, from the familiar to the outrageous, flowed in a way that made me realize that in stepping in out of the rain that evening, I had made a transition from one form of liquidity to another, just as rain and water from the kitchen faucets and the violin solo from "Summertime" had blended in my mind when I woke up on that long-ago morning in Ireland, in a remote valley called Glenaskeogh.

I am writing in praise of a quality at once so basic and so elusive I am hard-pressed to find a word for it. "Hybridity" and "eclecticism" come to mind. The thesaurus is a guide not only to words but to ideas, and when I try to make a start by looking up the word "hybrid," I find that my old *Roget's Thesaurus of English Words and Phrases* records it under "mixture," taking a rather disapproving tone and listing it with the following gallimaufry of words:

> cross-breed, mongrel; half-blood, half-breed, half-caste; mestizo, mustee; Eurasian, Cape-coloured, mulatto; quadroon, octaroon; sambo, griff, griffin; mule, hinny.

This list constitutes a musty little museum of British racial nastiness from an earlier era. That my edition of *Roget* is outdated is suggested by the fact that Microsoft Word's spell-check turns up its nose at five of these seventeen words, underlining them in red as soon as I type them in. Don't even ask me what a griff is, or a hinny. I'm not sure I want to know. Roget seems to speak for that way of thinking that abhors change, puts its money into bonds, gets nervous when miscegenation is mentioned, and argues for what it regards as purity—on behalf, as Yeats puts it, of the "bankers, schoolmasters, and clergymen / The martyrs call the world."

What I am arguing for here might be called impurity by the world Yeats invokes. Music historians tell us that jazz began to be heard in New Orleans, a city whose culture is beautifully evoked by those enthralling words—"mulatto," "quadroon," "octoroon," with their hint of taboos and family secrets and the keys to a walk-up on the other side of town. It began to be played when African musicians got their hands on European instruments like the cornet, trombone, tuba, snare drum, and clarinet and bent the notes and rhythms of marching-band music to resemble the music of the countries they had been abducted from. Jazz may be the most human of all musics, because like the human race itself, jazz is about adaptation.

That night in Babylon, Caroline and I had found our way, in the polyglot city of Istanbul, right to the heart of Pera with its ethnic mixture that goes back to the beginnings of the civilized era—an American and a Scotswoman transported by a gypsy violinist from Romania who earns his living in Paris playing jazz. My guide to this musical awakening would have to be a gypsy, wouldn't it, from the ancient, feared, and despised tribe of Romany. Millions of their number were exterminated by the Nazis, but still they park their raffish caravans by the sides of roads all over Europe, tell fortunes, run a thriving carboot business in electronic equipment, irritate the citizenry of several nations, and flock once a year to the shrine of Les Saintes Maries de la Mer in the Aigues Mortes region of Provence to pay tribute to the Black Maria who sailed there from the Holy Land in a little boat with Mary Magdalene and Mary the Mother of God.

The gypsies on stage were not the only ones to find themselves far from their ancestral home that night in Babylon. How inexpressibly strange it seemed to me as someone who had grown up in Memphis, another Mississippi River city with its own racial complexities and subtleties, where as W. C. Handy wrote,

> If Beale Street could talk,
> If Beale Street could talk,
> Married men would have to take their beds and walk.
> Except one or two
> Who never drink booze
> And the blind man on the corner
> who sings the Beale Street Blues.

I tapped my foot and sang aloud in this crowd of Istanbulites listening to "Blue Suede Shoes," Carl Perkins' and then Elvis Presley's hit song from a time when I was young, being sung by a gypsy who couldn't get the words right. No one else cared, but I cared. I felt, to borrow Anaïs Nin's words, like "a spy in the house of love." I was honored to be in that number, to be a wanderer far from home and yet deeply at home, a spiritual half-breed, mongrel, and mulatto.

George Gershwin, son of Russian Jewish immigrants, based his opera *Porgy and Bess* on the white South Carolinian DuBose

Heyward's stories of African-American life on Catfish Row in Charleston, South Carolina. Jazz rises, by means of its very "impurity"—the mestizo quality of its sources and its sublime eclecticism—to a higher form of purity.

I started off by asking presumptuously what music is. Etymologically, from Greek, it means "the art of the Muses." If we accept the dictionary definition, "the art of organizing tones to produce a coherent sequence of sounds intended to elicit an aesthetic response in a listener," have we been led to an epiphany of understanding? I don't think so.

Climate change is probably the greatest danger the world faces, and I fear that environmental disasters will write the next chapter of human history. Yet as individuals we experience these shifting realities only as incidentals that register, if they register at all, on the periphery of our lives. A hot summer in Dublin, a dry reservoir in Tipperary. The rainstorm that filled our kitchen taps that long-ago morning is but a few drops compared to the deluge of Hurricane Katrina that drowned New Orleans, the city where jazz was born, swamped by the waters of the Mississippi River. And without the river, New Orleans never would have come into being in the first place.

In the meantime there is the life of what may be called the soul. For that entity, music is as basic and essential as water. The rivers of Babylon, the waters of Sliabh na mBan. When I listened to the violin music in my head and rain on the skylight and heard water from our reservoir coughing out of the kitchen faucets for morning tea, I felt that Robert Frost in his poem "Directive" was speaking straight to me when he wrote:

Here are your waters and your watering place.
Drink and be whole again beyond confusion.

OVERLAND TO INDIA AND NEPAL

From Berkeley
to the Khyber Pass

When I was thirty I went on pilgrimage. In Berkeley I had been medi-
tating and doing yoga, going on retreats with visiting spiritual teachers
when they came through town. At the time I wouldn't have blushed
at calling myself a seeker, or even saying I was "on the spiritual path."
I belonged to a group of American Sufis who met regularly under
the tutelage of Murshid Samuel Lewis in San Francisco and Marin
County, studying Hazrat Inayat Khan's writings, working with mantra
and breath exercises and doing the "turning" of the Mevlevi dervishes.

This Sufi order was tolerant and eclectic. The idea was that we
have something to learn from each of the world's great spiritual tradi-
tions. The *silsila*, or lineage, came through the Chishtis, a line of Sufis
that originated in what is now western Afghanistan and flourished
in India at the court of the Nizam of Hyderabad. Perhaps because of
the order's roots in the vast multi-ethnic subcontinent where, at the
best of times, the followers of several religious traditions lived side by

side in mutual tolerance and respect, these Sufis avoided the narrowness of their brothers in countries where Islam was the one and only religion.

I felt frustrated by having to experience those traditions at one remove. Reading the Hindu scriptures in translation I kept wondering: What does this really say—that is, if I could read it in the language it was written in? So I audited a Sanskrit class at the University of California, where I was a young assistant professor, and learned enough of the language to read the original dialogues between Krishna and his charioteer Arjuna in the Bhagavad Gita. I was no more enlightened, but at least I knew I was not being subjected to a translator's poeticizing, imperfect understanding or flights of fancy.

That same search for authenticity made me curious about those parts of the world where Sufism, Buddhism, and Hindu mysticism were practiced. What was it like to do *zikr* in a dervish lodge in Istanbul, hear the monks chant in a Buddhist monastery in Nepal, be inside a Hindu temple while a *puja* was being performed? (*Puja* is the worship service practiced by Hindus. *Zikr* is a ritualistic recitation of an Arabic phrase, accompanied by controlled breathing and head movements.) Doing zikr in a group for an hour or so produces mental clarity and a sense of exaltation. The state of mind is similar to that induced by meditation, but perhaps less cerebral because it involves the whole body.

My journey began in the summer of 1970 in the French Alps, where I was taking part in a meditation camp, the *Camp des Aigles,* a high-country outpost above Chamonix where we pitched our tents among the rocks and Alpine wildflowers of the French high country. My Sufi teacher Pir Vilayat Khan was training an eagle to fly to him when he whistled for it. The eagle would perch for a while, digging its talons into Pir's gloved knuckle, and then soar away on the thermals that ran through the valley opposite Mont Blanc.

There was at the time a train route still known as the Orient Express—not the luxury item that will cost you £3,000 for a four-night round trip from Paris to Venice in vintage sleeping cars, but a very ordinary rail journey that shuttled along from London or Paris to Venice, and then across former Yugoslavia and Bulgaria to Istanbul. No crystal champagne flutes rang at your place setting, no linen sheets were tucked under soft mattresses in the *couchettes* on this train—in fact, there were no sheets or blankets or mattresses or place settings or *couchettes* at all. You were lucky if you could find space on the dusty floor during the night to stretch out your sleeping bag for an hour or two of sleep.

The details of my journey's origin are hazy; this was over forty years ago. Was Geneva, the nearest big city, just over the border into Switzerland, where I boarded the Orient Express? I think so. I traveled third class in the rattly old carriages, and my luggage consisted of a green Kelty backpack. I lived out of that backpack for ten months.

Farhad, an Iranian man I met on the train, taught me some words in Farsi and showed me how to write my Sufi name in Persian script. When the train reached Istanbul the two of us set out in search of a cheap hotel. This was many decades before Istanbul became the tourist destination it now is. I remember the city being monotone gray, Balkan in aspect, more like Belgrade than Venice.

You changed money on the black market, in a little room behind a shop in the Kapalı Çarşı. Food was cheap. A plate of white bean salad with chopped onions and tomatoes, olive oil and lemon juice, and strong black olives—with a chunk of freshly baked bread and a couple of crinkly hot green peppers on the side, plus a bottle of water—cost fifty cents American. Then you could wander by the shores of the Sea of Marmara, smoking an oval Balkan Sobranie, with a view of the rusty tankers lined up waiting their turn to steam up the Bosphorus to the Black Sea.

The streets we tramped through, lugging heavy boxes filled with my Persian friend's TV set and other loot from his shopping trip in Europe, were paved with cobblestones. The first hotel we found was cheap enough, but bedbugs hid in the mattresses and blankets and didn't show themselves till after dark. That's when I learned to dust my lower legs with insect powder and to place the feet of the bed in tin cans filled with water and insecticide. After a few days I put Farhad on board the eastbound train out of Haydarpasha Station in Kadıköy, turreted like a castle on the Rhine. He invited me to visit him in Tabriz, and I waved goodbye as his train pulled away from the platform.

A few days after I saw Farhad off, a friend I had made at the Camp des Aigles named Jake turned up in Istanbul and suggested we make a trip together to Konya, headquarters of the Mevlevi dervishes. The founder of the order, Jalāl ad-Dīn Muhammad Rūmī, known in Turkey as Mevlana, Master or Teacher, was buried there.

Does the nameless have a name? In his own times the poet we know simply as Rumi would have been called Jalāl ad-Dīn Muhammad Balkhī. No wonder we prefer the simpler name! He was from Balkh, a province of ancient Khorasan that straddled modern-day Afghanistan and Tajikistan. In the early thirteenth century Rumi's father, a renowned scholar and teacher of theology called Baha ud-Din Walad, became alarmed by news of the Mongol invasion into Central Asia and decided to flee.

Baha ud-Din Walad's decision to leave was wise. The Mongols under Genghis Khan were not only uncommonly cruel and brutal (even in those times when the Byzantine Emperor Basil II put out the eyes of ninety-nine soldiers from every company in the conquered Bulgarian army of 15,000 and blinded only one eye of the hundredth so the half-blind man could lead them home)—the Mongols were also experts in the art of siege warfare, and it was not uncommon for them to sack and burn an entire city, taking the women and children as slaves and leaving behind only blood, smoke, and a pyramid of skulls. Baha ud-Din escaped with his family and set off on a journey west through Khorasan into the western provinces of the Persian Empire, finally accepting the invitation of the Seljuk ruler of Anatolia to settle in the city of Konya. Anatolia had been part of the Roman Empire, and this province was called Rum, or Rome.

Rumi's mausoleum, officially a museum, is one of the most visited places of pilgrimage in the Islamic world. Because of its strikingly beautiful turquoise-green ceramic tiles, the mausoleum is known as the Yeşil Türbe or Green Tomb. The morning after our arrival Jake and I walked through the shrine, at the center of which rests Rumi's catafalque, with the departed man's massive white turban coiled and resting at the head of the long box. Alongside him is placed the bier of his son, also a leader of the Mevlevi order, covered in green cloth, green being the sacred color of Islam.

In Muslim, Hindu, and Buddhist countries you come across holy places—often a saint's tomb like this one, around which a shrine has grown up. Other pilgrims, mostly Turks who had come to Konya from their villages and farms, walked through as though in a trance, their palms cupped upward to receive the baraka, or blessing. This was my first experience of the powerful sense of well-being and exaltation that emanates from the türbes, or tombs, of holy men. One felt uplifted and intoxicated just by virtue of being there.

At the shrine Jake and I met some Mevlevi dervishes, one of them a baker and one a cobbler. They took us to meet the sheikh of their order, an old gentleman named Süleyman Dede, or Grandfather Süleyman (Süleyman is the Turkish form of the name Solomon). Dede was the kindest of men. That was before I learned Turkish, but being in this man's presence, language hardly seemed to matter. He received us at his home, and with the help of one of the dervishes who spoke a little English, we conversed about Sufism. I am a grandfather myself now, with a half-Turkish grandson who calls me Dede, and I often think of that kindly old man in Konya.

Jake and I stayed in Konya for a week and were entertained by the sheikh and his followers. At the dervish lodge we performed namaz—Islam's ritual prayer service—with the group and were instructed in the art of turning. Sitting in a circle on the floor, we performed zikr. The word in Arabic means "remembrance." The dervishes wore close-fitting leather slippers, and Dede asked his cobbler dervish to measure my feet and make me a pair of soft leather, brick-red slippers, which I still have in Sewanee.

The dervish musicians played at a Thursday night sema while Jake and I were in Konya. A sema is an evening of music, recitation of Sufi poetry, and turning. The dervishes were dressed in street clothes, but before they got out on the highly polished wooden floor of the tekke, they threw other garments on top of these—soft woolen robes the color of cinnamon. On their feet were light leather slippers, and on their heads they wore the conical hat of their order, a brown elongated fez, tilted to one side, giving these plain men an appearance at the same time raffish and otherworldly.

Süleyman Dede stood at one end of the line, but he did not join in the turning. He stood there to guide and monitor—white bearded, dignified, and aloof. Each dervish bowed to the old man, arms crossed, a hand on each shoulder. Like the four directions themselves, the direction of any circular turning motion is significant, whether clockwise or counterclockwise, just as water swirls down a drain in the southern hemisphere in a different direction than in the northern.

These dancers turned to the left, counterclockwise. As I call up pictures of those whirling dervishes—the cobbler, the baker, the schoolteacher, the shop assistant, the policeman—so many years after the event, I find it impossible to imagine them turning to their right as they whirled. They moved as planets spinning like satellites around their sun, the elderly sheikh. Counterclockwise unwinds the clock, reverses incarnation in the direction of that which is uncreated and nameless, like the soul's journey toward reunion with its creator. The music, the dancing, the hospitality of these men, the kindness of the grandfatherly sheikh—all of this was a blessing, and the perfect way to begin one's journey.

THROUGH PERSIAN LANDS

I returned to Istanbul and was back at Haydarpasha Station myself within a few days, eastward bound. Seating myself in a compartment filled with a group of French New Age travelers, I had my first realization that what to me was a spiritual pilgrimage was, to others, the Hippie Trail to India. My newfound French companions' most frequent question to each other was "*Ou est la pipe?*" Hashish was their smoke of choice. And *les puces* were along for the ride, as I found out when I woke in the night with fleabites all up my arms.

When I finally arrived in Tabriz, Farhad, my friend from the Orient Express, received me hospitably into his home. Whenever I ventured into the kitchen, where Farhad's wife and mother-in-law sat cross-legged on the floor preparing the evening meal, they would hastily cover their heads with their filmy shawls. They smiled when they did so, as if it were a conspiratorial little joke we shared. "You're a man and not a member of our family, so," they seemed to be saying, "we have to play this little game of covering ourselves."

The main thing I knew about Tabriz was that it was the hometown of Shems-i-Tabriz, Rumi's friend and muse. I found both friendly curiosity and hostility in Tabriz. Little boys in the bazaar threw pebbles at me. It wasn't clear whether what they had against me was that I was a Westerner or that I looked like a hippie.

But standing in line to board a bus, fellow passengers often deferred to me and addressed me as "Sufi." I learned that in the popular imagination a Sufi was a bearded, ascetic-looking man. I guess I fit the description. As we left Tabriz the bus conductor went down the aisle with a clipboard, getting all the passengers' names. When he came to me halfway to the back of the bus, it seemed pointless to give the name Richard. He wouldn't have been able to write it down; so I gave him my Sufi name, which was Persian. Without blinking an eye or acting as if there was anything incongruous about a Westerner having a Persian name, he just jotted down "Jamshed" and moved along down the aisle.

‹‹‹‹‹‹‹‹

I was one of those rare travellers lucky enough to get into Iran before the Islamic revolution deposed the Shah. Even to someone like myself with no understanding of Iranian politics, it was clear that a revolution was brewing. In Tehran, soldiers with rifles and machine guns deployed on every street corner. The city abounded with spies and informers, and any foreigner, especially an American, was suspect, even a backpacking traveler with long hair and a beard. Paranoia and conspiracy theories are endemic in this part of the world. Maybe they are justified, considering America's record of interference in Iran's internal affairs.

One of the dervishes whose name I had obtained from Pir Vilayat met me in the center of the city and then drove me at breakneck speed on a circuitous route down side streets and alleys until we reached the *khanqah*, or dervish meeting hall. I was hospitably received by these kind men. Their khanqah adjoined the tomb of a Sufi saint, set in a beautiful garden, irrigated, planted with fragrant jasmine and roses.

Like most cities in this part of the world, Tehran was crowded and noisy. Air pollution made it difficult to breathe comfortably. I cooled off by drinking glasses of pomegranate juice squeezed by men who set up hand-pulled juicers on street corners. It was a relief to retreat from Tehran down to the garden city of Shiraz. Pir Vilayat had told me about the Haft Tanan garden there. The name means "the seven bodies," because seven Sufi saints are buried there.

All through the Islamic world people visit the tombs of saints, holy men, and other notable people to receive the *baraka*—the blessing or spiritual power—from the saint's presence. The Yeşil Türbe in Konya was my first experience of these extraordinary places. I am using the word saint—someone who would be called *aziz* in Turkish—though there are no saints as such in Islam. The holy man's body rests in a sarcophagus, covered with a green pall inside a little domed building, and one can look inside through windows protected by metal grilles.

The Haft Tanan is a museum now, but back then it was a park, and you could just walk in. I strolled around the garden through air fragrant with citrus blossoms, looking at the collection of stone carvings arranged there and admiring the mural paintings inside the small buildings. Persia boasts a civilization that predates Mohammad's religion. The Turks have a saying: "He who reads Persian loses half his religion." And there is some truth in that, in the sense that Iranian Shiism as interpreted by the Sufis sometimes makes fundamentalist Sunni Islam seem narrow minded, hard shelled, bumptious. Though there is no Koranic prohibition against it, Islam traditionally has shied away from images depicting the human figure. In Judaism this goes back to the second of the Ten Commandments with its prohibition against graven images.

The paintings, which I think date from the seventeenth-century reign of Shah Abbas, range from arabesque patterns whose floral designs approach abstraction to depictions of bearded holy men and dervishes to scenes from the Old Testament that Islam has adopted as part of its own traditions, including Abraham (*Ibrahim* in Arabic) preparing to follow God's commandment that he sacrifice his son Isaac. Then there are paintings of dervishes with outsized moustaches that project to their ears and beyond, and beards that would put ZZ Top to shame. Stone carvings render panels of ancient script, goats and other animals, soldiers, cavalrymen on horseback.

In the garden I came across a group of old men sitting quietly, talking and fingering their prayer beads. They welcomed me, asked me to sit with them and share their meal of *chelow kabab*, a rice pilaf with lamb. They kept a stash of food supplies and a little butane stove in one of the buildings to cook over. I still remember how the pilaf tasted. It was flavored with cinnamon, saffron, and freshly chopped parsley. After we had tea, one of the men set a thick volume of the poetry of Hafiz on a Qu'ran stand and sang the poems out loud, taking breaks to puff on his narghile, which was primed with some kind of brown stuff—opium or hashish I think. His singing was beautiful, melodic, and expressive, and all of us were weeping by the end of his recitation. It is no wonder that Hafiz is referred to as "the tongue of the invisible."

<<<<<<<

After Shiraz and Isfahan I rode buses again across vast eastern stretches of Iran all the way to the border with Afghanistan. Was I carrying any drugs with me?, the border guard asked. No, of course not, I replied. That's good, the man said, and he pointed out the little assemblage of VW buses and Land Rovers parked alongside the customs post. They had belonged to drug dealers who were summarily executed there, he said. What a good thing I am not that foolish, I replied.

On the main routes through Turkey, buses can be fast, clean, even luxurious. Many of them are air-conditioned, recorded music is played, tea and biscuits are served. The Hadiths say the Prophet loved scent, and his followers feel the same way about it. Turkish buses have a conductor, the driver's sidekick who keeps an eye on things, manages his passengers, and often passes down the aisle with a plastic bottle of lemon cologne which he offers to the passengers. You hold out your hands, palms upward, to receive it, and then splash it on your face to refresh yourself.

But further along the road, bus journeys in the Middle East make America's Greyhounds seem almost bourgeois. Many of them are gaily painted with fanciful landscape scenes, flowers, soulful-eyed veiled women, and almost all of them have *Maşallah*, "God Willing," painted somewhere on them. At prayer times, particularly in Afghanistan, people get out and lay their prayer rugs down on the sand at the bus stops to perform *namaz*.

There are no trains through the mountains, so everybody travels by bus. And when I say "everybody," I don't mean just human beings. If you have a couple of chickens you want to take to market in the next town, you tuck them under your arms and get on the bus. People bring baskets of food and share it around. On a trip I took in Afghanistan one of the passengers put his sheep on top of the bus. It was a hot day, but we had to close the windows because the rivulets of sheep urine that trickled down.

Certain moments stand out memorably. Once I was awakened at four in the morning in some village by the first call to prayer of the day. "Prayer is better than sleep," the muezzin sang. That wasn't going to get me out of bed, but I did look out my window onto a sky so blue it was almost violet, to see the dome and single minaret of the little mosque next door to my hotel, and hanging above it halfway down the sky, the crescent moon, lit with a pearly luminescence.

AMONG THE AFGHANIS

I was travel-weary at this stage of the journey, so I holed up to rest for three weeks in a hotel in Herat, a city in the far west of the big, mountainous country of Afghanistan. The only thing I remember about my hotel was the lavatory. Delhi Belly hit me even before I arrived in India, and I saw more of that little room than I would have liked. Excrement fell through an open hole to a spot about fifty feet down, where pigs were waiting. Efficient if unsavory.

I wish I had read Robert Byron's *The Road to Oxiana* before going to Afghanistan. Byron spent a month in Herat in 1933. His description of the place was still accurate forty years on, and I enjoy comparing his impressions to my own. The old town remained "a maze of narrow twisting streets enclosed by square ramparts," with the long tunnel of the covered bazaar cutting through it at a diagonal. The ateliers of the coppersmiths, "whose clang between dawn and sunset deters the guests from sloth," were just as active and noisy in my day as they had been in his.

I spent many of my days in those open-front shops, bargaining for Baluchi rugs, their dusty crimson and chocolate-brown fields scored with lozenge patterns in dark blue and black. It was pleasant to lounge there on cushions covered with old carpets, drinking strong cups of tea, listening to someone play melodies from the windswept northern plains on the plucked, three-string lute that is popular in those parts. In the forty years since Robert Byron's visit, dress had changed as little as had the layout of the town. Pashtun tribesmen took an eclectic and raffish approach to fashion. The occasional items of European clothing, "accompanied," in Byron's words, "by a turban as big as a heap of bedclothes, a cloak of parti-coloured blanket, and loose white peg-top trousers reaching down to gold-embroidered shoes of gondola shape, have an exotic gaiety, like an Indian shawl at the Opera."

Other styles that he notes, I don't recall seeing: Turcomans wearing "high black boots, long red coats, and busbies of silky black goats' curls. The most singular costume," he continues, like a writer on fashion, "is that of the neighbouring highlanders, who sail through the streets in surtouts of stiff white serge." I do remember what he calls their "dangling false sleeves, almost wings, that stretch to the back of the knee and are pierced in patterns like a stencil."

I bought one of these surtouts in the bazaar, as well as a warm vest made from the skin of a grey wolf. I wonder what has become of them? In whose attic or fancy-dress costume trunk do they now reside? There is one thing I know had not changed, and that was—and is—the burka, that unfortunate portable jail cell that Afghan women wear: "Now and then a calico beehive with a window at the top flits across the scene. This is a woman."

Afghanistan still had a king back then, and one day the university students marched through town demonstrating against the government. People in the streets, though, seemed pretty indifferent to politics. Things were more relaxed here than in Iran. I found Afghanis to be friendly, highly independent men who liked to joke around and have a good time. Up to that point in its history, Afghanistan had largely escaped from the domination of any empire, and I think that helped them avoid the sort of unctuous, servile behavior of people in some post-colonial societies.

Byron loved, as I loved, the dash and *élan* of these upland tribesmen: "Hawk-eyed and eagle-beaked, the swarthy loose-knit men swung through the dark bazaar with a devil-may-care self-confidence. They carry rifles to go shopping as Londoners carry umbrellas. Such ferocity is partly histrionic. The rifles might not go off."

As part of the Northwest Frontier of Britain's Indian empire, this mountain kingdom populated by warlike tribes was the focal point of the Great Game, the epic struggle between the British and the Russians in the nineteenth century. The British were afraid the Tsar would try to invade India through Afghanistan, and they fought and lost two wars in their attempt to secure the northwestern flank of their eastern empire. Like mountain people throughout the world, the Afghanis are self-reliant and independent. "Here at last," in Robert Byron's words, "is Asia without an inferiority complex."

>>>>>>>

When I was there, Herat's glorious past was scarcely visible. The Citadel, that enormous adobe fortress looming over the town, stood in ruins, its battlements eroded, looking like a child's sandcastle on a beach after the tide has washed over it. Its castellations that at one time intimidated would-be attackers now were toothless and forlorn. Herat had its moment of glory under the Timurid Empire of Tamurlane the Great and his successors.

The Mongols, Turkic nomads who were to conquer most of the lands through which they stormed on their westward migration from Central Asia, were leaving Chinese civilization behind, and Tamurlane led them to embrace Islam. His empire encompassed all the Mongol lands except for China and stretched westward across Iran to what is now Iraq, and to the southeast through what is now Pakistan, into parts of India. Herat lay at roughly the midpoint of this vast territory, ideally situated for the exchange of ideas and artistic trends. But

Tamurlane was not lucky in his descendants. They never established a fixed law of succession, so internecine feuds, murders, and poisonings were common. Many of them drank themselves to death.

On the other hand the Timurids were great patrons of the arts. Herat was known throughout the Islamic world as a center for miniature painting in the Persian and Mughal styles. The faces in these miniatures look Chinese, but the pleasures and pursuits pictured there are hedonistic and Persian, not austere and Confucian. Surprisingly, they even wrote in Turki, the common tongue, as opposed to Persian, the court language and literary medium. These poets' choice of the vernacular finds a parallel during the European thirteenth century in Dante's choice of Italian as opposed to the more literary and respectable Latin.

Herat at the beginning of the fifteenth century was acknowledged to be the greatest metropolis in Central Asia. Ambassadors were dispatched to its court from the Mamluk capital of Cairo, from the Byzantine emperor in Constantinople, and even from the Forbidden City in Beijing itself. Babur, one of Tamurlane's descendants, left Herat with great reluctance. Looking back from his new realms in India, he wrote: "The whole habitable world had not such a town as Herat had become under Sultan Hussein Mirza . . . Khorasan, and Herat above all, was filled with learned and matchless men. Whatever work a man took up, he aimed and aspired to bring it to perfection."

<<<<<<<<

I was one of the lucky ones to visit Afghanistan before the struggles-to-the-death that have ravaged the country since the Russian invasion in the winter of 1979. This was followed by the war of resistance fought by the Mujahidin, backed by America and the Gulf oil states— a struggle that led to Afghanistan's being dominated by jihadist fighters, the coming of the Taliban, and the American campaigns of the early twenty-first century, which proved to be just as bloody and no more successful than the Anglo-Afghan wars of the 1840s.

While in Afghanistan, I made two friends among fellow travelers. Both were American expats who had been traveling in India for years. One was a veteran of the Korean War from Arkansas who had renounced

America for good. Once a year he flew to London to spend a week with his mother, who flew there from Little Rock to join him. He liked things in the East and had no intention of going home. The three of us stayed in the same cheap hotel. On one occasion we left the city behind and went up into the mountains to an oasis where there was a little spa renowned for its hot springs. There, you could stretch out in huge bathtubs where hot mineral water flowed in at one end and drained out the other.

One day while we were at the spa, I took a hike up above the oasis and eventually found myself on an ancient caravan trail. I was miles above and miles away from Herat. I had gone back several centuries, to a time when caravans traversing the Silk Road crossed this land in the kingdom of Khorasan, before the modern states of Iran, Afghanistan, and Pakistan came into existence. An old man plodded along leading a donkey. *As-salaam Aleikhum*, I greeted him, using the salutation that is common currency throughout the world of Islam. Instead of coming back at me with *Wa-Aleikhum As-Salaam* as expected, the old man's only reply sounded like a grunt. Or perhaps he was speaking some language older than Arabic in these parts.

Another time, as we were sitting at a table outside a restaurant we liked, an Afghani man approached us. *Yahudi?* he asked one of my friends. Jewish? We knew only a few words of Farsi, but my friend knew enough to say *Baleh*, Yes. The young Afghani explained that his family were caretakers at the Yu Aw Synagogue in the Mahalla-yi Musahiya, "Neighborhood of the Jews" (literally "Followers of Moses") in Herat. The intrepid twelfth-century Jewish traveler and trader, Benjamin of Tudela, who left a written account of his travels through the Middle East, reported that in his day 80,000 Jews lived in what is now Afghanistan. There was greater tolerance there than in neighboring Iran. The Jewish population in Herat back then was large enough to support a synagogue. Now there were no Jews left.

Thus we were honored guests, and for a few hours I became an honorary Jew. Our host dusted off a little case containing the tools he used for butchering animals according to kosher specifications. Though he had no way of knowing, he was doing this for two vegetarians, one of whom was not even Jewish, one of us Jewish but not observant. He grabbed one of the chickens that were running around in the yard and slit its throat in the prescribed manner. The notion that an animal was being killed for our benefit was not only unpleasant—it was also slightly sickening. But we kept smiling, and soon we found ourselves sitting around the family dinner table having a delicious meal of spicy chicken—the only meat I ate for months.

TO THE KHYBER PASS

I was reluctant to leave Herat, but eventually I did move on. Along the way to the Khyber Pass I stayed for the night at a *khan* or caravanserai. A stout wall built of rough stone enclosed the place, with a dirt floor inside, swept bare, and arcades around its four sides where pack animals were stabled. It is high in the mountains, and the night was cold.

We were a motley crew that night in the caravanserai: one or two travellers like myself, one or two truck drivers and camel drivers and a shady group of men who may have been smugglers. These latter kept to themselves. The rest of us scavenged firewood outside the walls and threw together a rough blaze on the dirt floor. At some point one of the men brought out a water pipe, and we sat around it by the fire. They filled the bowl with shag tobacco, then laid a big coal extracted with tongs from the fire on top of the tobacco. When the lung-searing tobacco was alight, they laid a chunk of fresh hashish from Balkh on top of it, and we took turns bringing the hashish alight with huge inhalations of breath. The old men coughed horribly.

Until late in the evening the gates of the caravanserai stood open. Scavenger dogs slinked in, gnawing bone-scraps. But when it got dark they chased the dogs out and secured a massive iron padlock onto the ancient doors, which were studded with iron twenty-penny nails. I gathered straw to cushion my bedroll and threw some wood on the fire. Then I stretched out with my backpack as a headrest and gazed up in wonder at the searingly bright constellations that wheeled overhead.

‹‹‹‹‹‹‹

Kabul was a peaceful enough city in those days before the cataclysms that were to come. Like Kathmandu, which I was to see a few months later, Kabul was a high-country city built on a plateau with views of the Hindu Kush mountains to the north and east. Even in the city Afghans think tribally, and they live in family compounds with adobe walls around them. I liked to walk out through the city's broad boulevards and past these spacious compounds into the countryside.

After a week in Kabul I was on a bus again, heading east along what was once the Silk Road through the Khyber Pass into the Indian subcontinent. Darius the First of Persia, Alexander the Great, and Genghis Khan had passed through here. The road winds through steep switchbacks among cliffs and rocky ridges, dropping precipitously toward the Indian plain. The traveler hardly needs a history book, because the lands through which he travels have their own story to tell.

Around every bend in the mountainous road were nineteenth-century monuments to British regiments that perished here during the Anglo-Afghan Wars of the 1840s. The slaughter had been terrible. The British tried to fight their way upward into the mountains, and snipers among the Afghan tribesmen in their turbans and shawls, firing antique muskets, waited to pick the redcoats off as they tried to ascend.

When the bus stopped at a dusty wayside tea shop beside a store selling weapons, I walked to the top of the ridge and gazed over the plain that stretched out before me on the next leg of my journey. Unsmiling border guards with AK-47s slung across their shoulders kept watch over the road. A derelict Buddhist *stupa* and abandoned railroad tracks from a line built by the British stood off to the side of the road. Brown haze stretched horizontally across the valley below. It looked like smog but did not smell of factory smokestacks or automobile emissions. It rose from cooking fires on the plains below, where people burned whatever wood they could scrounge, as well as from the dried round cakes of dung I would see slapped onto the walls of houses to dry in the sun. I had come this far. Below me, Pakistan and India awaited.

Days and Nights at a Sufi Khanqah in Pakistan

Picture a scattering of small impromptu buildings spread out under shade trees among grasslands. A well and a pump for washing, an open-air prayer space swept in the very early morning and sprinkled with water to keep the dust down. Some of the structures here were fashioned of saplings bent and lashed together to form frames over which cloth could be thrown to provide shelter from the sun or a tarp to keep off the rain. This was Darul Ehsan, the khanqah of Sufi Barkat Ali in Faisalabad, a short drive from the Pakistani city of Lahore, in the midst of a farming area where sugarcane was grown.

I am calling it a khanqah, but that implies a monastic atmosphere, which Darul Ehsan did not have. It was more of a community center with religious underpinnings. I am tempted to use the word "compound" to describe the place, but that implies a fenced-in area. Sufi Barkat Ali's headquarters had no fixed boundaries; it sprawled out into the fields that surrounded it. It was a kind of camp.

Boardwalks had been constructed around the place to connect the different parts of the khanqah with small platforms where visitors and travelers could stay and where *mureeds* could go on retreats, including the rigorous forty-day retreat that involves isolation, day-long fasting and long sessions of zikr. A mureed is an initiate into a Sufi order or *tarikat*.

Barkat Ali was Murshid Samuel Lewis's teacher, and I had a letter of introduction to him through Murshid Sam. In the Indian subcontinent holy men—whether Muslim, Hindu, or Buddhist—hold court, and coming to the khanqah was like visiting a royal court. That's the word: this was Sufi Barkat Ali's court. Some of Sufi Barkat Ali's followers stayed at the khanqah, while others visited from the city and the surrounding farms.

As a visitor from faraway America, I was accorded a warm welcome. One of the mureeds who worked as a tailor made me a suit of homespun local clothes to wear. I was assigned a platform of my own where I rolled out my sleeping bag and slept under the stars. No ambient light out there in the countryside interfered with the light of the heavens, and the stars and planets burned through the pitch-black sky in piercing darts of apple-green, red, and pure-diamond brilliance. In Turkish the Milky Way is called the *hacılar yolu*, the pilgrims' way, and that phrase resonated with me during my time at Darul Ehsan. While there I wrote, somewhat fancifully since I did not arrive on horseback:

> Dismount, set down your bundle.
> Here's straw to cushion your bedroll,
> deadfall oak from the forest for your cooking fire.
> Your horse can munch the fallen apples in the orchard
> while you stretch out after supper and smoke your pipe
> under the astonishment of the constellations,
> those legend-threaded pathways through the dark.

Though you were surrounded by friends, you felt you were out there on your own at the edge of the round and turning earth. Mornings came early, because we got up for *Fajr*, the pre-dawn prayer, when Muslims begin the day with the remembrance of God. Sometimes one of the mureeds would bring you a clay cup of steaming milky chai to help you wake up.

I have never been good at remembering strings of words in languages I don't understand, and as I don't understand Arabic, I could never succeed in getting the Muslim prayers by heart. So I performed the ritual movements and mumbled under my breath words in English that meant something to me—poetry, the 23rd Psalm.

I did understand enough to know that when the muezzin sang *Allah ho Akbar*, this didn't just mean "Allah is great," but implied that God, by whatever name you chose to call Him, or It, is greater than all other presumed deities, that contemplation of divinity trumps other aspects of life that may involve and entangle us. I knew that somewhere in the string of repeated words in the pre-dawn call to prayer, believers were being told *Haya ala Assala*, "Gather in prayer," and *Haya ala Alfalah*, "Gather in goodness."

〈〈〈〈〈〈〈

Sufi Barkat Ali conducted his affairs much the same way as what I would later experience with the Hindu holy men and Tibetan lamas I visited on my pilgrimage. His court functioned as a clearing house within the community. If he were a Hindu he might be called Baba and thought of as a guru, but this concept does not exist in Islam. Turks or other Muslim Sufis would have called him a sheikh. His followers came to him to seek advice, ask him to be an arbiter in family disputes, or simply because they wished to spend a day in the presence of this wise and pious man. Every day people came who simply needed something to eat. Often his followers gave him offerings of money, and it was a hard-and-fast rule with him that all moneys received during the day had to be dispersed before nightfall that same day.

Barkat Ali gave money and food to those who needed it, helped support charities, and ran a free clinic at the khanqah to treat diseases of the eyes, which were common in rural Pakistan. He had authority. People went to him as in biblical days they might have gone to Solomon. In spite of his grey flowing beard and the skullcap or turban he wore, the man had a military bearing and conducted himself with soldierly briskness. When you watched the way he dealt with the petitions and requests brought before him, it was not hard to picture the spit-and-polish officer he would have been, handling regimental affairs. Pakistan is ruled by the military, and Barkat Ali's followers must have found his masterful bearing reassuring.

I later learned that the Sufi—born under the Raj during the first year of the reign of George V, King of Great Britain and Ireland and Emperor of India, before the cataclysmic split between Hindus and Muslims that accompanied Partition in 1949 and produced the state of Pakistan—had in fact been an officer in the Indian Army. He attended the military academy in Dehradun, earned his commission, and served for fifteen years with the Royal Corps of Engineers, leaving the service in 1945.

>>>>>>>>

Three sister religions—Hinduism, Buddhism and Islam—have lived side by side on the subcontinent for centuries, though not always peacefully, it's true. One thing they share is a belief in the capacity of inanimate objects to carry *baraka*. Sufi Barkat Ali wore a homespun woolen robe, basically a thick woolen blanket hemmed at both ends, with a neck hole cut into the fabric so it could be worn as a kind of poncho. The Sufi also often wrote receipts, directives for how a certain fund of money was to be spent, letters to the authorities on behalf of his flock, and so forth.

For these writings he used a steel-nibbed pen that he dipped into a bottle of ink. After writing, he would sling the unused ink onto his robe. That transferred the *baraka* of his written words onto his robe. One day while we were talking, he took off his robe and put it over my head, which was regarded as a mark of favor. From that day forth I was treated with special regard at the khanqah. I had risen in the hierarchy, though it was not clear to me exactly why. They warned me not to have the robe washed or dry-cleaned—that would remove the *baraka* implanted in it by the Sufi's ink.

>>>>>>>>

I had heard the Arabic word *madzoub* among the Sufis back in San Francisco. I supposed the word to mean a "God-intoxicated madman," someone possessed of what the renegade Tibetan lama Chögyam Trungpa called crazy wisdom. At night at Darul Ehsan I would hear a sheep baa-ing late into the night—only this wasn't a sheep, it was a man who thought he was a sheep. Everyone referred to him as "the *madzoub*." Back in America it would be assumed that he was just nuts. He was a follower of Sufi Barkat Ali's and, like me, he had been given his own platform out on the edge of the camp where he could set up a tent and baa to his heart's content.

Providing refuge to the man who thought he was a sheep, giving hospitality to pilgrims and travellers, assisting in the economy of the region, setting up a clinic to treat eye diseases, all this was part of the work of this extraordinary Sufi, a God-intoxicated man who was at the same time attuned to human suffering and human needs in a practical way.

The Police Chief
of Mustafabad

Old Delhi was smoky with wood fires. Dozens of men and women in dhotis and saris who had slept out under the shelter of the train-station roof were performing their morning ablutions, brushing their teeth with twigs, having a wash, chewing *paan*, hawking and spitting, smoking *bidis* and brewing up chai. Just the day before, when I took the train to Delhi from the Pakistani border, war had been declared between the two neighboring countries. More unsettling for me was that the pouch where I kept my passport, shot records, and other travel documents had gone missing, plus seven one-hundred-dollar bills. In India in the early 1970s, seven hundred dollars was a lot of money.

I had traveled overland from London through the Low Countries and France across the Alps, boarding the Orient Express in Venice, bound for Istanbul. From Istanbul I continued across Turkey and then through the fragrant and fraught kingdom of Iran. The Shah was still on his throne back then, and Americans could get travel visas. Next I crossed through mountainous Afghanistan, a refuge of hospitality and goodwill unaware of the cataclysms that awaited it. A precipitous bus trip down the Khyber Pass brought me into Pakistan, where I had stayed at the khanqah of Sufi Barkat Ali near Lahore.

But those miles were behind me now. My Pakistani friends had pleaded with me not to travel to India. It was a treacherous place, they insisted, populated by untrustworthy people. In Lahore, crowds marched through the streets demanding war. But I was on pilgrimage, and India, Mother India, was the object of that pilgrimage. I was not to be deterred.

I took a bus to the border and walked the hundred yards across no man's land into India. A blackout was on. I changed some of my money into rupees, bought a train ticket to Delhi, checked my backpack at left luggage and strolled around the darkened town, buying chapattis and potato curry from street vendors before boarding the train. The weak light of lanterns, cooking fires, and spirit lamps illuminated the small, unpaved streets of the little border town. It was not until I was seated on the train that I felt under my shirt for my passport and money and found to my horror that the pouch was not there.

I spent a restless night. Even under the best of circumstances it would not have been easy to get to sleep on the wooden third-class bench I shared with five other men. Once outside the station I hired a bicycle rickshaw to take me to the home of a friend of a friend where I was to stay. My hostess, a Dutchwoman, welcomed me warmly, paid for my cab after arguing vociferously over the fare with the rickshaw *wallah*, and did not seem overly anxious when I explained to her my predicament. In India these things happened, her manner seemed to suggest. An official at the American Embassy later in the day shrugged at my plight and gave me some forms to fill out.

I had enough rupees left from the money I had changed to take rickshaws where I wanted to go and to eat cheaply, and I saw a bit of Delhi. One evening I returned to my lodgings to be told that a man had turned up asking for me. My Dutch lady could be abrupt, and it seemed she had scared the man off without learning much about why he had come.

Two days later an official-looking letter arrived asking me to turn up at the police station in a little town eighty miles from Delhi—let's call it Mustafabad—and ask for the chief of police. Feeling like a character in a Sherlock Holmes story about India during the Raj, I paid for a ride in a shared car and made my way to Mustafabad, where I presented myself at the station. The clerk on duty told me the chief was at his home just then, so I walked to his little villa at the edge of town. He greeted me with a sober cordiality. A servant brought lunch to us at a table on the lawn.

My host and I chatted unhurriedly about our two countries, my travels, this war. Finally he opened a folder and produced my passport and documents, as well as the seven crisp one-hundred-dollar bills. Someone had turned the pouch in with the contents intact, the policeman said matter-of-factly. He would just ask me to verify my identity and then to write out the serial numbers of the bills and sign a document attesting that the money had been returned to me. I was seven thousand miles from home, and for the past week I had had no document, no scrap of paper, to prove who I was. You could have knocked me over with a feather.

I guessed from the chief of police's name that he was a Muslim, and after I had tucked my pouch away and we were finishing off our meal with fruit compote and tea, I asked him about being a Muslim in a majority Hindu country. First he acted surprised that I knew enough to tell a Muslim name from a Hindu name, which shows how little foreigners are reckoned to know in this part of the world. He talked about having to be circumspect. He never suggested that by returning my money he might have just given witness to something exemplary about his religion.

If he had said that the hundred-dollar bills were missing when the pouch was brought to the station, there would have been no way to disprove it. I thanked this honest man for the lunch and for the kindness he had showed to a stranger. Even today, these many years later, when Islam is mentioned, I remember the police chief of Mustafabad.

On Pilgrimage in India

THE STREETS OF DELHI

So many people live out on the streets of Delhi that only a God who numbers the hairs of our heads and knows the fall of the sparrow could count them all. Here on Earth we have our words for this: poverty, destitution. When it comes to money, these people are poor to a degree almost unimaginable. But if you have reached India via the overland route, you will have been travelling through places where material possessions do not define life, and by this point you might be rethinking the meaning of the word poverty. The lives of people I encountered along the road through Turkey, Iran, Afghanistan, and Pakistan did not seem any less complete or fulfilled just because they did not own a vacuum cleaner or an automobile. As a result, street life in Delhi did not send me into shock when I arrived in 1970. But still it made its impression.

Some of the poor managed, with resourcefulness and by maintaining a sense of family and community, to get by. Women in brilliantly colored saris simmered their curries over open fires and scrubbed out brass cooking pots using water that flowed brightly down the gutters of cobbled streets. A scatter of children, their nappies draggling down behind them, played their games in the spaces between where pedestrians passed. Girls sat on the pavement braiding each other's long black hair. Boys kicked soccer balls in and out of passing traffic.

They patched together makeshift huts from cardboard boxes and made little homes for themselves. Some of these families even got their children washed, brushed, into school uniforms, and off to school, though how they managed it is beyond me. On mats spread at the doors of shacks sat dark-skinned heads of families, mouths stained crimson from chewing betel leaf-wrapped paan. They smoked bidis, drank chai, and talked of this and that while watching the multitudinous world parade before them, heedless of the fat and contemptuous rich riding past in their chauffeur-driven Mercedes, masters of all they surveyed.

India seized control of me and altered my sense not only of poverty but of time. Getting anything accomplished here, from buying a train ticket to changing money on the black market to getting your visa renewed or having a prescription filled, could and would take hours of your time. In cases where you guessed a few rupees discreetly placed in the right hands might speed things up, it was hard to decide precisely how this should be done, or whether a fumbling attempt might just make things more difficult.

The hippie rule of thumb was that if you could get one thing done in a day, you should be satisfied. Once I learned the fares between different parts of the city, I loved riding through Delhi in a motorbike rickshaw. These conveyances posted no set fares and had no meters—none, at least, that functioned. The fares were a matter of prior knowledge on everyone's part. God be with the first-time passenger who had to negotiate payment!

In the flimsy passenger seat, you rode closer to the swarm of traffic—motorized, pedestrian, on two feet or four, surging through the streets at all hours—than you could ever be if you were inside a car. You were a fish in the sea of traffic. You could smell the rickshaw *wallah's* sweat and garlic and the areca-nut tang of the paan he nursed against his gums, spitting the crimson juice over his shoulder. Antiquated double-decker buses strained under their human burden, puffing out clouds of diesel exhaust and sharing the road with all manner of transportation—bicycles, pedestrians, ox carts, and rickshaws.

You scrunched your long American legs in so close to the driver that his loose white shirt flapped up against you as he guided his scooter through traffic dodging taxis, sputtering and wheezing around lorries painted with scenes from the Ramayana—blue-skinned Krishna with Radha clinging to his side, Hamuman the monkey god, many-armed Shiva.

Travels around the city suggested that while some of the poor were brave, tough, and resourceful enough not only to survive but to make a decent life for themselves and their families, for others the burden of poverty had become intolerable. Gray cows, hollow-looking skins blown up with air, lumbered impassively through the teeming crowds—aware, seemingly, of their status as sacred and protected creatures, munching on whatever fodder they could find, from vegetable scraps and refuse to discarded newspapers, brushing with their ribs ox-carts, taxis and lorries, men and women on foot in their shawls and saris, dhotis and lungis.

A little girl shepherded a pig that rooted up filth from cracks in the pavement. Outside the city stretched mountains of garbage swarmed over by seagulls, crows, and spectral kites, frightening with their scrawny necks, crone-like visages, and angel-of-death wings, and by human scavengers too, all of them fighting for scraps.

Christ's words, "Blessed are the poor," sometimes came uninvited to mind. Here those words came freighted with irony. Into this city flocked the unfortunate in great numbers, lightly clothed, building fires on the streets outside their tarpaper and corrugated-tin shacks, caring for their young haphazardly, brewing up spicy chai, smoking chillums stoked with hashish, sometimes getting drunk on cheap bootleg. Occasionally I saw a TV set, its blue screen aglow in the gloom. The white moon rode above Delhi, its edges sharp as broken glass.

TRAINS AND MONEY

When you went to the station to buy a train ticket, no matter how early you got there you had to be prepared for the hyper-excited rush that would ensue once the clerk opened his ticket window. The British left their mark on the subcontinent in many ways that included building an impressive rail system, but one thing they never succeeded in teaching the Indians was the etiquette of queuing, which is essential to the British sense of fair play. Perhaps this cultural difference owes something to the innate Indian understanding that, no, life is not fair—who would be so naïve as to think such a thing? According to the caste system, you were born to a particular station, and your privileges, your expectations, were determined from birth.

Vendors moved among the crowds in the station hawking chapattis, steaming chai, vegetable and potato curries in banana-leaf bowls, curdy yogurt in little clay pots that could be discarded anywhere, thrown out the train window to smash on the tracks, where they would be recycled into the earth whence they came. India had a recycling system for centuries before the concept was introduced to the consumer societies of the West. As for trains, the system of first, second, and third-class compartments fit the caste system as well as it had fit the European class system for which it was designed.

I never traveled first class, so I can't speak to the atmosphere or comfort of those carriages; but as for second and third class, they almost seemed designed for the relative body sizes of the prosperous and the poor. In third class five skinny men jammed together on one bench, whereas in second, generally speaking, only two people could fit on one bench. These two people tended to be a *nouveau riche* merchant and his wife, broad-beamed and sleek. It was a mark of a person's wealth that if you could afford to eat and eat, you ate and ate.

In many train stations a hotel was built in. There were "railway retiring rooms" you could rent by the hour to get some rest while waiting for the next train. I liked staying in railway hotels, retiring to the comfort of my room and then venturing out among the crowds, sampling food from the vendors, drinking hot cups of chai, and watching the parade of humanity crowding to their trains—trains with names like "Grand Trunk Express," "Amravati Tirupati Super Fast Express," "Grand Diamond Express." When a train pulled into the station, the place became suddenly animated. Porters swarmed around the new arrivals, vendors pressed their wares on disembarking passengers. When a train was pulling out, scores of men would rush it and try to clamber in through the windows.

Changing money on the black market in Delhi was much like changing money in Istanbul, Tehran, or Kabul. You went to a certain shop in the bazaar, usually a shop selling the gold rings, earrings, and necklaces with which Indian women like to ornament themselves. The proprietors of these shops were usually turbaned and bearded Sikhs. Once it was ascertained that the coast was clear, you would be ushered through a curtain screening off the back of the premises, where you would hand over dollars or traveler's checks to a man who would gravely count out a stack of rupees for you, and then you were on your way.

SHIVA CITY

The Ganges issues from cold springs in the Nepalese Himalayas and flows downstream across northern India to its mouth in Bangladesh on the Bay of Bengal. Along with David, a friend from the Sufi community in San Francisco, I took the train from Delhi to Varanasi, and together we rented a sparsely furnished houseboat on the sacred river.

Devout Hindus will tell you that no harm can come from the waters of the sacred river, and would that this were true. One day when I was bathing alongside the houseboat, a decomposing body floated by. It had burned only partially and they must have just thrown it into the river when they were raking out the funeral pyres. The carcass was swollen and charred, and parts of it were missing.

To avoid getting sick in India you would need to stay at one of the better hotels, drink bottled water, make sure fruits and vegetables had been peeled or washed properly. I did none of these things. Careless about hygiene, I liked sampling street food, and I did get sick. You could call this going native, or just being stupid. When I returned to Berkeley it took a few rounds of pills to flush out the intestinal parasites.

The prow of our houseboat was carved and brightly painted with representations of the Hindu gods and goddesses, and it docked near the burning *ghats*. The *ghats* were closed to tourists, but by now we had transcended that category. We were travelers and pilgrims. After dark we pulled our shawls over our heads and ventured down to the Manikarnika Ghat along the banks of river.

Life in Varanasi, as in Venice and Amsterdam, takes place on the water. Life and death inevitably find their way to the banks of the Ganges. Devout Hindus come to Varanasi from all over India, believing that to die here can set one free from the cycle of death and rebirth. Old people sew coins into the hems of their garments to pay for cremation in case they die suddenly.

We saw porters dressed in saffron yellow, with bad-looking bloodshot eyes, their skinny legs wiry and muscular, carrying litters, trotting over the hard-packed dirt of winding lanes past tough-rooted old ghosts of trees. Those litters held bodies—insubstantial bundles of orange cloth roped onto stretchers lashed together from green saplings. When the wind turned around and blew up off the river, it carried a smell of burning flesh from fires that incinerated the dead. Kites and vultures floated on the heavy air. Boats loaded to the gunwales with firewood docked along shore, the far bank of the river obscured by brown haze.

Attendants circled the blazes, men the missionaries never met—long poles in their hands to crack bones, harsh, glittering cymbals crashing in the hands of tranced musicians who accompanied the chanting, faces chapped by fire and painted with puja marks, yellow hundreds of candles blazing, eyes shiny, black, unfocused. They stoked up their *ganja* pipes with live coals off the funeral pyres. Gongs beat the thick air. The skulls of the dead exploded with loud pops, like gunshots.

And when skulls did not crack from the heat of the fires, the men who circled the blazes smashed them with long poles to speed up the incineration. Power surged on and off through low-voltage bulbs in banana trees, throwing dark rainbows into the steamy night. Lives were terminated in those fires—or did the greasy smoke and incense, the funeral coins clutched in dead hands, the weird chants of holy widows from riverbank temples carry them clear over the wide, bending river?

Nighttime was burning time. They strung up loudspeakers on poles along the river and sang *bhajans*—repetitive Hindu call-and-response devotional songs—past midnight and into the morning hours, long after we had returned from the ghats, stunned, ears ringing, heads full of unbelievable images and sounds. Hours of singing *bhajan* put the singers into altered states too. There was something crazed and scary about their voices. You would hear the praises of Krishna and Rama with repeated hypnotic phrases like *Guru Deva* and *Hari Hari* when you woke in the night in your sleeping bag on the houseboat, rocked by the lapping water of the Ganges, hearing the clandestine rustlings of water rats.

‹‹‹‹‹‹‹‹

Along the riverbanks were temples devoted to Kali, the black goddess, the scariest deity of them all. Despite our adventuresomeness and curiosity, David and I shied away from these places. Who knew what kinds of ritual sacrifice were practiced in Kali's precincts? Hinduism embraces death. Shiva is the destroyer, the god of change, and Kali is one of his wives. My name for Varanasi was Shiva City. In representations of Kali, the old girl is pictured naked and hideous, her red tongue lolling out obscenely, a necklace of skulls around her neck, her bloodshot eyes staring straight out at you, daring you to turn aside from her gaze. I have adopted Shiva as my patron saint, because of many changes and upheavals in my life. I have a little bronze statue of him in my house in Tennessee, dancing inside the wheel of karma. But I steer clear of Kali. She terrifies me.

North into the Foothills

Overloaded with impressions, shell-shocked and shaky, my friend David and I left Varanasi behind us—though you can never really leave the burning ghats behind. No one returns unchanged from Shiva City.

We headed north into the foothills of the Himalayas, just as generations in search of relief from the heat and the crowds in the cities have done, following in the footsteps of the British military and civil service folk who built the alpine chateaus and Carpenter Gothic summer cottages of the hill stations that climb the lower mountain slopes. Even though the Raj was gone, signs of it were everywhere—in the clapboard cottages of government employees on leave from their desks, in barracks and parade grounds, in the majestic government buildings built by Sir Edward Lutyens along Rajpath in Delhi, and in India's Victorian railroad stations, in the government rest houses and bungalows I sometimes stayed in, where on the doors of the rooms little slots had been fitted for residents to post their calling cards.

Like the severe, under-heated Protestant churches stranded in post-colonial Catholic Ireland, their memorial plaques polished with brasso by underpaid sextons and honoring officers who had fallen in far-flung outposts of empire from Africa to Burma, India's hill stations memorialize the receding tide of empire. Congregations in these plain pews shrank to a few arthritic widows and retired colonels in stiff tweeds and pressed flannels, and then, when this remnant died off, owls came to nest in the limestone steeples of those stiff, sparse houses of worship. Now the churches stand deserted among encroaching nettles and blackthorn, gravestones untended in the tall grass and rendered illegible by moss and brambles.

An English friend took me one day to an Indian club for retired officers in Delhi that accorded him guest privileges as a member of a club in St. James, London. Assembling an acceptable outfit to wear was not easy, since I had given or traded away all my Western clothes. The manager of my hotel lent me a necktie. The club members were all Indian by now, or Eurasian, but how British they looked and acted, with their whisky-and-sodas and their grousing about how things had gone downhill since the British pulled out in 1949! "Nothing works in this country since the British left," a kindly old Sikh colonel from a Punjab regiment confided in me as we smoked our cigars.

The government rest houses, where members of the public could stay now, offered a view of how the colonial ruling class had traveled in its high and palmy imperial days, and the kinds of digs they stayed in when they shut down their offices in Delhi and Calcutta for the summer. The rooms in these places were absurdly spacious, their ceilings impossibly high. Big fans turned at a stately pace, safe drinking water awaited in cut-glass decanters on Sheffield salvers, four-poster beds stood draped with mosquito netting riffled by the breeze, their windows opening from floor to ceiling onto terraces broad enough to accommodate a buffet supper for an entire regiment, wives and sweethearts included.

Beyond their terraces stretched views of a lake, or a vista over the immensity of the Himalayas, white row on blue row of snowy ridges and peaks extending north past the Indian tribal lands and princely kingdoms all the way into neighboring Kashmir, Nepal, and Tibet with their Northwest Frontier enclaves, their nomads, lamas, and un-governable high-country folk.

HILL STATIONS AND ASHRAMS

Like other pilgrims and seekers, we made our way north, glad to find relief in the breezy, uncrowded hill stations from the press of numbers in Delhi and the stench of death along the Ganges in Vara-nasi. At this altitude the air catches you by surprise and delights you with a freshness that blows off the high peaks. The nights are cool. In Rishikesh the Ganges drops out of the mountains and starts to level out and flow toward the sea. The river has not yet broadened into the mile-wide flood carrying topsoil, ashes, trees, bodies, and refuse that powers through Varanasi. Here it is a vigorous mountain stream with groves of trees on its banks, and ashrams where spiritual seekers stay, contributing in whatever way they can to the life of the community.

We often sojourned at these havens of tranquility and good will, eating the nutritious vegetarian fare on offer to pilgrims, meditating, doing yoga, and singing kirtans with other ashramites. Performing the *asanas* of Hatha yoga in the open air and heat of India, you knew you had found the right place for it. Many were the holy men who held court in these ashrams. Two years earlier, the Beatles had come here at the same time as Mia Farrow to stay at the ashram of Maharishi Mahesh Yogi. John Lennon paid ambiguous tribute to the Maharishi in his song "Sexy Sadie" from the Beatles' *White Album*.

Something I liked very much about Rishikesh was the *sadhus*. I had heard the word sadhu, or else I had read it somewhere, and while I grasped the principle of wandering, free-spirited ascetics, I had not been able to picture what these men looked like. Many of them wore diaper-like breech-cloths cut from voluminous lengths of fabric, and their faces were smeared with ash or chalked with I knew not what caste or Hindu ritual marks.

The sadhus are Hinduism's dervishes. Or else dervishes are Islam's sadhus. It seems the ancient world of traditional religions has always had a place for wandering seekers like these, too unorthodox and restless to be part of a regular monastic order, perhaps too unstable to stay within bounds of any kind.

One might be forgiven for thinking the sadhus went to some lengths to look just as far-out as possible. Strange as it might seem among men for whom worldly matters were not supposed to matter, I think there *was* a chic factor in the way they turned out.

As devotees of Shiva, fire played a prominent role in their lives. Their clothing was scanty, so they were always building little camp-fires to warm up around, to brew up tea. And they also liked to fire up their clay chillums, intoning lengthy prayers, ritually raising the chillum up to the crown of the head before taking monster, steamboat-whistle tokes.

NAINITAL & GURUS

David and I fell in with the entourage surrounding Baba Ram Dass. Ram Dass was the former Richard Alpert, PhD, psychedelic pioneer and former colleague of Timothy Leary at Harvard. He went to India on a spiritual quest and became a disciple of the man he and many other people called Maharaj-ji, also known as Neem Karoli Baba.

The beauty of the name Maharaj-ji is that while literally it means something like "Great King," in daily use it is an honorific so ubiquitous that it means almost nothing specific—like "Captain" or "Chief" or "Boss." Now that Maharaj-ji is no longer numbered among the living, the name allows him to slip back under the radar, to be almost anonymous in retrospect. Legends surround his memory. It was said that he worked wonders. In Vrindavan, where he lived for many years, he was known as *Chamatkari Baba*, "Miracle Baba." He was known by many names in the many different towns where he resided, and to some extent he remains a man of mystery. I can add almost nothing to what little is known about him.

Maharaj-ji would have struck many observers as little more than a toothless old man with a smile on his face, wrapped in a blanket. In Allahabad, where I first came into the holy man's presence, Ram Dass was allowed to sit by his side. He was smiling too, blissed out in the presence of his guru. One of the Hindu spiritual paths is known as *Bhakti Yoga*—the path of devotion—and this was Ram Dass's way. Neem Karoli Baba regarded himself as a devotee of Hanuman, the monkey god, the god of service, and his mission was to serve mankind. Ram Dass, like Timothy Leary, was good at slogans, and "Love, Serve, Remember" was one of his more memorable mottos.

Up to this point the phrase "hanging out" has not appeared in this narrative. But now I must use it, because in the life of spiritual devotees in India, hanging out is a lot of what one does. There is blessing, it is felt, in the presence of an evolved soul, and so you go where he is and hang out with the *satsang,* the company of those who gather around him for the guru's *darhsan. Darshan* refers to the blessing conveyed by a holy man's glance. I am using the word "blessing," but it seems a tepid word to suggest the power and understanding that can be conveyed through a glance.

Prosperous Hindu families used to come to Allahabad from the cities to spend time with their spiritual guide, loaded down with boxes of pastries and delicacies such as candy covered in gold and silver foil as offerings. The old man would pass the sweets around to those of us who sat with him. Those Brahmin families who regarded Neem Karoli Baba as their spiritual guide hosted us at their homes and served us meals, but since we were not Brahmins we had to eat separately from them.

One day David and I found ourselves on a bus going up to Nainital with Ram Dass and his entourage. How this came about, I forget. The group of us stayed in a small, family-run hotel on the lake there. If you wanted to take a bath you ordered buckets of hot water at half a rupee per bucket from the kitchen. A boy brought them up to your room.

I liked being part of Ram Dass's circle, but I never really "got" Maharaj-ji, just as Ram Dass never "got" my Sufi teachers. That is to say, meeting Neem Karoli Baba was not a life-changing event for me. He was famous within the spiritual wing of the counterculture because of Ram Dass's book, *Be Here Now.* Handset and hand-printed copies of *Be Here Now,* the pages sewn together with rough twine, were produced by a team of artists, printers, and volunteers at the Lama Foundation, a long-lived commune in the mountains outside Taos, New Mexico. Steve Durkee at Lama, also known as Nur and other names, an old friend and running buddy of mine in Chamonix, Taos, and Marin County, was the genius behind this communal project. The phrase *Be Here Now* became a mantra for our generation.

The legend and lore of Neem Karoli Baba was backstory to my days with Ram Dass and his crowd in the hill country of northern India. Ram Dass tells his story well. Prominently featured in *Be Here Now* is Maharaj-ji's clairvoyance, his ability to see into Richard Alpert's heart and learn intimate details of his life. Once Ram Dass gave some LSD-25 to Maharaj-ji, a dose large enough to put most people over the moon, or so the story goes. The disciples sat with him all afternoon, and nothing changed in Maharaj-ji's demeanor. It was as if he had ingested nothing, as though 1000 micrograms of Sandoz's finest had no more effect on his system than an aspirin tablet would have on yours or mine.

I'm not sure I ever whole-heartedly bought into the guru idea. Looking back it is clear that on the spiritual path I was never more than a temporary traveler anyway. Though I thought of Pir Vilayat Khan as my spiritual guide, my real mentors were not holy men but other writers, people like Robert Lowell and Andrew Lytle. Even writers I know only through their books, like Patrick Leigh Fermor, Edward Thomas, Karen Blixen—and Robert Byron, whose work I hadn't yet read back then. One time at Chamonix they had a hard time getting me out of my tent to perform some duty at the camp like teach a meditation class. I was inside my tent reading Gabriel García Márquez's *One Hundred Years of Solitude* and pretended not to hear them. I couldn't tear myself away from that book.

AWAY IN A MANGER

Visitors came to Nainital, dropping out of nowhere into life at the well-run little hotel by the lake. Usually they came to see Ram Dass. R. D. Laing was one of these visitors. I knew him from his books, *The Divided Self, The Self and Others,* and *The Politics of Experience.* Laing was from Scotland, one of a group of innovative psychiatric practitioners at the Tavistock Clinic in London, a place where it was hard to tell the patients from the doctors, or so people said.

Laing argued that psychiatric episodes, going mad, having a nervous breakdown—call it what you will—were best handled by letting the patient go completely through the process, the journey. Laing likened it to the story Coleridge tells in *The Ancient Mariner*. The analogy to psychedelic trips suggested itself as well.

The Scotsman had got in over his head in London. I couldn't help but think he was exaggerating, but he told me he had been taking acid and drinking half a bottle of Scotch, and sometimes the whole bottle, every day at the clinic. So you could say Laing came to India to dry out. As he saw it, he had come to find a guru. The man to whom he apprenticed himself lived nearby in Nainital, and since he meditated in a reclining position, it was hard to tell whether he was meditating or napping. It was cold in the foothills that winter, and Laing's guru's house was heated with a charcoal brazier they would let burn in the room until the room filled up with smoke. Then the windows would have to be opened, and the place got cold again.

R. D. Laing *listened* in a stronger, more emphatic way than anyone I have ever met. I put the word in italics because with Laing the quality of listening merited a completely different verb. I could see why he must have been a great doctor of the mind. He listened to what people were saying, and not only listened to what they were saying but heard what lay below the words. We celebrated Christmas at Nainital while R. D. Laing was there.

There are two tunes to "Away in a Manger," and it was the older, simpler British tune that Laing sang on Christmas morning. His clear but unemphatic voice and accent expressed compassion for the actors in that long-ago scene in Bethlehem, compassion for us all. The singer's deep loneliness made the manger scene stand out in a highlighted, mythic way, almost as if it were being pictured in a Byzantine icon.

GREEN TARA

A girlfriend of mine back in Sonoma County once embroidered, at my request, a picture of a skull onto the black *zafu* I used for sitting. Many in our *satsang* in Nainital were drawn to bare-bones, stripped-down disciplines like Vipassana meditation. Vipassana, like Zen, is about mindfulness, clarity, and attention to the moment. The tradition comes from Southeast Asia. The teacher I studied with in Bodh Gaya was Burmese. If Zen is the mountains, Vipassana is the lowlands.

Vipassana clears the mind. But was there any room among the minimal brushstrokes of Zen sensibility or in the silences of the Burmese meditation hall for the dramas of human passion, the fire of romantic poetry? Pilgrims on the spiritual path sometimes acknowledged these fires and passions, but only as part of their colorful pasts. St. Augustine sowed his wild oats and later wrote about them in his *Confessions*. Bob Dylan's song, "Tangled Up in Blue," has always spoken to me, with its story of a lifelong, on-again-off-again romance:

> She opened up a book of poems
> And handed it to me
> Written by an Italian poet
> From the thirteenth century.
> And every one of them words ran true
> And glowed like burning coals,
> Pouring off of every page
> Like it was written in my soul,
> Brought me to you,
> Tangled up in blue.

Poetry, romantic love, a sense of destiny—did they have any place on the spiritual path? Buddhism doesn't even admit the existence of the individual soul, does it? Everything is part of—what? Universal mind, energy? How could two people be soul mates if there is no such thing as the soul? For me the severity of the religion of the Awakened One is leavened by female figures in Tibetan Buddhism like the Green Tara and the Chinese Kwan Yin, goddess of mercy.

The austerities of Islamic doctrine and practice are humanized too—somewhat—by the romance of the stories that surround the life of the Prophet, his wives, and his children, and unattested stories and sayings recorded in the Hadiths. The mystical writings of Ibn al-Arabi and Jelal-ad-din Rumī present the dance of creation itself as a romance. Rumi's idea that God only discovers himself as we, his creatures and extensions of his consciousness, discover ourselves, is appealing. David the Psalmist, in Rumi's poem, asks God why he cre-

ated the world. "I was a hidden treasure," the Lord replies, "and I cre-
ated a world in order that I might be known."

BHARAT AND INDIA

Ram Dass used to say that he had not come to India, he had come to
Bharat—in other words to mythical India, spiritual India, land of sad-
hus and yogis. Bhārata was the ancient Hindu name for the subconti-
nent, for what is now India, Pakistan, and Bangladesh. In the days of
the great Muslim empires these lands were called Hindustan. I think
I also preferred Bharat, but that ideal land was illusory, more a state
of mind than a place. The Raj was a living presence for me, and I was
also drawn to ghostly places like the British cemetery outside Dehra-
dun, the spooky deserted Mughal palace at Fatehpur Sikri, and the Taj
Mahal. David and I went to Agra to see the Taj at the full of the moon.

Shah Jehan built the Taj Mahal of marble as translucent as alabas-
ter, and his architect engineered it as much for acoustics as for the
beauty of its appearance. It glows in the moonlight almost as though
it were made of moonlight itself, as though the moonlight in Agra
had formed itself into a shapely, domed temple that vibrated at just
the right pitch.

I doubt, though, if it had the right vibration for our rickshaw *wal-
lah*'s cough. The one who cycled us out to the Taj. He was so skinny,
his legs looked like birds' legs. He had no spare flesh on his body to
keep off the chill. I won't try to say I forgot the rickshaw *wallah* while I
was inside the famous monument of the Empress Mumtaz Mahal. In-
side, the place was lit up with moonlight and everyone was delighted
to be there, shyly and tentatively singing different tones and tunes
that echoed in those moonlit marble spaces.

When we left the Taj hours later, there was our rickshaw *wallah*
waiting to pedal us back into town. Part of the route climbed a steep
hill, so steep that we got out and walked. At the end of our journey
David gave his cashmere shawl to the man. Even with that, we didn't
feel good; we felt like a burden. We had entered the world of India,
and we didn't like the role we played in the equation of rich and poor,
poor and rich.

»»»»»»

Once, in Rishikesh, we spent part of the afternoon with a sadhu we called Chillum Baba and afterward took a walk along the Ganges to a part of town we had never seen before. As we strolled along the unpaved road I was mildly puzzled to see, among the usual chai stands and food stalls where spicy pakoras and fried dal were cooked and the air was drenched with their oily fragrance, blankets spread out with big pyramids of almost worthless small-denomination coins, meticulously stacked. One rupee would buy a whole stack of these coins, oddly shaped, some of them, and minted from light, flimsy tin. It didn't occur to me to wonder greatly about this. One sees incongruous and inexplicable things all the time in India.

As we kept walking we came across people sitting on blankets spread out beside the path, swaddled in shawls and scarves. As we passed one such blanket a man raised one of his limbs. And without being able to see that blighted appendage—he kept it covered with his shawl—suddenly we knew what this place was. We had wandered into a leper colony. That was what the pyramids of small coins were all about—for visitors to give to the afflicted ones. The place must have been run by some Hindu charity.

One woman with parts of her face missing set up a regular keening wail from which there was no escaping. The first importuning sick man who had raised his stricken limb was but the first of many, and we were on this little road or track from which there were only two ways out: turn back or keep going. We kept going. It was hard. No—what it was, was horrifying. These people wanted our attention, and of course our charity. Too bad we hadn't spent a few rupees back along the path and picked up pocketsful of those flimsy coins. I wonder if in the colony itself, or in the surrounding town even, those coins could buy anything worth buying. Or was collecting the coins something more like collecting glass beads thrown from the floats at some ghastly Mardi Gras?

Finally, after what seemed an eternity, after having given away our rupees, we made it through. We were in shock, and joking about it didn't help. But we were right beside the Ganges as it churned between its banks, the water blue-gray with the limestone that was in it. We both waded in, and splashed the mountain-cold water on our faces and arms to try to wash away the shock of it all.

A SLAP UPSIDE THE HEAD

"Love, Serve, Remember" is not the writer's motto. True, we all need love. Life doesn't make sense without it. But do writers serve? Maybe some feel they do: Kipling probably felt that way. I think the writer lives to make connections and to communicate. Above all, his mission is to make things—to make shapely constructions out of words. He is a maker. He shares with the devotees of Hanuman the injunction to remember, though he uses memory not to inspire good works, but to make something—a poem, a work of fiction, an essay, a newspaper article, a song.

When I told Ram Dass about my fantasy of returning from India to California and taking up my romance with an old flame, he said that was *maya,* the world of illusion. But my life was stubbornly making its claims on me in a way that would not be clear to someone like Ram Dass. The writer has to live in the world of phenomena, illusory or not. He has to get tangled up in blue. At the time I didn't understand my own path well enough to explain that it was not under the star of Hanuman that poets live. Our guiding spirit, our harbor, the Penelope at the end of our journey, is the White Goddess, the Green Tara, the Muse.

On our way north, David and I spent a few days in Dehradun, where we had been told to look up an old Brahmin who performed puja in a Hindu temple there. We found the man, known to us only as Baba, and went to the temple every day to discourse with him. I loved listening to Baba, loved the temple, loved its human dimension, the way people came and went as it suited them, buying garlands from the flower sellers on the temple steps to drape around the necks of the statues of the gods and goddesses, lighting a stick of incense, pouring ghee over the Shiva lingam. Monkeys scampered in and out trying to steal the fruit people left as offerings.

Everyone was welcome at the temple. There was no formal service, as there would be in a church or a mosque. The pujas looked spontaneous and chaotic, the hand drums and tinkling bells and crashing cymbals guided by an invisible score. During one of our discourses over in a corner of the temple my mind must have wandered, because Baba suddenly looked hard at me and demanded, "Do you understand? Do you understand?" Then he slapped me hard on the side of my head. And yes, suddenly I understood.

Eastward Bound,
Across a Storied Landscape

Leaving Portland, with its microbreweries, drive-through coffee stations, Pacific Rim restaurants, and lumberjack chic, I drove east along the Columbia River Gorge on the first leg of a four-thousand-mile trip that would take me to northern Michigan and then down to South Carolina and Tennessee. The Gorge's mist-wreathed granite cliffs, rising above the onrush of the Columbia River, looked as though they could have been painted by a Chinese landscape artist from the Tang Dynasty. In late-afternoon light the stone took on a purple glow. From the look of things, Taoist hermits might be meditating in caves up in those hills.

Above White Salmon in the state of Washington, where I spent my first night, it seemed that pioneer days had not ended. As I drove up precipitous roads that reached up from the Columbia River, some of the hillsides had that desolate shredded look that follows clear-cutting. One little house, a shack really, was flanked on one side by a pile of rough-cut logs, each about the length of a big American car

69

from the fifties. It looked as though the householder had wrangled them there for sizing into smaller chunks as fuel was needed during the long winter. The month was May, but a sharp wind sliced across the hills. My nephew Richard and I took his son, six years old, to his baseball game down in White Salmon. The diamond, with its boys' and girls' coach-pitch three-inning game, and the pure Americanness of the scene, was thrown into perspective by the massive hills towering above, verdant with the spring rains.

The following morning I woke at five in the rough-hewn guest house my nephew had built behind his vegetable garden. No one in the household was stirring; the rooster crowed as I pulled out. Once I had descended the hill to White Salmon, I drove along the Columbia River on Interstate 84 with a cup of tea from Starbucks in the cup holder between the seats of my Honda and morning news from National Public Radio as a soundtrack, then veered south on US-97, free of traffic except for the occasional truck. Vast acreage, big ranches with sparse cattle grazing the big rounded hills. Somewhere along the way I became aware that the needle on my gas gauge was dropping low. The day was cold and rain whipped across the highway as I turned into what looked like a filling station beside the road where a yellow school bus was fueling.

The bus left just as I pulled in beside a truck with "Explosives. Drilling Equipment" painted on the driver's door. The driver was a rough-looking man in his fifties with a broad gray moustache who was talking on his cellphone. "Naw," he was saying loudly to the person on the other end of the conversation, "You have to yank out right smart on the throttle as soon as you start her." As he stepped out of the cab to talk to me, I could not help but notice the large box of Trojans on the seat beside him, and I thought about their relevance to the business the writing on his truck advertised.

This man cheerfully informed me that the gas pumps were accessible only if you had a certain kind of card which entitled you to use them, which I did not have. How far was the nearest gas station? In Madras, he said, hitting the first syllable hard, pronouncing the name in a way purely innocent of the city in India. How far is that? I pursued. Forty miles south. Oh hell, I said confidently, I can go forty miles, and got back in the Honda, leaving him to his cell phone and his Trojans.

It was not reassuring to see a sign less than a mile further along that read "Madras, 56 miles." The needle touched empty. I began to worry, alternating with periods where I was able to convince myself of the beauty of living in the moment. And the scenery *was* gorgeous—vast ranchland with few houses of any description other than the occasional stock pen fashioned from fieldstone and rough-cut logs, gates opening here and there onto roads that appeared to lead nowhere except off into the empty hills. A sign announced, "Elk Crossing."

Not a good place to run out of gas. Elk appeared to be the theme, as an Adopt-A-Highway sign let drivers know that this stretch of road was cared for by the Madras Elks Club. Good to know. My low-fuel indicator lit up just then, and I started trying to calculate how much gas I really did have left. After climbing to a considerable altitude, the road began to slope downhill, and I cut my engine, put the Honda in neutral, and coasted. I have seldom been so glad to see a town as I was to see Madras, which I now delightedly pronounced to myself in the vernacular. Before I gassed up, only a tenth of a gallon was left in my tank.

Just north of Bend, the terrain became high desert—barren fields with wind-stunted cedars, sagebrush, and rocky outcroppings. I turned east through the pleasant, prosperous town of Bend on US Highway 20, a two-lane blacktop that bisects the state laterally all the way to the Idaho border. Rain whipped across the road, and then— what were those broad, feathery drops? Snowflakes? Yes, snowflakes, and this was the 22nd of May. Then peppery shots of sleet, or was that hail? Whatever it was, I didn't like the look of it, even with good tires and a full tank of gas. This is not the sort of place you'd want to have to cope with a blizzard—easily possible, common even, in the high desert.

The road climbed to over forty-five hundred feet. I was glad to reach Burns, the only town of any size along this stretch of Highway 20. This is cattle country, and into the McDonald's where I was having lunch three ranch hands in cowboy boots asserted themselves, jeans stained with mud, one in a weather-beaten cowboy hat, the other two

wearing the baseball cap that is part of the national costume through-
out most of North America.

A NIGHT IN BURNS

Like many American communities, Burns appears to have been the
creation of one man. An early settler and merchant called George
McGowan named the town not after himself, as he might have felt
entitled to do, but after Robert Burns, whom McGowan admired as a
poet of the common man. Within its first decade Burns had acquired
stores, a post office, and a couple of hotels, and McGowan was the
town's first postmaster. In its early years, mining and lumber brought
settlers to this remote part of Oregon. But cattle ranching was intro-
duced to the region as early as the 1860s and flourished after passage
of the Desert Land Act of 1877, which made 320-acre plots available to
hardy souls willing to "reclaim, irrigate, and cultivate" the land. The
town was incorporated in the 1880s. Cattle, hay, and horses remain
the main commodities bought and sold in Burns.

I stopped for the night at the Silver Spur, mainly because of the
name. When I opened the little rear window of my motel room, I
found I was looking into someone's back yard. A old man who walked
with difficulty was splitting kindling on the stump of what once must
have been a huge tree right behind his house—a frontier dwelling
faced with rough-cut sections of logs chinked inexpertly with ce-
ment, the roof shingled with rusty sections of tin nailed on so that
they overlapped one another.

Projecting from the back of the house proper was a shed, older
than the house itself, fashioned of big blocks of the same stone used in
the stock shelters I saw along the highway. I am guessing that the stone
shed was built first, then the log house was added later. To satisfy my
curiosity, the next morning before leaving Burns I drove around to
the little street behind the motel. From that vantage point the house I
saw through the back window of the motel turned out to be, in front,
a comparatively modern-looking clapboard structure. The house rep-
resented a museum of Burns's modest architectural history.

Bikers like Highway 20, and the Silver Spur is a popular hostelry for them. As I sat there typing, several rugged shaved-head men roared up. When they dismounted, I saw that one man was missing a leg. King of the road on his Harley, he walked unmounted with an aluminum crutch—none the less cocky though, a blue bandanna wrapped around his neck, smart-looking in his gray goatee and studded leather jacket emblazoned with his club's standard, a red heart out of which emerged the spokes of a wheel.

Every now and then one stumbles into a really good restaurant along the road. The one where I ate that night was a throwback to the 1950s. First the sexy waitress brought out a little shrimp cocktail with pink shrimp on a bed of shredded iceberg lettuce served with a sauce sharply redolent of horseradish. Next she served up a bowl of peppery chili. Then an undistinguished salad—forgivable within the context of the cold IPA they had on draft, which I drank cold pints of—followed by a twelve-ounce, top-round steak, seared but genuinely rare, next to a big baked potato topped with sour cream and butter. The best kind of old-fashioned American restaurant meal.

Back in my car to my room at the Silver Spur. After that meal, I figured a baseball game would be just the thing. Instead I found a TV show called "Unsolved." UFOs. Seems that a Frisbee-shaped aircraft came down from the sky and landed on a remote blacktop road in New Mexico. A local couple witnessed the landing, which left a circular burned spot on the pavement. When they went there the next day with their camera for a second look, what do you think they found? Well, someone had come along with a truckload of asphalt and re-paved the road. There was no sign at all of the landing. My goodness!

WAGONHOUND ROAD

The West is its own distinct place. As you drive from progressive coastal Oregon and Washington, the political climate shades from blue to red. "Get the US out of the UN," a billboard demands. Proceeding east on four-lane interstate highways through Oregon, Idaho, and Wyoming, one is retracing—moving in the opposite direction—

the route that Lewis and Clark took on their expedition, the route that later became the Oregon Trail. The trail was so steep in places that pioneers lashed ropes to trees and laboriously lowered their wagons down hills hand over hand. Life was hard, existence bristled with dangers. Stinkingwater Creek and Bitter Creek tell a tale of thirst in an arid land.

Place names along the highway indicate that those days are not so very far behind us. Massacre Rocks near American Falls in Idaho, now a state park that runs along the south bank of the Snake River, was also known as the "Gate of Death" or "Devil's Gate." Passage through here was narrow, and emigrants making their way through on the Oregon Trail feared ambush by Indians. Settlers traveling in a convoy of five covered-wagon trains were attacked by Shoshone on August 9–10, 1862. Ten emigrants died in the fight.

Place names like Lodgepole and Medicine Bow are encrypted with the conflicting histories of settlers and Indians. Laramie takes its name from a French trader, Jacques LaRamie, who disappeared into these hills in 1810 and was never heard from again. Cheyenne takes its name from a Native American tribe, but it is a cowboy town. These are names to conjure with. Even a tourist-focused billboard for Cheyenne acknowledges the myth of the West. "Live the Legend," the sign advises. Another billboard announces "We Buy Antlers. Top Dollar Paid." There's a toll-free number to call.

I descended from mountainous Idaho into Wyoming. Where did Wagonhound Road in western Wyoming get its name from? A little research told me the territory around Wagonhound Road has played a role in western transportation since the earliest days of human activity in the Rocky Mountain West. Teepee rings from 10,000 years ago indicate that people have camped here for centuries. In the 1850s a Captain Howard Stansbury led an expedition through to scout out potential routes for the Union Pacific Railroad. In the 1860s a stagecoach route followed the trail from Elk Mountain through Rattlesnake Pass on the mountain's north flank. But why "Wagonhound"? From the sound of it, the name must be a corruption of some other word, German maybe. Yet when you see the word, don't you picture a hungry dog slinking around the wagon trains looking for food?

To get a feeling for the history of Oregon, Idaho, and Wyoming, and even of Nebraska farther to the east, I was traveling in the wrong direction. American history is a westward-moving phenomenon, and the distances are so great that roads become both necessities and icons. It is a horizontal landscape. Freight trains rattle through, long and frequent. High desert terrain gives way eastward to high plains, to arable land planted with alfalfa and winter wheat. Tractors plowing for the spring planting kick up clouds of dust.

As you cross over into Wyoming, you become more aware of the sky. It stretches vast and broad as the landscape flattens out. Annie Proulx is the writer who has most distinctively put her stamp on this part of the West. I thought of one of her paragraphs as I drove east along I-80:

> The country appeared as empty ground, big sagebrush, rabbitbrush, intricate sky, flocks of small birds like packs of cards thrown up in the air, and a faint track drifting toward the red-walled horizon. Graves were unmarked, fallen house timbers and corrals burned up in old campfires. Nothing much but weather and distance, the distance punctuated once in a while by ranch gates, and to the north the endless murmur and sun-flash of semis rolling along the interstate.

Driving these distances as part of that endless murmur and sun-flash, you provide your own soundtrack, either from local radio or your iPod. Coming down US-97 through Oregon I listened to Neil Young. His western intonation, the beautiful naïveté of his high register—it all fit the countryside I was driving through. And at a certain point during any road trip I started to feel like listening to Willie Nelson. Quint-essential American road music. Once or twice on these trips I have even managed to synchronize listening to the Band singing "Across the Great Divide" with crossing the Continental Divide. Gram Parsons is another musical presence for me whenever I get out on the highway:

> I headed west to grow up with the country,
> Crossed those prairies with those waves of grain.
> And I saw my devil, and I saw my deep blue sea,
> And I thought about a calico bonnet from Cheyenne
>   to Tennessee.

We flew straight across that river bridge
Last night half-past two.
The switchman waved his lantern goodbye and good day
As we went rolling through.
Billboards and truck stops passed by the grievous angel—
And now I know just what I have to do.

But classical music fits this majestic landscape too, perhaps even better than songs about roads and highways and trucks and bridges. There's nothing like passing eighteen-wheelers at ninety miles per hour while listening to the last movement of Beethoven's Ninth. My early-morning drive east out of Oregon from Burns was accompanied by Brahms's String Sextet No. 1 in B-flat major, first published in 1862. Europe and America—two very different places. While we were fighting our Civil War, Vienna and Paris were listening to new chamber music by Brahms.

BIG NOSE GEORGE

I limped into Rawlins, Wyoming late one afternoon after driving four or five hundred miles—hot, dehydrated, unshaven, and road-weary. Once I had found a motel and had a wash, I set out to see what kind of town I had fetched up in. Rawlins, it turns out, was named for John Aaron Rawlins, a general in the Civil War, who camped there a couple of years after the Union victory, having moved west in search of dryer air on account of his tuberculosis.

General Rawlins, who had no military training of any kind, played a peculiar role in the Civil War. Ulysses S. Grant was a good general when sober, but he had a weakness for the bottle, and Rawlins, his closest friend and confidant, served as aide-de-camp and Chief of Staff, keeping an eye on Grant and making sure he stayed away from alcohol. After the war, Grant appointed him Secretary of War, but Rawlins died from tuberculosis a few months into his term. A photograph shows him and Grant on campaign, with a private standing at attention behind them. Rawlins, in an unmilitary-looking, high-crowned hat, has his eyes fixed sternly on his superior, as if he is afraid to let the general out of his sight. The photograph is amusing if you know the backstory.

I learned that the town of Rawlins provided a stage for the last act in the life of George Parrott, "Big Nose George," who also went by the names George Manuse and George Warden. It's a story so truly western and bizarre that a Hollywood scriptwriter sitting by the pool in Beverly Hills would have been hard pressed to make it up. Big Nose George was an outlaw and cattle rustler who was hanged by a lynch mob in Rawlins in 1881, the year of the town's founding. Perhaps the town's incorporation and the rough justice administered to the outlaw were signs of Rawlins's coming of age as a civilized community. Or, as we shall see, perhaps not.

‹‹‹‹‹‹‹‹

In 1878, Parrott and his gang murdered two law enforcement officers—Wyoming deputy sheriff Robert Widdowfield and Tip Vincent, a detective for the Union Pacific Railway—while trying to escape after robbing a train on a remote stretch of track along the Medicine Bow River. On orders to track down Parrott's gang, Widdowfield and Vincent found the outlaws camped on a hot August day at Rattlesnake Canyon, not far from Wagonhound Road near Elk Mountain. One of the gang who had been posted as a lookout saw the lawmen coming and alerted his companions. The robbers stamped out their campfire and hid in the brush, guns drawn.

When Widdowfield and Vincent arrived at the scene and had a look around, they discovered that the ashes of the fire were still hot. Just as they started to look for the outlaws, the gang opened fire and Widdowfield was shot in the face. Vincent tried to escape, but was shot in the back before he made it out of the canyon. The gang stole both men's weapons and horses, then covered up the bodies and fled. The murder of the two lawmen came to light and a ten-thousand-dollar reward was offered for their capture.

In February 1879, Big Nose George and his cohort found themselves in Milestown, Montana. Word got around the saloons, livery stables, and whorehouses of Milestone that a man named Morris Cahn, a local merchant, would be taking money east on a buying trip to replenish his stock of merchandise. Cahn was traveling in a heavily armed convoy with an ambulance and a wagon from Fort Keogh, guarded by fifteen soldiers and two officers on their way to collect the army payroll. Big Nose George, his sidekick Charlie Burris, also known as "Dutch Charlie," and two other outlaws managed to ambush and overpower this formidable assemblage in a deep ravine now known as Cahn's Coulee, near a crossing of the Powder River in Montana.

Soldiers, ambulance, and wagon got strung out along the trail. The gang, wearing masks, were waiting at a bend in the trail at the bottom of the coulee. They surprised and captured the vanguard of soldiers, then seized the ambulance containing Cahn and the officers. Having accomplished this, they lay in wait with the wagon for the rest of the soldiers. Accounts vary, but it appears that Big Nose George relieved Cahn of somewhere between $3,600 and $14,000—a lot of money back in those days.

In 1880, following the robbery, the law caught up with Big Nose George Parrott and Charlie Burris in Miles City after Big Nose and Dutch Charlie got drunk and boasted of killing the two lawmen. Parrott was brought back to face murder charges in Wyoming, and a jury sentenced him to hang on April 2, 1881, but—always resourceful— George tried to escape while being held at a jail in Rawlins. He filed the rivets of the heavy shackles on his ankles, using a pocket knife and a piece of sandstone. Having removed his shackles, he hid in the wash- room until the jailor, a man named Rankin, came to check on him. Parrott struck the jailor over the head with his shackles, fracturing his skull. Rankin managed to fight back and call to his wife, Rosa, for help.

Flourishing a pistol, Rosa forced Parrott back into his cell. Once news of the escape attempt spread through Rawlins, a crowd assem- bled. While Rankin lay recovering, masked men brandishing pistols burst into the jail. Holding the jailer at gunpoint, they took his keys, then dragged Parrott from his cell and strung him up from a tele- graph pole. Charlie Burris met with a similar fate not long after his capture. He was being returned to Rawlins for trial when a group of locals found him hiding in a baggage compartment and hanged him from the crossbeam of a nearby telegraph pole.

But the story does not end there. The doctors who took possession of the corpse decided they wanted to study Big Nose's brain in hopes of gaining insight into the mind of an outlaw. So they sawed off the top of Parrott's skull, the cap of which they presented to fifteen-year-old Lillian Heath, who was then a medical assistant to one of the doctors in town. Heath went on to become the first female doctor in Wyoming and is said to have used the cap—depending on her mood, I suppose— as an ashtray, pen holder, and doorstop. Someone also made a death mask of Parrott, and skin from his thighs and chest was removed.

The skin—including, we are told, the dead man's nipples—was sent to a tannery in Denver, where an enterprising leather worker made it into a pair of shoes and a medical bag. These items were kept by one of the doctors, John Eugene Osborne, who wore the shoes to his inaugural ball after being elected as the first Democratic Governer of Colorado. But no, it didn't stop there. Parrott's dismembered body was stored in a whiskey barrel filled with a salt solution for about a year while these resourceful medical men continued to run experiments on him, until finally he was buried in the yard behind the doctor's office.

In 1950, while working on the Rawlins National Bank on Cedar Street in Rawlins, construction workers unearthed a whiskey barrel filled with bones. Inside the barrel was a skull with the top sawed off, and the shoes made from skin from Parrott's thighs. Dr. Lillian Heath, then in her eighties, was contacted and the skull cap from her office was sent to the scene. It was found to fit the skull in the barrel perfectly. DNA testing later confirmed that the remains were indeed those of Big Nose George.

Today the shoes fashioned from the skin of Big Nose George are on display at the Carbon County Museum in Rawlins, together with the bottom part of the outlaw's skull and Big Nose George's earless death mask. The shackles used during the hanging of the outlaw, as well as the skull cap, are on display at the Union Pacific Museum in Omaha. The medicine bag made from his skin has never been found.

THE WEST AND THE MIDWEST

Well into May the mountain peaks are dusted with snow, but the journey east is a descent, and not just topographically. One feels a certain sadness about leaving behind the heroic and bizarre history of the Old West. The heroic West of pioneers on the Oregon Trail, the outlandish West of outlaws and lawmen, receded as I drove eastward through Nebraska. No more rock formations, no more sand and sagebrush, no more bizarre stories about big-nosed outlaws, no more cowboys having lunch at McDonald's, no more blast and drilling equipment men driving the hills of eastern Oregon with a box of Trojans on the seat beside them.

Spring gave way to summer as I drove, and with summer came the big Midwestern rains. The pastures glowed emerald green, and in fields that had already been sown, the young plants, too, were green. I felt more relaxed now that I had passed beyond the rocky aridity of the West. Spring greenery refreshes the traveler's spirit; the highway is easier to drive. Pickup trucks with gun racks and horse trailers give way to cars with "Baby On Board" stickers on their rear windshields.

More cars. Traffic. There is still something untamed about Nebraska, at least through its western reaches. Nebraska is, after all, the home state of John Wayne. But here the West gives way, with great sadness it seems to me, to the Midwest. As I travelled east on I-80, I saw that more land was plowed now. Grain elevators rose into the cloudless sky, and suddenly my nostrils were assaulted by a noxious stench. A few hundred yards further along, I found the source of it. Penned-up cattle, several acres of them, milled dispiritedly around inside their fences. One of the worst smells in the West. Beef for Eastern steakhouses.

Passing from Iowa into western Illinois, I crossed the Mississippi River. Cole Porter's "Don't Fence Me In," which my mother used to play on the piano, includes the lines, "I want to ride to the ridge where the west commences, / Gaze at the moon till I lose my senses." Run that sentiment backward and you're on the freeway in Illinois, skirting the edge of Chicago through ever-coagulating traffic, heading sensibly east.

IRELAND AND
THE WORLD

A Village on Galway Bay

Kinvara perches on the shores of Galway Bay at the southern edge of the County Galway. Nine pubs address the thirst of its four hundred inhabitants. Well past its prime as a fishing village but still a lovely spot, the town stands at the edge of the Burren, a limestone moonscape combed by deep fissures out of which an epiphany of wildflowers emerges in May. Kinvara is the center of a farming community where the milk and meat of pasture, root crops and loads of hay, come by hoof or wagon down to market. In bygone days turf boats sailed over from Connemara, loaded to the gunwales with fuel. Firewood is scarce here.

The salt-stung, rain-cleansed air thickens with a smudge of turf smoke. White seagulls glide overhead, and in the convent beeches above the road, rooks croak, jackdaws chatter. High tide pounds stone walls along the harbor and throws sea-spray up onto the road.

The town's main street presents a vista of broad-shouldered Georgian row-houses. Three and four stories tall, fashioned of limestone in the eighteenth and nineteenth centuries, some of these buildings are faced in plaster and painted bright pastels, their slate roofs rain-slick, aglow with creeper and the green brilliance of mosses. Against the elemental energies of the sea they rise defiantly in the face of wet weather and gale-force winds off the Atlantic, taking a stand on behalf of human existence. These rooted verticals hold a fleshy hand, palm outward, against what Robert Lowell called "the earth-shaker, green, unwearied, chaste / In his steel scales." No force off the Atlantic, one feels, could threaten their angles or budge their masses.

One of the best places in Ireland to listen to traditional music, Kinvara is also home to a community of artists, writers, scholars, gardeners, and musicians who have brought new energy to a village that at one time was dying, its population depleted by immigration. Many of these people are blow-ins, some from other towns and counties in Ireland, some Dutch, some English, some German, even a scattering of Americans.

Poets and musicians, organic growers, practitioners of homeopathic medicine live here. John Prine keeps a house near Kinvara. Liadain O'Donovan, Frank O'Connor's daughter, moved here decades ago from San Francisco and lives in a thatched cottage just above the town on the Galway road. Caoilte Breathnach, a folklorist and singer of traditional songs, lives up the Gort Road with his Dutch wife.

Until his death, the Irish ceramicist John ffrench had a home on the nearby Doorus Peninsula, which juts out into Galway Bay. John brought a Mediterranean sense of color to Irish pottery, and even to his house, which stood out among the traditional farmhouses and newly built holiday homes. He and his American wife Primm painted the trim of their whitewashed cottage powder blue and the corrugated tin roof of John's studio lemon-yellow. Since these happen to be the colors of the Clare football side, locals referred to John and Primm's place as "the Clare house."

On the Doorus Peninsula an excellent public house, the Travellers Inn, serves as an informal community center for the journalists, photographers, and authors who live among the farmers and the fishermen. Jeff O'Connell, the dean of local historians, lives in Doorus. When I moved my family to Kinvara for a year in the early nineties, Jeff and I became friends. We used to venture out to look at out-of-the-way churches, or talk our way into Anglo-Irish castles, wrapping up our day in a country pub.

Kinvara and the countryside surrounding it are dotted with holy wells, the ruins of big houses from Anglo-Irish days, prehistoric monuments, "fairy rings," and suchlike. Jeff published a set of maps of the area, carefully drawn and illustrated by Anne Korff, a German artist who also lives out on the peninsula. Folded many a time, taped together again after coming apart with hard use, some of my copies of these maps still stand on the bookshelves in my house in Tennessee, firing pangs of nostalgia and a desire to return.

The Kinvara community is close and caring, and my family and I were welcomed into the heart of it. We are not Catholics, but my wife Mary sang in the church choir, and my children attended the national school in the village. My two younger boys, Andrew and Charles, ran wild with lads from the town, joining the warring "armies" that reen-acted battles from the Troubles up at High Rock, a settlement aban-doned during the famine, where they played IRA vs. Black and Tans.

At the national school my daughter Julia attended, she learned firsthand about Irish class consciousness and the rigidity of a pecking order not visible to outsiders. While corporal punishment was legally forbidden in the schools, it was still practiced, though selectively. The headmaster never laid a hand on the children of locally prominent citizens such as the strong farmers, publicans, grocers, and other tradesmen—and certainly not the offspring of a visiting American poet who wrote occasionally for *The Irish Times*. But rude farm boys from hardscrabble mountainy acres felt the back of the headmaster's hand.

‹‹‹‹‹‹‹‹

A decade ago, before the Irish housing bubble burst, I revisited Kin-vara and found that many changes had occurred. Development and pollution of the bay were common topics of conversation. Traffic on Main Street had become formidable; Kinvara had now acquired both a morning and an evening rush hour. The attractive and well-constructed houses in Mike Burke's luxury Cuan An Óir (Gold Coast) development were on the market for one million euro and more, yet long-time residents owning land outside the town were having difficulty getting planning permission.

Some feared that Kinvara's unique character and quality of life might be lost if no one but the rich could afford to live there. Houses bought as second homes stood empty much of the year in what are called, with the Irish gift for turning a phrase, "ghost estates." Many people lamented the absence of any provision for new low-income housing. Others, such as publican Michael Connolly, welcomed the new development. "When I left school," he told me once, "eleven out of fourteen in my class had to go abroad. The place was dead."

Jeff O'Connell recalls that when he first moved to Kinvara in 1974 there was no butcher, no place to buy groceries other than a few canned goods and a loaf of bread in Tully's, a small combination shop and pub on the main street. People bought necessities from the traveling grocer who drove around the countryside in his truck. Yet, even with the new prosperity, few of my friends' children could afford to live in Kinvara. There were few jobs outside tourism.

On the cover of the Cuan An Óir brochure, a locally-built Galway hooker, the Mac Duach, floats on tranquil Kinvara Bay with Dungaire Castle in the background. There's no more beautiful sight in Ireland. Kinvara is known far and wide for its Cruinniú na mBád, the festival of the boats, which takes place every year in August. But until recently, all has not been well beneath the surface of the bay. Sewage treatment facilities were, for mysterious reasons, not required of new developments. The town's raw sewage—seventy thousand gallons a day—issued directly into the bay through a pipe only about forty yards in length. A release valve designed to shut off at low tide had corroded and was stuck in the "open" position. If you sailed from Crushua to Kinvara, you could see a line of raw sewage coming out into the bay. It was not a pretty sight.

Kinvara Bay is a basin, partially but not completely flushed out by the tides. A brackish underground river empties into the saltwater bay, bringing agricultural run-off into already polluted water. The resultant eutrophication, or artificial enrichment, causes algae to grow.

When algae die they turn brown and give off a sulfurous smell. Seen from above, the demarcation between the brown waters of Kinvara Bay and the blue waters of Galway Bay made a startling contrast. Finally the Irish government responded to Kinvara's concerns about the quality of its water, and a sewage treatment plant is in place.

<<<<<<<<

In Ireland as elsewhere, places are becoming non-places. Perhaps it's a normal process. As cities grow, towns and villages merge and then become neighborhoods of the encroaching city. Urban sprawl in Galway City, seventeen miles up the road, creeps closer every day. Oranmore has effectively disappeared as a separate entity. If the Bucks of Oranmore of the traditional reel were to return to their old home today, they would not recognize the place. My heart sank as I drove past the barrack-like rows of houses in a treeless development called Oak Wood outside Ballindereen. "Oak Wood" ironically echoes the town's Irish name, *Baile an Doirín*, "townland of the little oak grove."

For many years, Winkles Hotel on the square was the only hostelry in Kinvara. Tiffy Winkle was one of west of Ireland's great characters, and both Peter O'Toole and Robert Mitchum could do imitations of her. Conversing with a stranger, she would interject questions such as "And would those be your own teeth?" or "What do you call that color your hair is now?"

Winkles did not have the snugs made of natural wood, the Old World coziness of what we think of as the traditional Irish pub. "Traditional" is a contested concept. Some people suggest that an Irish pub is not traditional unless it has a TV over the bar showing horse races or football. That's the kind of place Winkles was: black formica instead of pine, 1950s Irish modern, redolent of years of tobacco smoke and porter.

Where Winkles once stood, a shopping mall had gone up on the square. It occupied half a block. Before the wrecking ball went to work, I peeked through the windows of Winkles, where Niamh Parsons and Seán and Dolores Keane once sang, where Seán Smyth,

Brendan Larrissey, and Frankie Gavin played the fiddle, along with button-accordion players Jackie Daly, Charlie Piggott, and Sharon Shannon when she was still an unknown. The wooden floor for set dancing was littered with builders' debris. The limestone fireplace-surround that came from an old house in the country and installed here had been ripped out of the wall.

The Dead Alive and Busy

Books speak with the living voices of those who have written them, whether recently or years ago. In significant ways, their authors live forever. This must have been what Shakespeare meant when he wrote, "Not marble nor the gilded monuments / Of princes shall outlive this powerful rhyme." Everything written forms part of a historical palimpsest, with more accretions than erasures. The seventeenth-century poet Henry Vaughan, in a poem called "To His Books," compares books to the inextinguishable stars in the sky: "Bright books . . . The tracks of fled souls, and their Milky Way, / The dead alive and busy."

Georgian row-houses in Kinvara, ruined abbeys and churches scattered throughout the countryside in Clare and Galway—who built them? I used to wonder as I walked around the town and hiked out into the countryside. And when, and why? And why did so many churches and abbeys now stand roofless and windowless? The answers to these questions take one back to the Middle Ages and the British conquest of Ireland in the sixteenth century when the monastic system was eliminated under Henry VIII. Monastic buildings throughout the British Isles—not just in Ireland—were robbed, by order of the king, of their treasures and endowments and left to the mercy of the relentless wind and rain that sweeps through these islands off the farthest northwestern edge of Europe.

H. G. Leask's three-volume work, *Irish Churches and Monastic Buildings,* which I ordered by post, arrived at the little shopfront post office in Kinvara from the publisher in Dublin, smelling faintly of mildew—a smell the volumes have managed to retain for twenty-five years. I love the blocky pen-and-ink drawings in the book and the detailed plans of buildings like Cormac's Chapel on the Rock of Cashel, built in the Germanic Romanesque style, and another little gem, much less well known, the church of Kilmakadar on Slea Head on the Dingle Peninsula in Kerry, which Leask thought was probably built by the same craftsmen who built Cormac's Chapel. These craftsmen were probably itinerant stonecutters who traveled from parish to parish throughout Ireland carrying their satchels of chisels and saws and hammers on pack animals, trying to drum up work for themselves.

With Leask's books as my guide, I visited both Cormac's Chapel and Kilmakadar during the year I spent in Ireland in the early nineties, and later, when I lived for five years in County Tipperary and Cashel was about an hour's drive away. In the front parlor of the Bishop's Palace in Cashel—an early eighteenth-century mansion in the Queen Anne style, now a comfortable hotel—I used to round off an afternoon of prowling around the Rock by enjoying a cup of tea by a turf fire.

In the late Middle Ages the spiritual empire of Christendom overrode national boundaries, and the influence of the Irish church spread over all of Europe. Irish monks sailed their little coracles across the choppy Irish Sea and built a monastery on the island of Iona in the Inner Hebrides. They brought their learning and piety to places as far afield as Germany and Switzerland.

In the twelfth century an Irish priest called Dirmicius, abbot of the monastery of Regensburg in Germany, sent two of his carpenters to help build this chapel on the Rock of Cashel, given to the church by King Cormac Mac Carthaigh, or Cormac McCarthy in its Anglicized form. Except for Kilmakadar, no other church in Ireland looks quite like Cormac's Chapel. Its steeply pitched roof, blind arcading, and square twin towers on either side of the junction of the nave and chapel, if they could talk, would speak German.

Kilmakadar lies in an Irish-speaking part of County Kerry close to Ventry, where I used to go every summer for a week at the seashore, and it made a nice excursion when one tired of walking on the windy beach. But I had discovered Kilmakadar years before. When two friends and I went to Kerry to see the church one stormy day in the early nineties, we pulled our rental car off the road, covered ourselves as best we could from the rain, and trudged through the graveyard that surrounds the ruined church. A funeral had just concluded and people were filing out through the churchyard. The mourners greeted us in Irish, and we did our halting best to reply in kind. I felt we had traveled back in time.

Curiosity and a bit of acquired knowledge about history and architecture had conspired to enrich our lives that afternoon, to frame and enlarge them. Leask led us there, in the same spirit as Frank O'Connor's wonderful little book, *Irish Miles,* which describes his cycling journeys around Ireland decades earlier in search of the same kinds of experiences.

H. G. Leask died in 1966, but I was introduced to his widow in the early nineties at Moyne Park, George MacBeth's house. Who would not respond to the reminiscence written about Professor Leask by A. T. Lucas for the *Journal of the Royal Society of Antiquaries of Ireland*?

> . . . on the last of the innumerable excursions which he had guided throughout the length and breadth of the country, that held on Sept. 29, 1962, to visit Trim Castle, Rathmore Church, and Bective Abbey, he had, despite failing health, advanced years, and the well-intentioned persuasions of several of the party to omit the last stop, insisted on completing the day's programme by speaking at the Abbey in a downpour whipped by a biting wind. If at the end of a long day and near the end of a long life (he was born on Nov. 7, 1882), there had been something of the routine in what he said or the way he said it, his audience would have been sympathetically understanding, but he spoke with the enthusiasm of a young man eager to communicate his enthusiasm to others, and the gale and the rain were temporarily forgotten by his hearers.

The dead are tireless.

George MacBeth
at Moyne Park

The first time I clapped eyes on George MacBeth, he was standing outside a reception at Kennys bookshop on Middle Street in Galway. The year was 1990. At George's side was his skinny beautiful wife Penny, who was wearing a fur coat. I think of that period as Galway's golden age. Perhaps that's because I was new to the city then. The upsurge of creative energy from the Druid and Macnas theatre companies, the wave of irreverent new comedians trying out their routines in rooms around the city, the thriving art scene, the vitality of traditional music sessions where young fiddlers and box players played their tunes—and above all, the excitement of conversation in pubs like Mick Taylor's, The Quays, and Neachtain's spilled out into the little streets of that neighborhood *The New York Times* called "Ireland's Left Bank."

Even in a scene so vibrant and amongst a crowd that threw off such bright sparks into the West-of-Ireland night, George was a man you would notice. He wore a striped cricket blazer and was leaning on a silver-headed cane. Two years later he would be dead. But that night in Galway, with his longish, salt-and-pepper hair and gray moustache, George's amused, tolerant face, with eyes that took in everything going on around him, seemed to say, "Yes, perhaps there *is* a bit of a pose about me, but so what? This old world is a colorless enough place on the best of days. Why not try to brighten it up?" I was in Ireland looking for a house where my family and I could live for the coming year. As soon as I saw this striking couple, I knew I wanted to know them better.

A few years before, George and Penny had bought Moyne Park, a big house in County Galway near Tuam. They were looking for someone to rent their annex, and so on the off-chance that it might be suitable for my family—it turned out not to be—they invited me to follow them out to Moyne Park after the reception at Kennys. George drove a vintage Jaguar saloon car, the only one I have seen before or since that was painted gold. I squeezed into my little rental car and followed them out to their house.

I'll never forget that drive. Ireland was new to me at the time. Driving on the left-hand side of bendy roads with nettles and cow parsley swishing and slapping against the fenders and hubcaps was still a novelty. I had only one cassette in the car, the *Famous Blue Raincoat* album, Jennifer Warnes singing the songs of Leonard Cohen. When I think of Moyne Park and George and Penny, I hear the sultry notes of the tenor saxophone in "Famous Blue Raincoat" while my Toyota sloshes along behind the Jaguar, the windscreen wipers doing their best to make the road visible through the lashing rain. Whiffs of turf smoke blew into the car from cottage fires along the way.

Moyne Park was an Irish manor house straight off the pages of one of those oversized coffee-table books you see on the front tables of bookshops—a Georgian block of grey limestone set down in the midst of pastureland, cattle munching away all round it. It may even have had, as people used to say about houses this size, "a window for every day in the year." No matter. It was very large and like all country houses I've visited in the British Isles, very cold. I remember being told it was built in the 1820s, and at one time the Church had converted the place into a sanatorium for alcoholic priests. Perhaps some of the big rooms had been pieced up to form cells for those poor souls struggling with the drink. Certainly many lavatories had been added: the house boasted a score of them. The British singer Donovan was a previous owner of the place—Donovan whose song "Mellow Yellow" had motivated many in my generation to try drying a banana peel in the oven, then rolling it up and smoking it. (It doesn't work.)

Penny was thin as a whippet, and susceptible to drafts. When we came to visit, she would answer the front doorbell wearing her mink coat. Paradoxically for someone who lived in such a large house, Penny painted miniatures, and had adapted a tiny room upstairs as her studio. She had painted and redecorated the interior of the house herself. George MacBeth, in keeping with the largeness of his personality, did his writing in a Gothic Revival library on the ground floor. On the same floor as Penny's studio was a double parlor with a fireplace at either end. The MacBeths kept fires of turf and logs burning in both fireplaces, and it was a lovely room to be in. They also made much use of the kitchen in Moyne Park's magnificent vaulted cellar, another cozy refuge in this enormous house.

Perhaps because George was a Scot and Penny was Welsh and Italian by parentage, or perhaps simply because George was the most humane and tolerant of men, he didn't see the big houses in terms of an English-Irish duality. To George these hulking manses were not English impositions on the native Irish landscape and culture. He would have reminded you that the masterpieces of big-house architecture, their workmanship and materials, were first and foremost Irish. A few years after we first met I read his poem, "A Conversation with Grandfather," in that amazing late book of his called *Trespassing,* which chronicles his years in his adopted country. The poem gives a most balanced and mellow treatment of Anglo-Irish history during the Troubles of the 1920s. Here it is:

And where were you the night
We burned Mount Sion? Were
You in the passing crowd, or safe
At home in Ballyruin?

That's me in the cloth cap, Declan,
Your old father's father, seventy years

Back, near as damn it. I was
Up there by the colonnades.

   I remember,
I remember, all those beer-flushed faces,
James and Paddy, Rush and Edwards, all
Ploughed under like the landlords.

   Who
Was there, was Jimmy Daly, Jimmy from the forge? Was
He there?

   I don't know, lad. I
Remember curtains blazing, plaster breaking, taken
All in all, it was a fine night, better
Than a football riot.

Meanwhile, far away in London,
Lord and Lady Simper-Footwell stuffed their hearts
With spit and mustard, largely ignorant
Of what was happening, idle at some Chelsea Ball.

Good riddance to them. Yes, I'm sorry
For those bricks and mortar, crashing joists
And ancient floorboards. Houses don't have feelings,
Do they? Lucky for us that they don't.

Ruining two centuries' handwork, Irish masons
Laid the stones, Irish work and Irish genius
Pissed on for a night of spite.

Still, it happened. It's forgotten,
It's remembered. Well, who cares?

Lord and Lady Simper-Footwell and the men
Who burned their mansion, all

Except your poor old Grandad,
Roast in hell, or roost in heaven. Give

Or take another five years, you can
Spread manure on
What's left. Fallen arches, twisted ivy,
Holes in walls that stood for pride.

Have another Guinness, Declan. I'd not
Rack your pretty head with bothering
About an old war. That, or any other. Drink, and smile.

For all their considerable style, the MacBeths did not just swan
around striking attractive poses; they were engaged, productive peo-
ple. Penny, in addition to being an artist, was a serious amateur musi-
cian. Sunday afternoons, she and George would get into the Jag and
motor down to Kinvara, where Mary and I ended up living for the year,
to play early-music trios with the fiddler Bartley O'Donnell and Tracy
Harris, the fiddler Frankie Gavin's wife, in the parlor of Winkles Hotel.

Poets can't live on their earnings from verse: few have been able
to since the days when people stood on chairs to see Lord Tennyson.
One of the most celebrated British poets of his generation, known for
the edginess of his verse, George had been a stalwart of the London
literary scene in his heyday, a novelist, anthologist, author of chil-
dren's books, producer of poetry programs for the BBC. More than
once I've turned up second-hand copies of his books in places like
Charlie Byrne's bookshop in Galway and wondered whose library
they came out of.

George MacBeth was rumored to have written, under a pseud-
onym, a string of profitable novels you wouldn't want to leave lying
around where the kids might find them. I've never read *The Samurai*,
published under his own name, but an online bookseller who has a
first edition available for $18.50 lets it be known that "The Samurai is an
all-out assault on the senses, an exuberant and witty adventure story, a
frank tale of erotica, and an exploration of the nature and ideals of obe-
dience." I think that book made George some serious money; I know
he kept a samurai sword on his writing desk. But then so did Yeats.

《《《《《《《

George and Penny liked to entertain, and none of us who knew them
will soon forget the parties and special events they hosted at Moyne
Park. They were proud of their house and knew what a splashy setting
it made. The MacBeths took naturally to playing lord and lady of the
manor. Their parties set the stage for high-spirited evenings in the grand

manner and brought together people who might not otherwise have met. I remember one evening of music and poetry in particular that they organized. George, Mary O'Malley, and I read, and the tin whistle master Seán Ryan provided the music. Some of the best things that happen in Ireland result from hasty puddings whipped up from an unlikely variety of ingredients, and that evening in an Irish big house with entertainment provided by a Scotsman, a Welsh-Italian Englishwoman, a fisherman's daughter from Connemara, an American blow-in, and one of Ireland's finest traditional musicians was only one of many.

For their Midsummer's Night fancy dress party, Penny drew up invitations with "Carriages at Dawn" printed at the bottom of the card. As Mary and I drove up the long approach to Moyne Park dressed as Oberon and Titania, we were shouted at by one of George's friends, an English lord, in the sackcloth of a medieval hermit, shaking a staff and hectoring us with warnings to repent our evil ways. George and Penny never did anything halfway. That night's bonfire, fueled by an enormous pile of scrap lumber, felled trees, old furniture, and God knows what else, reached the height of a small house, and when kerosene and matches were applied to it, must have been visible as far away as Athlone. We danced all night, fell into bed in one of Moyne Park's many bedrooms as dawn was streaking the sky over the surrounding farms, and woke to eat an enormous late breakfast in the cellar kitchen.

>>>>>>>>

You might be forgiven if you picture George, with his silver-knobbed cane, cricket blazer, gold Jaguar, and "carriages at dawn" stylishness as some kind of late twentieth-century *grand seigneur*. But that would be to confuse the surface with what lay beneath. If he was one of nature's aristocrats, he was also wonderfully warm and humane. According to the *Encyclopedia Brittanica*, George was born the son of a miner, as D. H. Lawrence was. His mother was the daughter of an antiques dealer. True to his calling as poet and fiction writer, George's greatest fiction was the role he created for himself as the squire of Moyne Park, and he had great fun playing the role.

But he never fancied that by dint of owning his big house he had become one of the Anglo-Irish gentry. In fact he studied the last of that dying breed like an anthropologist and used to regale us with the stories he brought back from meetings of the Irish Georgian Society. Back in the 1960s George had been one of the first performance poets, though that term was not used at the time. He performed the following poem for a small group of us in the double parlour at his house, with an exaggeratedly plummy accent, a lisp and a stutter, and a deranged glint in his eye:

The Twilight of the Ascendancy

Good afternoon. So good
Of you to have come. Here we all are.

This is Fiona, my grand-daughter, she's
Making a box
For her douroucouli.

This is Alaric, my grand-father, he's
Cleaning his pipe
Into a jam-jar. He's rather deaf, I'm afraid.
AREN'T YOU, OLD FELLOW?

This is Edwina, my wife's
Lady's maid, she's
Percolating coffee, in a colander. Will you
Have some?

This is Hengist, my
Faithful hound, actually
He's a bit of a mongrel, a bit manky.

And what's he doing? I think he must be
Spring-cleaning his equipment.

Who is this, darling? Ah yes, this
Is Roger Longrod, who
Does the drains. Thank you, Roger.

There's no need to shake hands.

And this is Pipistrelle, the
Baby-sitter, she
Rocks Fiona to sleep every night
With her krumhorn.

This is the drawing-room, and this
Is the room
For folding newspapers. Mind the drip.

That's Edgar, paring his nails. A cousin, yes.

Anyway, there you have it. Lorimer Hall
In all its glory. I look
Forward to your book, especially the photographs
Of the dove-cotes and the footmen's loo.

Mind the caravan, as you leave,
In the drive. We have a visit
From Oonagh, my mother-in-law.

And this is her family, yes. They deal
In scrap metal. All fourteen of them.

Sorry about the mess
And your exhaust. But they're easily replaceable,
Aren't they?

Do come again, when you've time
And the energy. We'll do the cow-byres, too.

It was hard not to respond to George's good-natured sense of humanity. The delicacy with which he navigated his position in his adopted country made an impression on everyone. The travelers—dealers in scrap metal like the ones in the poem—who squatted in the outbuildings around Moyne Park paid him the compliment of not stealing from him. Matt the postman, a Republican of the first water who never missed an issue of *An Phoblacht*, amiably engaged George in an ongoing political debate as he delivered the daily post. George even wrote a poem about him, "The Postman," which was included in *Trespassing*:

Past a green hole in the wall
With E VII on it,
He drives his orange van.

"In the 1930s
you wore a bottle round your neck,
if you couldn't speak English."

Is that so? Thus Matt,
The Republican postman
Who brings me letters from England,

Smiles through dark glasses,
His peaked cap
A reminder of military glory.

Nothing smiles more easily than victory
On the former landlords

Who still wash their Jaguars
Before the portals
Of an Irish excellence.

But who cares? Not me
Nor the educated postman
Who remembers Patrick Pearse,

And can recite his poems
In a language
Neither Yeats nor Wilde could speak.

Life seems to have a way of being particularly cruel to those who
least deserve its cruelty. The silver cane George leaned on when I first
saw him that evening outside Kennys, which seemed at the time a
charming affectation, like the cricket blazer and the silk scarf knotted
at his throat, was one of the first signs of what would be diagnosed
as motor neuron disease. First the disease rendered him unsteady on
his feet, then there came a point where, when we visited Moyne Park,
George would greet us from a wheelchair. When his speech began to
slur, at first I thought he must have been drinking. Finally the disease
took away all his strength and power. By this time I had gone back to
live in America and was never able to visit him in hospital or witness
the agony the loss of his powers must have been for him and Penny,
isolated in that big drafty house in north Galway. George died in 1992.

He approached his fate like the thoroughgoing professional he
was. In the period when his health was deteriorating rapidly, he was

writing poetry about it. Sonnets. The struggle involved in mastering the strict rules of the form must have given him a grim satisfaction. Here is one of those harrowing poems, "The Worst Fear":

Some days I do feel better. Then I know
It couldn't come to this, it never would.
I'm much the same as I was long ago
When I could walk two thousand yards, and stand

Upright at parties, chatting. When the men
At petrol stations understood
The words I mouthed. Now is the same as then.
It isn't, though. These are the days when food

Falls from my grip, drink chokes me in my throat
And I'm a nervous nuisance, prone to tears.
The time has come when I put on my coat
With fumbling fingers, grappling with my fears

Of God knows what. Well, I know one that's worse
Than all the rest. My wife's become my nurse.

My address book is becoming increasingly full of names and telephone numbers of people who are dead. I don't have the heart to weed them out. I rang George's number by mistake once a few summers back. "Moyne Park," an efficient, secretary-like voice answered. Before I hung up the phone, I could hear her voice echo in that drafty emptiness.

From Venice to Tipperary: Architecture and Empire

November. The wind roars across this hillside acre. The wind wants to wrench my garden-shed studio clear off its foundations and scatter the pine boards across the face of Sliabh na mBan. I live on a mountainside in a remote corner of remotest Tipperary, at the end of an unmarked lane, three miles from the nearest stop sign, four miles from any shop where you can buy a newspaper or a bottle of milk. Even when the wind drops, there is no traffic noise—no sirens, no horns. If one hears a motor, usually it means one of the neighbors is driving his tractor up the lane bringing hay to the cattle. When a solitary airplane flies overhead, its silent passing is a singular enough event to make one look up and follow its progress across the sky.

The wind is relentless. It whispers, whistles, swoops and swerves, rattles gutters and window panes. The rain-saturated meadows out the window glow emerald green, and the pines that grow along the demarcations between fields wear a velvety denseness. Here and there the ghostly gray trunk of a beech tree shows through, and black and white Friesian cattle decorate a field. The only color other than natural tones is the red car parked in front of the house.

But someplace else fills my mind's eye tonight. We have just returned from Venice. While we were gone a gale blew the hinges off the henhouse door, then blew the door off, and the fox killed one of our chickens. This morning when I got up I saw him out there, trying to sniff out another opening. He pranced away when he saw me, looking for all the world like a Renaissance dandy in a russet-colored tunic, his gorgeous tail pluming behind him. He was light on his feet and carried himself with the style of young courtiers in paintings by Carpaccio in the Accademia Gallery.

EUROPE IN THE MIDDLE AGES

One goes to Venice for the intoxication of spending a few days in a place utterly beautiful. By comparison with many parts of the world, I already live in such a place, even though Ireland is changing every day, and not necessarily for the better. It has been many years since anyone could with a straight face call Ireland the land of saints and scholars.

Both Venice and the Irish hinterland carry some flavor of life in Europe during the Middle Ages. Contemplating both of these ancient cultures raises us for a few moments above the day's trivia. By the eighth century, when Venice first established herself in her lagoon as a city-state with a more or less secure foundation, trading for salt and grain between the mainland of Lombardy and the Byzantine Empire to the east, Ireland had already achieved a rich monastic culture that produced illuminated manuscripts like the Book of Kells. The Irish church dispatched missionaries to nearby Scotland and England, as well as to Germany and Switzerland on the Continent. The first Viking invasions lay a century or so in the future, and Irish monastic culture was thriving. The monks can hardly have suspected their way of life was about to be ravaged by predators sailing fast ships down from the northern fjords.

After the breakup of the Roman Empire, the problem for cultures all over Europe was how to sustain commerce, trade, prayer, the fashioning of art and artifacts in the way all this had been carried on under the Romans, and at the same time to keep it safe from marauders like the Vikings in northern Europe, the Goths, Visigoths, and Huns in Central Europe and Italy, the barbarians at the borders of the Byzantine Empire—the New Rome which had supplanted the old imperium. Protected from outside interference by its remoteness, Ireland never had the Romans to deal with either as conquerors or as overlords who could provide a garrison of centurions to keep watch over the sea while a monk shaped the capital letter at the beginning of the book of John into an eagle, or applied gold leaf to the facade of a mansion in paradise.

Julius Caesar conquered Britain but must never have thought it worth his while to cross the Irish Sea. Perhaps he never thought there was anything here worth having. To the Romans, Ireland was Hibernia, the land of winter. The recent excavation of a Roman camp north of Dublin suggests the imperial army must at least have sent a party over to reconnoiter, but little has surfaced to show they came here other than a few coins and a rusty belt buckle or two. Unaccountably a Roman doctor's kit has been discovered at the Rock of Cashel here in County Tipperary. No one knows how it got there.

In the annals of Irish piety, Christianity reached this island in the person of the British slave who became St. Patrick. The monasteries with their scriptoria where manuscripts were copied out and illuminated, the round towers where bells and chalices wrought in bronze, silver, and gold by local artisans were stashed for safekeeping and a ladder pulled up behind them when local warlords or invading Vikings threatened, had somehow to survive on their own remoteness and integrity. Even before the Vikings got wind of treasures to be plundered, the monasteries were not safe: the local Irish lords and petty kings themselves raided these sanctuaries from time to time.

<<<<<<<<

The Venetians with all their glory and wealth knew some of the same insecurities that typified life in Ireland. That they began their communal life as refugees was something I had not contemplated before reading John Ruskin's *Stones of Venice*. Ruskin saves us from being blinded by the city's dazzling magnificence by taking us back to the Venetian lagoon before a city was built there:

> In order to know what it was once, let the traveller follow in his boat at evening the windings of some unfrequented channel far into the midst of the melancholy plain; let him remove, in his imagination, the brightness of the great city that still extends itself in the distance, and the walls and towers from the islands that are near; and so wait, until the bright investiture and sweet warmth of the sunset are withdrawn from the waters, and the black desert of their shore lies in its nakedness beneath the night, pathless, comfortless, infirm, lost in dark languor and fearful silence, except where the salt runlets plash into the tideless pools, or the sea-birds flit from their margins with a questioning cry; and he will be enabled to enter in some sort into the horror of heart with which this solitude was anciently chosen by man for his habitation. They little thought, who first drove the stakes into the sand, and strewed the ocean reeds for their rest, that their children were to be the princes of that ocean, and their palaces its pride . . .

Consider a few of the terms Ruskin uses to invoke a vision of the city in its magnificence: its brightness, its walls and towers, its princes, palaces, and pride. One may apply any of these six nouns to Ireland, but when one does, they immediately begin to suggest sadness and irony, if not bitterness—the sorrow, the irony, the bitterness of history.

TRADERS AND CRUSADERS

Ruskin defines his subject in the *Seven Lamps of Architecture* as "the art which so disposes and adorns the edifices raised by man, for whatsoever uses, that the sight of them may contribute to his mental health, power, and pleasure." I think of architecture as the one art everyone has an opinion about, stated or unstated. You don't have to open a book, pop a CD into your disk drive, or buy a ticket for the theatre or cinema—you have only to walk down the street and you will see buildings that engage, soothe, or assault the eye.

The longer one looks, the more one starts to distinguish certain features: columns, with their different orders—Doric, Ionic, Corinthian; pointed Gothic or round Romanesque arches; roofs that are flat, gabled, or hipped; the fanlight over a Georgian doorway; different kinds and colors of stone—marble, limestone, sandstone, granite, slate. Looking at architecture also has something to do with apprehending geometry and balance in the non-abstract world. An old Irish proverb puts it well: "What fills the eye delights the heart."

Venice, perhaps more than any other city in the world, represents the triumph of architecture. It is a *constructed* place, the work not of nature but of the architect, the builder, and the patron who paid them. For the city to come into being and serve as the foundation for an empire, nature had to be conquered and dwellings, churches, arcades, palaces built in a tidal lagoon. Think, by contrast, of the United States as celebrated in the anthem "America the Beautiful," which we learned as children: "Oh beautiful for spacious skies / For amber waves of grain. / For purple mountain majesty / Above the fruited plain."

Venice luxuriates in the green of its surrounding waters, delights in the sea breeze that mitigates the ancient stench of the canals in August and keeps the mosquitoes from settling. It relishes the mists and fogs of autumn, and enjoys at any time of year the dazzle of sunlight on the walls of its *palazzi*. But the city does not glory in its natural setting the way America and England and Ireland do. When one thinks of Venice, the overall impression is of a unified, deliberately constructed magnificence.

In the Cathedral of San Marco the merchant princes created a Byzantine basilica to rival the pomp of Haghia Sophia and the fabled Church of the Holy Apostles in Constantinople. In the Doge's Palace, Venetian architects brought the Gothic genius of northern Europe to the Adriatic. A few gems like the church of Santa Maria dei Miracoli embody the Renaissance spirit.

《《《《《《《

In the fourth century AD, as the Roman Empire's western capital staggered under repeated assaults by barbarian invaders—Goths, Huns, Avars, Herulians, and Lombards coming one after the other—the Emperor Constantine established a new Rome, a *Nova Roma*

Constantinopolitana, on the site of the Greek town of Byzantion on the Bosporus. Citizens of the old Roman Empire, with order and stability disappearing, lived in dread of barbarian incursions. Venice as an independent state got its start as a satellite outpost of Byzantium at the mouth of the Adriatic, expediting commerce between the high civilization of the Byzantine Middle East and a Europe that was then but a primitive feudal farming society.

As the New Rome in its turn began to totter, weakened by border wars and the growing instability of its subject territories in southeastern Europe and Asia Minor, the Venetians thrived, standing poised to supplant their former patrons. To complicate matters, the Byzantines were starting to grow hostile toward Venice, suspicious of its growing power, and they began tightening up trade policies that had previously been favorable.

Conveniently for Venice, this was the time when waves of Crusader knights from Northern Europe were setting off toward the Holy Land, with the joint aims of attaining salvation and freeing Jerusalem from the Saracens. Whether or not they achieved the former, I couldn't say. They did not even attempt the latter. In 1202 the Crusaders' emissaries brought the following message to Doge Enrico (or Henricus) Dandolo:

> We come in the name of the noblest barons of France. No other power on earth can aid us as you can; therefore they implore you, in God's name, to have compassion on the Holy Land, and to join them in avenging the contempt of Jesus Christ by furnishing them with the ships and other necessaries, so that they may pass the seas.

The doge's hard-headed riposte was, "On what terms?" The Venetians always arranged things on terms of maximum advantage to themselves. Not only did they fit the Crusaders out with ships and provisions and convince them to subdue a couple of rebellious Venetian tributaries along the Dalmatian Coast, they joined in with these bumptious Western Europeans on their adventure. With the ninety-year-old doge himself at the head of the armies, they succeeded in storming the legendary four hundred towers of Constantinople and deposing the emperor. Then they loaded down their ships with booty and divided the empire among themselves.

This Crusade never did reach Jerusalem. Constantinople was too juicy a plum to leave unpicked. The Europeans led mules into the Church of Haghia Sophia, making it easier to load them down with jewel-encrusted Eucharistic vessels and the gold and silver they stripped from the altar and the walls. They even tore the lead roofs off churches and melted the metal down to sell. Constantinople's fabled relics, including the head of John the Baptist, were divvied up, traded, sold, or taken back to Europe.

One of the choicest relics, the Crown of Thorns, the Venetians took custody of as surety on a loan of 13,134 gold pieces they made to the Crusaders. Deposing the Byzantine emperor, these Europeans, whom the Byzantines called Franks, set up one of their own in his place. When his empire fell on hard times through inept management and a scanty tax base, the Latin emperor, Baldwin II, bought the Crown of Thorns back from the Venetians and sold it to St. Louis, King of France, who built the Sainte-Chapelle in Paris to display it.

As for the Venetians, they became, in archaic wording that is both picturesque and precise, "Lords and Masters of a Quarter and a Half-quarter of the Roman Empire," bringing back, along with relics, gold, and treasure, four gilded bronze horses from the Hippodrome in Constantinople. These they strapped on board their galleys and shipped home. Many of these things may now be seen in the Basilica of San Marco. In Heraklion or Candia, Corfu, Rhodos—in whatever port you sail into across the eastern Mediterranean, from Corfu to Leros, the stone lion of St. Mark's will be there to greet you.

At another time Venice commissioned the sumptuous Pala d'Oro—"such a form," as Yeats would write in "Sailing to Byzantium," "as Grecian goldsmiths make / Of hammered gold and gold enamelling"—now on display behind the high altar of Saint Mark's. The Venetians never stop devising ways to make money. Once you have paid your way into St. Mark's Cathedral you can pay the Procuratoria della Basilica di San Marco another €1.50 to see the Pala d'Oro.

The two very different narratives of Venice and Ireland are both stories of empire. The ancestors of those Venetian Lords and Masters whom Ruskin invokes were at first simply residents of an obscure province of the Roman Empire at some distance from the center of imperial grandeur. The decline of Roman power in northeastern Italy allowed invaders to sweep down and terrorize the residents of this defenseless province as early as the fifth century. The invasion motivated the original Venetians, those who in Ruskin's words "first drove the stakes into the sand, and strewed the ocean reeds for their rest," to make their home in the lagoon.

The story is awe inspiring. These terrorized refugees proved themselves possessed of a remarkable resourcefulness that reached its peak when they joined up with the Crusaders to ravage Constantinople. But their audacity had displayed itself even earlier. In 828 Venetian merchants were able to smuggle the body of St. Mark out of the port of Alexandria, stealing it from under the noses of the Arabs, so the story goes, by concealing the body between layers of pork, guaranteeing that Muslims would not go near it.

They brought the saint's body to their city and consecrated his cathedral in 832. The building has had an eventful history, with many additions and embellishments, changes wrought by the coming of new architectural and artistic styles. When the church was rebuilt in the tenth century following a fire, the saint's body somehow went missing, only to be miraculously rediscovered by Doge Vitale Falier in 1094. The saint's arm burst from inside a column, revealing the location of the sacred relic.

The Venetians were very rich, and they spent many ducats beautifying their cathedral. It was the symbol of who they were and who they wanted to be. Ruskin characterizes the basilica as "a Book of Common Prayer, a vast illuminated missal, bound with alabaster instead of parchment, studded with porphyry pillars instead of jewels, and written within and without in letters of enamel and gold." The metaphor is a subtle one, because while it invokes prayer and devotion, it is really about the church as a work of art.

When I first saw St. Mark's fifty years ago, I was disappointed. My idea of a cathedral was Gothic—something tall and soaring, with spires that reached to the sky. I was on the American college student's version of the grand tour and had just come from seeing the cathedral of Notre Dame in Paris with its Gothic arches and being dazzled by the stained glass of the Sainte-Chapelle. My eye had not been trained to look at domes or rounded arches.

I didn't learn how to look at St. Mark's until I had seen the mosques of Istanbul and Bursa and the Orthodox churches of Greece, Serbia, and Macedonia. St. Mark's hugs the ground from which its domes harmoniously rise. As such, it is well suited to its place in the flat Venetian lagoon. The best way to approach San Marco is the one suggested by Ruskin. Come up one of the narrow passageways through the maze of crowded shopping streets on the west side of the piazza, then emerge into the open, so that your first glimpse of the church is full on:

> A multitude of pillars and white domes, clustered into a long low pyramid of coloured light; a treasure-heap, it seems, partly of gold, and partly of opal and mother-of-pearl, hollowed beneath into five great vaulted porches, ceiled with fair mosaic, and beset with sculpture of alabaster, clear as amber and delicate as ivory,—sculpture fantastic and involved, of palm leaves and lilies, and grapes and pomegranates, and birds clinging and fluttering among the branches, all twined together into an endless network of buds and plumes; and in the midst of it, the solemn forms of angels, sceptred, and robed to the feet, and leaning to each other across the gates, their figures indistinct among the gleaming of the golden ground through the leaves beside them, interrupted and dim, like the morning light as it faded back among the branches of Eden, when first its gates were angel-guarded long ago.

The range of entryways on offer as one approaches this profusion of ornamentation is reminiscent, on a slightly smaller scale, of the approach to Haghia Sophia in Constantinople. The tympanum over each of the five doorways is decorated, as Ruskin says, with "fair mosaic." Unfortunately only those mosaics above the doorway on the far left as you face the church are original to the medieval basilica. In these survivors from the church as it once was, one can appreciate the dignity, the hieratic stillness that is the genius of Byzantine art.

Here as elsewhere in the church, you need to stand still, stand up close, and let your eye drink in the properties of the marble columns. I can recognize porphyry and *verd antique* when I see them, but beyond those stones I am out of my depth. One of my guidebooks identifies some of the others as "red Phrygian marble, Iassian, with slanting veins of blood red on livid white." Many of these amazing marbles must have been salvaged or plundered from the Greek churches of Constantinople, where in turn they would have been salvaged or plundered from pagan temples.

It is hard to stay focused on what you are looking at as the tour groups sweep across the piazza, their guides lecturing in Italian, French, German, English, Japanese, and Chinese. The architectural pilgrim needs an inner stillness to let his unhurried eye fall placidly on the marble revetments with which the church is decorated and to appreciate the beauty of these blocks of fine stone sawn in such a way as to display the patterning of the grain. There are also fine and simple carvings of peacocks and vases, allegorical trees, and fountains, which the Venetians either pried off the walls of Byzantine churches in Constantinople or other parts of the empire, or else commissioned their own stone carvers to copy. One wants the leisure time to return to this marvelous building early in the morning, when the marbles drink a gray coolness from the sea mist, or at sunset, when they glow with a mysterious fire.

SUNLIT GOTHIC

Gothic architecture began, so art historians say, when a French abbot named Suger began redesigning the abbey church of St. Denis outside Paris in 1137 after fire gutted the old church. The abbot found an architect and craftsmen who brought a new grace, lyricism, and sumptuousness to Romanesque forms—the forms, that is to say, that were inherited and imitated from the architecture of the Romans.

Travelers—the Crusaders among them—who reached the Middle East and Muslim Spain would have seen the pointed arches and

Moorish extravagance of the infidels' architecture and slowly found ways to adapt its flair and airiness to their own new buildings. In his book *Understanding Architecture,* Leland Roth writes, "It is no mere coincidence that cathedral building started shortly after the 1st Crusade ended and the Crusaders returned home." From St. Denis, from Paris, from France, the style spread across Europe and made its transformative influence felt in the airy fan-vaulting of Henry VII's chapel in Westminster Abbey, in the glorious cathedral at Toledo in Spain, and finally in thousands of churches, universities, libraries and other buildings the world over.

Something happened to Gothic when it reached Italy. It lost its sense of spiritual aspiration, and yet at the same time it reinvented itself as a style in some ways more beautiful than what it had been in northern Europe. The technical lessons—what needed to be known about how to engineer an arch so as to carry a certain amount of weight, how high a traceried window could soar without collapsing, what percentage of a wall could consist of glass before it needed to be braced by buttresses—these lessons had been learned, applied, and tested before the style made its way across the Alps into Italy, where the issue became how daring and gorgeous windows and doors, balconies, and arches could become. Fourteenth-century Italian cathedrals like those at Siena and Orvieto used the Gothic style as pure decoration.

No one would deny that the Italians have a flair for fashion. These churches are cloissoné jewelry boxes executed on a large scale. The cathedral at Milano is an exercise in beautiful excess. W. B. Yeats called it "Nottingham lace architecture." The technical, mathematical challenges of engineering have long since been assimilated. Any spiritual meaning relating to the soul's aspiration toward God would seem bumptious and rude in the land where the worldliness of the Renaissance was budded up, poised to flower.

And if a largely ornamental Italian approach infused the Gothic style in provincial cities like Siena and Orvieto, think what happened to it in worldly, cynical Venice. For John Ruskin, the Doge's Palace is the quintessential Gothic building in the city, though I confess it is not a building I warm to. Its massiveness, its box-like chunkiness, the unwieldy look it has as it balances its rectangular block on the ground-floor arcades makes it look top-heavy.

It seems visually to symbolize the quasi-Stalinist apparatus of the Venetian state in its time of greatest power. Despite the delicate patterning of white Istrian and pink Verona marble that lightens the massive facade stretching around three sides of the palace, the Palazzo Ducale has power but not grace. And yet it is a building that cannot be ignored. As one travels down the Grand Canal and passes the piazza on a *vaporetto* taking pictures, one can hardly keep one's eyes off it.

The Gothic style in northern Europe is associated with fortresses and ecclesiastical buildings. It was left to the Venetians to adapt the pointed arches and the graceful columns that support them to the palaces their aristocracy built along the canals. In northern Europe, Gothic buildings are usually limestone gray; whatever color appears in them comes in the form of stained glass. The charm of Venetian Gothic owes something to Mediterranean weather and the affinity of Italian culture to the natural world. Venice is the city for sitting out on the terrace of a *trattoria* on a summer night, drinking the house wine and dining on dishes like fresh zucchini with the blossoms still attached, breaded and lightly fried, or rabbit cooked with young artichokes.

The owners of Venetian *palazzi* know how to slap a coat of dusky pink or lemon or umber onto their plaster facades and then let the sunlight, along with corrosive salt air and dampness off the lagoon, illuminate while it mellows and fades these colors. The old Veneto-Byzantine *palazzi* are studded with bezants of marble and lapis lazuli set into the plaster, giving these palaces their look of restraint and elegance. Lapping against the feet of these buildings is the cat's-eye green of tidal seawater. Stick a couple of poles alongside the boat dock in front of your sea-door where gondolas and *motoscafi* tie up, paint them with swirling stripes like barber poles—except these are cerulean blue and white—and this is Venetian Gothic at its most winning.

That otherworldliness the Gothic style embodied in northern Europe has been transmuted into an agreeable harmony and sense of well-being. The broad arch of a sea door at canal level rhymes with the ogee arches crowning balcony windows through which one sees the lights of a crystal chandelier—all of it part of a total effect composed of sea, sun, and the soft buzz of life along the canals, the cries of seagulls, continuum of a motorboat, the soft calls of gondoliers drumming up business from passing tourists: *Gondola! Gondola! Gondola!*

SAINT MARY OF THE MIRACLES

In Venice's early days, Gothic was the order of the day, but then things changed. The old style no longer pleased. The *Quattrocento* fell in love with the forms and ideas of a past more distant than the Middle Ages—the classical past, Greece and Rome—and made something new. The Renaissance wished away hundreds of years of barbarism, instability, chaos and irrationality that had descended like a plague on quiet parishes all over Europe when the Roman Empire lost its grip. At the same time that they worked to create a new world of vision, order, and intellect, the poets, artists, and architects of the Renaissance began to read works of antiquity preserved in monastic libraries and private collections. When they came to build, they imitated the rational proportions of Greek and Roman temples.

Santa Maria dei Miracoli, built between 1481 and 1489 by Pietro Lombardo, is a most beguiling building. Pietro, a painter and sculptor, patriarch of a family of versatile artists and craftsmen, was commissioned to build this church to house a highly revered icon of the Virgin Mary. Tall and narrow, its north wall thrown right up against a canal because of the constraints of its location, the Church of Saint Mary of the Miracles is itself a late fifteenth-century miracle.

How strange that Santa Maria dei Miracoli, built in a revolutionary style, was designed to house an old icon—and not only an old icon but an icon felt to have miraculous powers. As the story goes, the *Virgin and Child* by Niccolò da Pietro initially looked out on the passing world from a wayside niche near where the church is today. These shrines stand at street crossings all over Venice. Catholicism in Italy is different from Catholicism in Ireland. In Ireland religious pictures all seem to be about pain and suffering—the bony, angular crucified Christ, his baleful look and lacerated heart. In Italy the icons of Our Lady are earthy, womanly, accepting.

The icon by Niccolò da Pietro was affixed at first to the corner of a house, and the votive lamp at the base of it lit up the street by night. Later someone built a little wooden chapel to house the icon. Niccolò da Pietro's Santa Maria performed miracles—miracles of healing most of all. From the perspective of the twenty-first century, a belief in religious magic would seem to have nothing to do with the new ideas of the Renaissance. In any case, no medieval rudeness or Gothic cragginess was allowed here by an architect working in a style that would have been thought of as avant-garde in the fifteenth century. The church exudes serenity and effortlessness.

Santa Maria dei Miracoli looks more temple than church. The builders of sacred Byzantine buildings liked to cover exterior walls with revetments of marble, and that is what Pietro Lombardo has done here. Yet with its classical symmetry and logic, its allusions to Greek and Roman forms, this church is a pure product of the Renaissance. According to legend, Pietro Lombardo recycled materials discarded after the stonemasons finished their work on the Cathedral of San Marco, using marble that had been warehoused after San Marco was built. The building's purity of design owes much to the materials with which it is faced: symmetrical panels of white Carrara marble edged with pipings of blue-gray stone. When the sun hits the milky white marble, veined with seams of bluish gray, the stone takes on a dusky peach tone.

The church rises steeply from the pavement of the campo in four recognizable stages. The first of these is faced with simple rectangular panels of creamy white marble, punctuated by pilasters that support an architrave. Each rectangle divides into four parts with a cross of red Verona marble in the center of each, now faded to rose. It is as though someone has taken a pink ribbon from a gift package and wound it around the first level of the church, binding it together visually. The architect's design invites the viewer's eye to move back and forth between the whole and the parts. The serene uniformity of the marble revetments and the elaborate Corinthian capitals of the pilasters give a fillip of ornamentation to the austere surface.

The next level is taller by a third. Its round arches give the building a plain elegance. Because only every other arch opens into a window—half of them are what are called blind arches—the unfenestrated effect contributes to the unity of the structure by allowing the glow of white marble to seduce the eye into moving upward, undistracted by the intricacy of design found in Gothic churches.

The facades on all four sides of the building are each crowned with a semicircular gable that both echoes the round arches on the level immediately below and provides a sweeping transition from the sense of rectangularity produced by the lower part of the building. On each of the building's four sides, these gables are pierced by a simple round window that, if this were a Gothic church, might be thought of as a rose window. Here, in keeping with the classical lines of the church, no elaborate tracery associated with rose windows in the Gothic style complicates the round window's simple circle.

Perched above all this sits a square platform from the top of which an elegant dome rises. This dome is designed in the same style as the several domes of St. Mark's, lighted by eight round-arched windows and finished with a delicate lantern, its small dome supported by a circle of arches. Nestled into the side of the church is a graceful octagonal tower that rises in five stages, and it too is crowned by a dome of its own, supported by an arcade of eight columns. Everyone loves a tower, and this dreamy one is fit to grace the dollhouse of any little girl in the world.

‹‹‹‹‹‹‹‹

Saint Mary of the Miracles is just as serene and unified inside as out, but infinitely more sumptuous. The plan of the church takes after Roman basilicas, and so it gladly forgoes the distractions of side aisles or subsidiary chapels. The nave, which looks longer than the building's exterior size would allow, is roofed with a barrel-vaulted ceiling whose intricate interlocking pattern is stunning. Multiple paintings of saints are woven together by a gilded maze of framing set against a dark background. The simplicity of the ceiling overhead keeps viewers from getting sidetracked. The darkness, almost the blackness of it, sets off the brilliant white marble of the apse and the clear light that breaks through its windows.

The architect has made a church with one purpose and one purpose only: to put us in the presence of the holy icon. If that is not our business here, we can stay below in the nave. But if we want to see it and pray to it and ask it to bless our marriage or our children or our business or our art, then we have to walk straight up the narrow nave—its slimness emphasized by the tunnel-like effect produced by the vaulting—and then mount the stairs to where the icon is displayed on the high altar set inside the apse, framed by an elaborately carved arch supported by pilasters crowned with tall Corinthian capitals. Pietro Lombardo and his son Tullio carved an elegant marble balustrade for this raised area. The last time I was there, a florist was decorating the railings with dozens of creamy white roses for a wedding.

>>>>>>>>

The east end of Santa Maria dei Miracoli is one of the most beautiful things made by the hand of man. In contrast to the pointed shapes that characterize Gothic, this amazing building is all about circles, Romanesque arches, and semicircles. Set into the wall behind the altar, two round-headed windows flank a cross formed from circles of jade-green and amethyst marble. At the next level up, three round windows have been cut into tympanums that support the semi-dome of the apse. All these—all the windows in the church, in fact, but one—are glazed with clear glass articulated in a pattern of small round panes, like panes of glass with the blown-glass bottoms of wine bottles set into them. The one piece of stained glass in the church is a small window depicting Christ, surrounded by an almost violet blue, bluer than any sky, even here in the Veneto.

On the high altar is displayed the *Madonna and Child*, for which the church was built. Art historians date the painting to 1408. Visitors are discouraged by a little warning notice from approaching close enough to the altar to get a good look, but I found that a ten-euro note placed discreetly in the hand of the man who was arranging flowers on the altar did the trick.

To my eye the icon is not particularly striking. Dating from the first years of the *Quattrocento*, it belongs to that period of Italian painting when artists still followed Byzantine models but had begun to move away from the static, ritualistic portraiture that is both the beauty and the limitation of the older art. This Virgin reminds me of the anonymous Madonna at the center of the iconostasis in the basilica at Torcello, the little island forty-five minutes by boat from Venice. The Torcello Madonna is dated "fourteenth or fifteenth century," which is not very helpful. Both are modestly shawled in white and robed in blue, though the Miracoli Maria's robe is embroidered in thread of gold and the painting's frame is encrusted with jewels.

Both Madonnas have a fleshy quality. Both lack the forbidding ascetic aspect of paintings of the Virgin done both in the Byzantine tradition and by a Gothic master like Simone Martini, who painted the murals in Assisi. They are soft, human, medieval—not strikingly beautiful either aesthetically or spiritually. They do not impress us with anything like the beauty of Botticelli's women or the intelligence and complexity of Leonardo's. Robert Lowell's words describing the shrine of Our Lady of Walsingham in England come to mind: "Expressionless, she expresses God."

Whenever I am in Venice I like to sit in the café in the campo across the narrow canal from Santa Maria dei Miracoli, drink coffee, and look at the building in different lights. The literary critic Steven Greenblatt begins his book *Shakespearean Negotiations* by saying, "I began with a desire to speak with the dead." I would love to have sat at the Lombardos' supper table when Pietro discussed this project with his sons, to have broken bread with these remarkable artists and artisans.

"BARE RUINED CHOIRS"

Outside the windows of my studio here on the mountainside, no blue sky appears, no sunlight shimmers, no sherbety tones radiate from sun-warmed plaster. No doges or emperors, no hammered gold or gold enameling. No bezants of lapis and porphyry have been set into the side of the shed, which was built to house cattle. The Renaissance never reached the misty hills of Tipperary. The Mediterranean is well over the horizon. Our cottage and out-buildings sport the traditional angles and dignified beauty of vernacular farmhouse architecture. From the buff-colored sandstone of the house and barn to the steely sky and the rain that lashes through the fields outside, what I see are muted gradations of brown, gray, and green.

When one ventures forth to look at architecture in the Irish countryside, its very limitations, its imperfections, are what there are to contemplate. Ireland's history was ruinous and troubled for centuries, and this can be glimpsed in ruined abbeys and churches, crumbling tower houses, the bastions of what little security could be achieved on this embattled island amidst the chaos of medieval life. Venetian sunlight fades to Northern European darkness. Glory gives way to embattlement.

It takes an act of imagination to see the old structures as they must have been in their prime. Just about every building of note in Ireland from before the eighteenth century has been at least partially destroyed by fire, war, neglect, or a combination of all three. While Venice has been preserved as a world treasure, pre-modern Ireland is a country of ruins. Architectural pilgrims who take the trouble to drive or cycle around the island are rewarded with discoveries of a very different nature from what one experiences in Venice, where crowds often get in the way—not to mention the humbling realization that as far as someone else is concerned, you yourself may be in the way, blocking other people's views of the mosaics in San Marco or the Carpaccios in the Scuola di San Giorgio.

In the Irish countryside it is a pleasure to pull on your wellington boots and muck through a cow pasture to look at a well-carved sedilia in a roofless church or fragments of cloisters in what was once a thriving abbey or priory—"bare ruined choirs," as Shakespeare wrote, "where late the sweet birds sang." Most often, few others are in the hunt, and on the rare occasions one encounters them, their presence is more good company than annoyance.

When I was living in Kinvara on Galway Bay, I drove out one fine July day to look at the nearby complex of ecclesiastical buildings at Kilmacduagh near Gort. The monks abandoned it after Henry VIII dissolved the monasteries. The buildings became neglected; the Irish weather made them unsound. The roofs caved and rotted. No one was around with a key that day, so I climbed the wall of the O'Heyne's

Church and jumped down into the roofless nave for a view of the lovely paired east windows. I sat there soaking up the rare winter sunlight and looking at the carved stonework. Tall, round-headed windows, delicately splayed, were crowned with twin hood-moldings. I heard voices outside and soon enough a young man climbed up and jumped over just as I had done.

"Anything of interest?" a cultivated older voice called from outside.

"Two windows," the young man called back. "You should see them."

"Romanesque or Transitional?"

"Transitional," the young man answered without a moment's hesitation. All on a summer's morning. Every moment is transitional, but here you can see it carved in stone.

VENICE AND TIPPERARY

Wandering through the Doge's Palace in Venice one day, I came across a room whose walls were painted with old murals of maps, very detailed maps, of the world. There Damascus was, and Aleppo and Jaffa, Beirut and Jerusalem—all the cities, ports, and towns of the ancient Ottoman province of Palestine, ports of call all the way down the shores of the Persian Gulf to India and thence to China and beyond. The same detailed coverage was there for Europe. On our part of the continent, I would have expected to see London—it must have been a regular stop for Venetian ships—but did not expect to see indications that other parts of the British Isles were familiar to Italian sailors.

What surprised me was the detail with which Ireland was represented. Not just Dublin but Galway, Cork, and Waterford—even Kilkenny, just half an hour's drive up the road from where I am sitting. Ireland was on the map for Venice. Was Venice on the map for Ireland? Probably not, except as a legend of fabulous wealth. Venice's life-blood was trade and commerce, and the Venetians made it their business to know the world. The Irish worldview has tended to be, in a word, insular. Medieval Ireland was an inward-looking place whose energies were subsumed in warfare among local factions and resistance against foreign invasions.

Moving beyond the political sphere to architecture, the very different stories of Venice and Ireland are stories of rise and fall, wealth and poverty, perfection and imperfection. Lessons inhere in these two histories about what fosters a sense of beauty, what destroys and degrades it. History is a structure of irony. Even to equate the Venetians and the Irish as two peoples is misleading. Though the Venetians must originally, as residents of a Roman province, have had some kind of ethnic homogeneity—they were north Italians whose coloring and work habits speak more of Austria and the South Tyrol than of Naples and the *Mezzogiorno* (Southern Italy)—they were bound together by a sense of common enterprise.

When they fled from mainland to lagoon they were prompted by the most powerful human motive of all: survival. The primal terror felt by the founders of the Most Serene Republic comes to life in John Ruskin's *Stones of Venice*, in which he describes the cathedral in Torcello, one of the first islands in the lagoon where the refugees settled.

> [The cathedral] has evidently been built by men in flight and distress, who sought in the hurried erection of their island church such a shelter for their earnest and sorrowful worship as, on the one hand, could not attract the eyes of their enemies by its splendour, and yet, on the other, might not awaken too bitter feelings by its contrast with the churches which they had seen destroyed. The exterior is absolutely devoid of decoration. . . . while the massy stone shutters of the windows, turning on huge rings of stone, which answer the double purpose of stanchions and brackets, cause the whole building rather to resemble a refuge from Alpine storm than the cathedral of a populous city.

One day when I was at Torcello I examined these shutters. I tried to move them but found them too heavy. Clearly they were built so the inhabitants of the settlement could shut themselves inside the cathedral against attack. "If the stranger would yet learn in what spirit it was that the dominion of Venice was begun," Ruskin goes on, "let him not seek to estimate the wealth of her arsenals or number of her armies, nor look upon the pageantry of her palaces, nor enter into the secrets of her councils." He advises us rather to climb to the top of the little cathedral, and then, looking as the pilot did of old along the marble ribs of the goodly temple-ship, let him repeople its veined deck with the shadows of its dead mariners, and strive to feel in himself the strength of heart that was kindled within them, when first, the pillars of it had settled in the sand, and the roof of it had been closed against the angry sky that was still reddened by the fires of their homesteads.

Steeled by the racial memory of near extermination at the hands of marauding invaders, the Venetians went on to establish a city-state like the little kingdoms of Florence, Siena, Pisa, Bologna, Milano, and Urbino that the Italians built and defended in reaction to the chaos let loose by the collapse of Roman security. Each kingdom, within its own walls, was self-sustaining and self-defending. At the height of its power Venice operated along the lines of a highly profitable corporation run with ruthless efficiency by an impenetrable oligarchy.

Venice's is a story of four empires: Roman, Byzantine, Venetian, and Ottoman. A fifth even, if we count the French empire under Napoleon, who presided over its destruction in 1796. The ruthlessness with which the Venetians helped topple their erstwhile patrons by sponsoring and participating in the Fourth Crusade is typical of empire builders. With the rise of yet another empire, that of the Ottoman Turks, who supplanted Byzantium in the eastern Mediterranean, the Venetians fought only when they had no other choice, preferring to sign treaties, pay tribute to the Sultans, and carry on making a profit through trade.

When it came to religion, they were fortunate not to be caught up in battles during the Reformation between the old and new branches of Christianity. While Venice's was perhaps the first known ghetto, giving its name to Jewish and other ethnic enclaves throughout the world, Jewish merchants and bankers played an important role in the development of the Most Serene Republic. In dealing with the Byzantine Empire, Venice did not appear overly bothered by the schism between the Eastern and Western churches. Not, that is, until the Fourth Crusade, when suddenly it became convenient to think of the Byzantines as heretics, the easier to attack them with a clear conscience. Likewise Venice traded happily with Muslims when the Turks' time of ascendancy arrived in the eastern Mediterranean.

In terms of how Ireland is placed in relation to empire, the famous luck of the Irish has mostly been bad luck. The course of Irish history has been determined by the country's position as an island off the far north-western edge of Europe, next door to the capital of an empire on which the sun never set. Britain needed to control her neighboring island. Can you blame her? No sensible ruler of an island kingdom with pow-erful enemies on the continent of Europe was going to leave its western flank undefended. After the Reformation, when England emerged as a Protestant power at war with the Catholic powers on the Continent, the British had one more reason to distrust the Irish—and with good reason, because Irish history from the sixteenth to the twentieth cen-tury consists of an impressive list of wars, risings, and rebellions.

Because of its location, Ireland had only one real trading part-ner: Britain. She was unable to gain political independence until the twentieth century, when the British no longer deemed Ireland crucial to their own security. The Irish only achieved prosperity and fully emerged from the shadow of the British Empire when they joined another kind of empire, the European Union—with a level of pros-perity enhanced by its role as an offshore subsidiary of the American economic empire in the late twentieth century, when Ireland was able to put its well-educated, English-speaking work force into jobs con-nected with the burgeoning computer industry.

With a unity of purpose motivated by the need for self-defense, the desire to make money, and subsequently the business of run-ning a successful empire, the Venetians faced the world with a solid front. For the Irish it was different. Until the twentieth century Ire-land continued to be a country but not a nation, adhering to the old religion while its powerful neighbor fought under the standard of the reformed faith. Tribal rivalries kept Ireland in a state of chaos and in-security too easily exploited by foreigners—first the Vikings, then the Normans, and finally the British.

While the British colonized Ireland, controlled it militarily and economically, imposed English on the Irish-speaking population, dominated the smaller island in every respect, this relationship was not without benefits. The British and their allies among the Irish middle and upper classes made Dublin one of the great cities of the Empire, second in importance only to London. When ships flying the Union Jack filled the North Atlantic in the eighteenth century, the Irish economy flourished.

Whatever the Irish lost by having their native tongue replaced by English, if they still spoke Irish today, they would not be positioned to benefit from the computer boom, largely coming from another former British colony, the United States. And so while Venice was becoming a theme park for tourists, more museum than city, Ireland developed the fastest-growing economy in Europe, with a per capita income higher than that of the United States. Irish poets lament the loss of the language; businessmen and bankers do not.

HISTORY AND A LANE

Civilization is a great flurry and fuss, an expenditure of substance and energy, a heavy weight of deeds and accomplishments our species imposes upon the earth through ambition and restlessness, the desire for wealth, fame, and power. To contemplate a millennium and a half of European history can weary even as it delights. "The eye is not satisfied with seeing," Ecclesiastes says, "nor the ear filled with hearing." The sage goes on to say: "For in much wisdom is much grief; and he that increaseth knowledge increaseth sorrow." In the Book of Job, when God asks Satan, "Whence comest thou?" "From going to and fro in the earth," the Devil replies, "and from walking up and down in it."

The noble buildings, the hundreds of thousands of ducats spent on marble and gold leaf; the mind of the architect, the stonecutter's hand, John Ruskin's eye, the sheer life-force of that cunning old Doge of Venice, Henricus Dandolo; the skill and exquisite judgment of artists like Pietro and Tullio Lombardo—all of it seems far away today as I sit in this garden shed and look out at the placid countryside of South Tipperary.

Ireland and Venice—the rise and fall of their fortunes, the ironies of their histories, their relation to the wax and wane of empire, the glories and tragedies of their architecture. As someone not inclined to believe the civilized world will ever let Venice disappear beneath the waves, I am not so alarmist about the ultimate fate of the city, one of humankind's most sublime creations, as I reasonably should be. Still, in a world of rising sea levels, what chance does Venice realistically have of surviving catastrophe? Everything human beings build can and perhaps will be destroyed. In the present century we have seen what happened to the twin towers of the World Trade Center, whose fall prefigured one of those cyclical collapses global capitalism is prone to. In Ireland, evidence of the destruction of old civilizations lies all around.

>>>>>>>

An ancient lane runs through this acre of ground. No one knows how long the lane has been here. Too small to appear on a map I have seen from 1777 that shows the towns and a few widely scattered big houses in the neighborhood, this is a humble thoroughfare of little concern to the great world. For the local people it was a turf road, running along the brow of the hill and up the side of the mountain to the bog where they dug peat for fuel.

The land lies on a slope. On the high side of the lane, the road builders dug into the ground and reinforced the margin of their path with a stone wall inserted into the slope. On the downhill side they erected a dry-stone wall. In the 1930s the forestry department cut off the lane, put up a fence, and planted pine trees on the mountainside. Through the imposition of those non-indigenous trees and that barbed-wire fence, they interrupted the course of a road that had been here for centuries. Sometimes on full-moon nights I fancy that the spirits of the old ones walk down this lane and are puzzled when they find their way is blocked.

When those anonymous builders constructed their stone walls to delineate this boreen and divide it from the surrounding pasture land, they used no mortar, artfully positioning the pieces together instead, occasionally inserting a huge stone as the jewel in the crown of the wall. How did they manage to lift such huge pieces into place? Perhaps a group of men all struggled with the big stones, perhaps a donkey was pressed into service to drag them into place. Were they aware what a beautiful thing they were building, or were they simply building a road because they needed to get up the mountain to dig turf and cart it back down to their farms? The answer to these questions, it seems to me, is yes, and yes.

I think they knew what a lovely piece of work these walls were, perhaps even had a sense of what it would become as hedges grew up above the stones, fragrant and colorful with wild roses, foxgloves, stonecrop, primroses, and buttercups, musical with the songs of blackbirds, robins, wrens, and finches. A road is, in addition, a social space, particularly in the country. Conversations between neighbors ran along the lane, news was exchanged, games played. Lovers might meet on the lane away from the supervision at home. Even now it is not just a means of getting from one place to another.

The men who found, transported, lifted, and set these stones into place, the women (in those days before gender equality) who sewed their clothes, bore their sons and daughters, cooked their meals, and brought tea to them where they worked, were not the great ones of this world. They were the plain people of Ireland, unlettered subjects of the Kings of Munster and the Dukes of Ormond, "small people" who in Seamus Heaney's words desire only to "keep / the wick of self-respect from dying out," put bread on the table, and hope the calf won't be still-born, the newborn lamb won't have its eyes pecked out by the hooded crow or magpie, the chickens won't be killed by the fox. Yet like Pietro and Tullio Lombardo at Santa Maria dei Miracoli, they were builders. And what they built is a form of architecture.

It is comforting, in this world of exaltation and cataclysm, glory and decline, to walk along the modest lane those anonymous Irish farmers constructed. All the architecture I have written about today was built of stone, and the walls bordering my lane represent one of the humblest but not the most unworthy use to which stone may be put. The cathedral of San Marco, the church dedicated to Saint Mary of the Miracles, the Doge's Palace may all someday be drowned by the waters of the Adriatic. The walls of this ancient turf road endure. They never rose very high, but here they are.

Music along the Road

At home we get our music from the usual sources. For me it's the radio, my iPod, the CD player sometimes, the radio in the truck, the occasional concert, a night out at a bar where a band is playing. When I am traveling, it's a different story. Musical encounters on the road are less predictable, more random, and often more memorable. Take the Beatles' "Penny Lane."

I remember the first time I heard the song, with its stair-stepping trumpet obbligato. I was staying in a hotel in Rome just before Easter almost fifty years ago. The windows of my room opened onto an air shaft. Through opened windows, someone was playing a recording of "Penny Lane"—brand new back then. The air shaft provided perfect acoustics for that trumpet part. Even today, hearing the song carries me back to that first hearing, that warm and breezy hotel room in Rome. "Penny Lane is in my ears and in my eyes."

‹‹‹‹‹‹‹‹

Seven years later I went on a ten-day meditation retreat in India with the Burmese teacher, S. N. Goenka. It was pretty grueling. We practiced Vipassanā meditation for something like ten hours a day there at the Burmese Vihara in Bodhgaya. And we had agreed to observe silence for the duration of the retreat. The silence, the concentration of the practice, confinement for that length of time in a monastery, gave one a powerful reserve of energy and inwardness that transcended knees that ached beyond description from sitting cross-legged all day and into the evening and the bizarre kinds of free association that occur when the mind wanders during meditation.

When the retreat ended we walked down by the river with its slow-moving current and shady passages under big banyan trees— bodhi trees—with multiple trunks and snaky, vine-like appendages hanging down from their branches. A young American on the retreat had a guitar, and down by the river he sang "Imagine," John Lennon's song, which had just come out. I hadn't heard it before. Neither, I think, had the other people who had gathered at the monastery.

The silence had opened within us an enhanced receptiveness, and that amateur rendition beside that holy river remains powerfully lodged in memory. The song has achieved anthem status now—even contestants on "American Idol" sing it. But for me "Imagine" is about sitting on the ground in India under a bodhi tree, listening to this young man lilting John Lennon's words, "You may say I'm a dreamer, but I'm not the only one."

›››››››

Marcel Dupré used to be the resident organist at the church of Saint-Sulpice in Paris, and you could go there in the afternoons to hear him improvise. One day in particular I remember. The skies and streets of Paris were dull gray, the church almost empty. It was a comatose Saturday afternoon in this part of the sixth arrondissement, with its shops advertising *pompes funèbres,* the Gothic, formal, rather creepy accoutrements of old-fashioned French funerals. Like the bagpipe, the organ wants to be heard. It wants to be loud. This music seemed on a mission to enliven a gray quarter of Paris those winter afternoons.

Dupré must have been practicing for Sunday services that day. His Bach toccata and fugue was magisterial and uncompromising. He took hold of the stone walls of the church with the hands of his music and shook them. He didn't play the organ like the old man that he was by that point in his life. When he started to improvise, I felt I was a shaggy Caliban to this great musician's Prospero, who filled my ears with

> Sounds and sweet airs that give delight and hurt not.
> Sometimes a thousand twangling instruments
> Will hum about mine ears; and sometime voices
> That, if I then had waked after long sleep,
> Will make me sleep again; and then, in dreaming,
> The clouds methought would open and show riches
> Ready to drop upon me, that, when I waked,
> I cried to dream again.

My mother had a musical epiphany of her own on her first trip to Europe in 1930. She and the little group of friends from Memphis she was traveling with were staying at the Hôtel Bauer Grünwald on the Grand Canal. "After dinner," she writes in the travel diary she kept, "we dressed and went to the concert in the Square where, surrounded by thousands of music loving Italians, we heard with them, and intrigued by their fervor, one of their own singers—Gigli."

She loved the concert itself, but even better was what happened later: "In the early morning hours he passed our hotel in a gondola singing joyously and freely." Memphis has its own music and is known as the birthplace of the blues, but Beniamino Gigli, the premiere tenor of his day, singing from a gondola outside your hotel on the Grand Canal? Mother was transported.

‹‹‹‹‹‹‹‹

Can anyone claim truly to like the music of the bagpipe? *Is* there a proper setting for that nasal, insistent ear-torture? In Scotland they say that a gentleman is someone who can play the bagpipe, but refrains from doing so. I was in London once for the Trooping of the

Colors. Queen Elizabeth was on horseback reviewing her troops and Whitehall had become a parade ground for crack regiments in red coats, leather polished to a chestnut sheen, brass buttons agleam. When a Scottish regimental band marched by, bagpipes in full cry, their concatenation of bladder and reeded pipes seemed perfect. For this occasion nothing else would do.

My defining bagpipe moment was less formal. I was driving through Scotland, and when I geared down to enter a grimy lowland Scots town, I heard bagpipes. Saturday band practice, I suppose. Maybe some of the musicians were wearing kilts, but most of them had turned out in jeans, sweatshirts, and trainers. The children of the town ran along beside the marchers. The insistent, unsubtle wail of bagpipes filled the streets, exaggerated by the hangover I had, echoing off the hard surfaces of the pavement and the stone houses. I had met the bagpipe in its native habitat.

》》》》》》》

In my thirties I traveled several times from Europe to Istanbul by train on what was still officially called the Orient Express—though by my time it was its fabled self only on the wooden placards attached to the coaches. The Orient Express had become not much more than a local train that stopped at all stations as it crossed borders from France, Italy, former Yugoslavia, and Bulgaria into the European provinces of Turkey. The rattly old wooden carriages, badly in need of a good sweeping, were filled with guest workers returning home from Germany and *lumpen* travelers like myself with our backpacks and sleeping bags, sharing around our bread and cheese, our garlicky sausages, tomatoes, cigarettes, and wine.

On one of these trips I woke up at the border grumpy, stiff, and sleep deprived, in need of a shave and a wash. Once passport formalities had been dispatched, our train lumbered on its way, and at the first station inside Turkey, what should we see on the station platform but a band, like in a Fellini movie, uniformed in a ragtag way, playing a ragged march that perfectly fit my ragged mood. Why the band was there at all was obscure. Were they meeting some arriving dignitary, or was this just a convenient place to practice? Wheezing, thoroughly amateur, a little out of tune, their music made the journey a bit more cheerful, the morning a little less threadbare.

On that same trip a friend, Jake, and I took an overnight bus from Istanbul to Konya to visit the shrine of the Sufi poet Jelal-ad-din Rumi. Long, dusty bus trips are a way of life in the Turkish heartland of Anatolia. Konya was the Seljuk capital centuries ago, and it was here that Rumi founded the Mevlevi order of dervishes.

As soon as Jake and I got to Konya, we left our bags at our hotel and headed straight for Rumi's mausoleum. Topped by a fluted drum in the Seljuk style, clad in turquoise-colored ceramic tiles, the mausoleum ties, in its appearance, the ancient kingdom of Rum, a province of the eastern Roman Empire, to the Islamic kingdoms that once stretched westward across the Middle East from Samarkand and Bokhara and the kingdom of Khorasan to the shores of the Aegean in the west.

Shadows were lengthening, the dusty square in front of the shrine was deserted. From inside an adjacent building we heard flute music. This flute was the *ney*, that wooden instrument whose sound is heard in most dervish music. You blow into the *ney* through a wooden mouthpiece at the top, not through a hole along the side as is the case with the metal European variety. This dervish flute is the subject of some of Rumi's best known lines, sometimes called the "Song of the Reed," which opens his long poem in couplets, the *Mathnawi*. Here are the first eight verses from a very literal version Elif Şafak and I did in 2003:

> Listen how this flute complains, how it tells of estrangement.
> It says: Ever since they cut me from my reedy bed, men have
>   cried and wailed when I cried—and women too.
> I want a heart wounded by separation, so I can tell the pain
>   of longing.
> He who is cut off from his essence looks for the time
>   of reunion.
> I wept and moaned in every gathering, with the well-off and
>   the misfortunate.
> Everyone became my friend, each in his own way. Yet no one
>   wondered about the secrets I have inside of me.

My secret is no different from what I cry aloud; but the light to
     understand it is not found in the eye or in the ear.
The body is not hidden from the soul, nor is the soul a secret
     to the body; yet no one is permitted to see the soul.

Soon the *ney* Jake and I heard was joined by what sounded like a
fiddle—something I learned to know as the *kemençe*, a three-stringed
instrument the fiddler held on one knee and played with a bow. Then
a hand drum joined in. The music had a marching momentum. This
was the music of migration. I pictured the ancestors of the modern-
day Turks mounted on their shaggy steppe ponies, surrounded by
ragged flocks of sheep and goats, moving westward across Central
Asia. The *ney* and the *kemençe* sang of longing and separation, be-
fitting a people uprooted from their native land, on the move west-
ward—just as on my own journey I was on my way east.

Jake and I listened entranced and undetected for what must have
been two hours or more. Night fell as the sun dropped behind the ho-
rizon and suddenly the day's heat gave way to desert chill. The sliver
of a moon appeared. One of the musicians inside the room came to
the window and closed it. Though I am certain he did not see us sit-
ting underneath the window, it was as though he, or the music itself,
or whatever happenstance had led us here at this particular moment,
were saying, "Okay, that's it. That's all you get for now."

››››››››

Then there is music that does not call itself music. Seamus Heaney,
translating a phrase from the Irish, *Ceol an T'saol*, calls this "the mu-
sic of what happens." John Cage set up his tape recorder in a build-
ing on Sixth Avenue, recorded the sounds of the city, then played the
tape back as a concert piece. I wish I had packed a tape recorder in
my backpack when I was trekking in Nepal. I had set off west from
Pokhara Bazaar along the footpaths leading toward the valley of the
Tatopani River in the direction of the Tibetan province of Mustang,
spending the nights in Himalayan villages at *bhatti*, little inns that
serve a simple supper of rice and dal and give travelers a place to
stretch out a sleeping bag.

One day as I rested beside the trail, a breeze brought the tinkling of high-pitched bells. Then deeper bells in different registers. Then voices, and the rank, unmistakable stink of yaks. A caravan of Tibetan nomads was coming down into Nepal to trade skins and yak butter for barley and salt. These rough tribesmen, wearing heavy, fur-lined boots, whacked the sides of their pack animals and grunted at them, a boy on a pony played a modal tune on a wooden flute, the yaks activated their big, clunky cowbells, children skipped and darted along the flanks of the procession, chattering in words I could only guess at. It was not the kind of traffic John Cage heard on Sixth Avenue. This came from an earlier time and was carried by the ensemble music of bells, rough voices, animal sounds, flute music.

The Beatles, bagpipes, organ music in a Paris church, an Italian tenor singing in a gondola for the sheer joy of song, a Turkish marching band, dervish music in Anatolia, a caravan of Tibetan nomads— these are the sounds of the journey.

ENGLAND

Christmas in London

For someone with an eye for art and architecture and a head filled with English literature and history, London is a cornucopia of delights at any time of year. But the city really lights up at Christmastime. Christmas as we know it was more or less invented in Victorian England. We owe a lot of it to Victoria's consort, Prince Albert of Saxe-Coburg and Gotha. The Victorians adapted and popularized elements of the holiday as it was celebrated in Prince Albert's native Germany, with its Christmas tree, Yule Log, Christmas cards, boar's head on a platter, and the panoply of faux medieval fantasy that gives so much delight to so many people every year.

No writer has put his stamp on a holiday as Charles Dickens did with Christmas. As I walked the frigid streets last December, I found the words of Dickens's *Christmas Carol* running through my head:

> It was cold, bleak, biting weather: foggy withal: and [Scrooge] could hear the people in the court outside go wheezing up and down, beating their hands upon their breasts, and stamping their feet upon the

pavement stones to warm them. The city clocks had only just gone three, but it was quite dark already—it had not been light all day: and candles were flaring in the windows of the neighbouring offices, like ruddy smears upon the palpable brown air.

Back to Dickens later, and to *The Waste Land* of T. S. Eliot, another writer who imprinted his imagination upon London. But first to a visual artist who defined how we see England in the time of Henry VIII: Hans Holbein the Younger. Holbein is as central to our image of sixteenth-century England, when the Tudors consolidated their position in a country just coming into its own as a European power, as Dickens is to our sense of Victorian London.

Ours is a culture in which people like to be pictured smiling. Not so in Tudor England. Holbein's portraits emphasize his subjects' gravitas and solidity, their seriousness in the face of life and death. In garments, black was the color of choice. Inscribed on one portrait is a quotation from Job, 10:20: "Are not my days few?"

For courtiers, for theologians, for ministers of state such as Thomas More and John Fisher, for Henry VIII's six wives, England was a dangerous, even murderous place where speaking a wrong word, even being seen in the wrong company, could lead to imprisonment, torture, or execution. Those conditions persisted under Henry's daughter Elizabeth. Still, Tudor England was infinitely more secure, prosperous and self-confident than it had been during the fratricidal Wars of the Roses in the fifteenth century. And though in the sixteenth century England's imperial days lay in the distant future, one can sense in Holbein's art that she had already begun to consolidate her power.

Holbein is unsurpassed for Germanic phlegm and cold-roast-beef English rectitude. Like his later compatriot Handel, he brought to his English commissions a northern European seriousness that resonated perfectly with his patrons. Portraits notoriously flatter, but there is scant evidence of flattery here. Holbein's portraits of Henry VIII and powerful nobles like Thomas Howard, third Duke of Norfolk, are icons of masculine power that do not attempt to make these men look handsomer than they were or otherwise attempt to hide their ruthlessness. The exactitude of his portrayals makes you feel, "This man is telling the truth."

The unusual dual portrait of Thomas and John Goldsalve, father and son, reinforces Tudor England as the age of "the new man," as contemporary terminology had it. In order to secure their own power and wealth, the Tudors relentlessly undermined the power of the barons and replaced them with a meritocracy that would provide England with a new ruling class. Thomas, a wealthy Norfolk landowner, was clearly grooming his son to succeed him, and the son looks cognizant of his role as heir, impressed by the responsibilities he must prove fit to assume, and ready for the task.

As definitive as Holbein's oil paintings can be, he was also a dab hand with chalk, often using pink primed paper to suggest flesh tones, highlighting with pen and brush and adding watercolor washes. Among his chalk portraits, readers of sixteenth-century literature will recognize many names, if not faces. Sir Thomas Elyot was author of *The Book of the Governor,* a guide for rulers modeled on Castiglione's *Book of the Courtier.* Henry Howard, Earl of Surrey, is delicately portrayed wearing the elegant floppy hat of the period, a slight difference between his two eyes suggesting complexity of personality.

Sir Thomas Wyatt, though rumored to have been Anne Boleyn's lover, managed not only to survive but to thrive in Henry's diplomatic service. Holbein even did Henry Wriothesley, Earl of Southampton, Shakespeare's patron, his introspective blue eyes rendered deftly with pastel chalk. What one wouldn't give to see a portrait of Shakespeare himself drawn with Holbein's unerring and truth-telling hand!

His portrait of the king's falconer, Robert Cheseman, gives his subject the same watchful gaze into the middle distance that the gyrfalcon he is holding would no doubt show if someone removed its blindfold. Holbein infuses the falconer with the tension and alertness of the raptor itself. Because this most restrained of painters uses color so sparingly, when it does appear it delights the eye as it would never do in the palette of a more profligate colorist. Cheseman's orange sleeves emerge from his fur-lined black cloak like the first crocuses of spring.

Perhaps because his artistic values compelled him to be strictly accurate as a portraitist, Holbein seems to turn with relief from age and gravity to youth and flair. His portrait of a twenty-nine-year-old German merchant with a gorgeously prominent Roman nose,

Herman von Wedigh, plays the young man's black surcoat off against a gorgeous turquoise background and seats him at a little table covered with a wasabi-green cloth. His *Lady with a Squirrel and a Starling*—the lady's modest white cap and shawl set against a sky-blue background, green foliage growing behind her—provides a welcome note of levity after the gravity of all those Establishment worthies. As the lady (probably someone called Anne Lowell) is plain, perhaps it was as compensation that Holbein added the squirrel, the starling, the foliage and the cerulean blue of the background.

A rare full-length portrait shows how well Holbein does when he moves away from the head-and-torso format he usually employs. The subject is Christina of Denmark, Duchess of Milan—already a widow at sixteen! This is one of a series Holbein painted of eligible young noblewomen who were prospective brides for Henry VIII, and though her feet are concealed beneath a long black gown, Christina gives the impression of stepping toward the viewer—gliding almost—with an intriguing little smile playing over her introspective yet sensuous face. Perhaps fortunately for her, she did not join Henry's roster of six wives.

A portrait of her at Hampton Court Palace makes her look less appealing—ugly even—which may give support to Holbein's reputation for making these marriageable young ladies appear more attractive than they were in the flesh. This would contradict what I have said above about Holbein's aesthetic of accuracy. According to popular legend, Henry agreed to marry Anne of Cleves on the strength of advice from his chief minister, Thomas Cromwell, reinforced by one of Holbein's pictures of the lady. In person Henry found Anne clumsy and not at all pretty. Calling her "a great Flanders mare," he bribed her to release him from his vows and then put Cromwell in the Tower and had him executed.

It was his royal portraits that made Holbein's name. Henry appointed him official court painter and Holbein's life-sized wall painting of Henry at Whitehall Palace, legs spread wide apart in a stance of dominance, his hand on the dagger at his belt, has become an iconic image of Tudor power. Even though the original was destroyed by fire in 1698 when Whitehall Palace burned, copies survive. Though richly appareled, Queen Jane Seymour shows none of Henry's hauteur; in fact, she looks timid—and well she should be, as the wife of this dangerous, capricious man.

Dying of complications from childbirth, Jane gave Henry his male heir, whom his father hailed as "this whole realm's most precious jewel," the future Edward VI. The young man would have one of the shortest reigns in English history, dying from a chest infection at the age of sixteen. Holbein's portrait of Edward as Prince of Wales, presented to Henry by the painter as a New Year's gift, is the most vibrant of Holbein's portraits and the only one in which he uses red extensively, a brilliant vermilion that, along with the gold he sets beside it, makes this portrait stand out among its more somber companions.

<<<<<<<<

London is a wonderful place to look at architecture. Just before Christmas I attended services at Westminster Abbey, where I was ushered into a choir stall with a magnificent view of the fan vaulting overhead, a triumph of English Gothic. And having immersed myself in Holbein's Tudors, it made sense to visit Hampton Court Palace, where so much of the drama surrounding Henry VIII played itself out, and where monastic medieval architecture began giving way to royal showiness. The Renaissance, slow in making its way to northern Europe, gradually brought baroque architecture to England.

While the cloisters and garths of the palace come straight from the layouts of monasteries, the royal apartments display the pomp of power. The Chapel Royal is a showy blend of Gothic and baroque. The flat surfaces of the chapel's fan-vaulted Tudor ceiling, with its massive, decorated bosses, are painted royal blue with gold stars, reminiscent of the thirteenth-century Sainte-Chapelle in Paris. Its neoclassical west wall, with Corinthian columns done in dark wood, looks forward to the eighteenth century.

The earliest attempts to build in England using neoclassical ideas are in some ways the most interesting. The relationship between architecture and the stage might seem remote at first glance, but Inigo Jones, England's first modern architect, got his start designing sets for the elaborate court masques in vogue during the Jacobean period. The Queen's House, which Jones built in Greenwich in the early seventeenth century, is in the words of Queen Henrietta Maria a "house of delights."

In view of how the Palladian style became a default setting for official buildings all over the world, it is a pleasure to see Palladio's ideas expressed in Greenwich and in the Banqueting House in Whitehall so purely and simply—when these ideas had the freshness of innovation and discovery to recommend them. By contrast it is hard to look at the rows of government buildings erected later along Whitehall in rote Palladian style without a yawn.

I decided to spend some time looking at a few choice buildings by other English architects who worked in the Palladian idiom: Christopher Wren, James Gibbs, and that enigmatic figure who was Wren's pupil, Nicholas Hawksmoor. Wren's masterpiece, St. Paul's Cathedral, iconic national symbol that it is, remains a victim of its own magnificence, over-decorated on the inside, a monument more impressive than endearing. But it is a great pleasure to look at his smaller churches, like St. Stephen Walbrook near the Bank of England, stopping for a glass at the pubs in the little lanes and courts among which Wren was commissioned to rebuild or repair churches damaged or destroyed in the great fire of 1666. *The Waste Land* takes a glimpse at Wren's church near the Thames dedicated to Magnus the Martyr:

> 'This music crept by me upon the waters'
> And along the Strand, up Queen Victoria Street.
> O City City, I can sometimes hear
> Beside a public bar in Lower Thames Street,
> The pleasant whining of a mandoline
> And a clatter and a chatter from within
> Where fishmen lounge at noon: where the walls
> Of Magnus Martyr hold
> Inexplicable splendour of Ionian white and gold.

If you know *The Waste Land*, a visit to St. Magnus Martyr evokes the resonance of the baroque last line of that splendid passage. And many another of these churches appears in London folklore—like the tradition that a Cockney is someone born within the sound of the bells of St. Mary-le-Bow, or the old song that begins "Oranges and lemons / Say the bells of St. Clement's." That's St. Clement Danes in the Strand—the Strand is one of London's oldest east-west thoroughfares—originally the parish church of London's Danish community in medieval days when the descendants of Vikings were a presence in the town. Under King Cnut in the early eleventh century, this peaceful trading community rebuilt their wooden church in stone.

After the earlier church was destroyed by fire, Wren rebuilt St. Clement Danes. James Gibbs later added one of his fantastic steeples—an articulated tower rising by stages atop a massive square dado, each stage pierced with differently shaped windows and capped with a slightly different cornice, becoming slimmer as the tower rises to an eight-sided cupola, from there to a cylinder with eight little round-headed windows cut into it, and finally up to the brass weathervane that rides the winds high above the Strand.

The geometrical rationality of the design, with its clear round windows, its rectangles and obelisks, makes the claim that London has now emerged from Gothic fancies and medieval darkness. I especially like the two elegant domes Wren placed above the two ends of the narthex that flank the entrance to the church. The effect is classical and Mediterranean, with a touch of the mosque or temple.

St. Clement Danes's sister church, St. Mary-le-Strand, was built by Gibbs a hundred meters west, so that the two buildings make a pair along the Strand. Before the Thames's riparian embankment was filled in, the Strand was literally the strand, the riverbank. Gibbs built his church in imitation of Santa Maria della Pace in Rome, where he learned neoclassical form. The round porch borrows directly from the church in Rome. This was one of the first commissions won by Gibbs, whose most visible monument in London is St. Martin-in-the-Fields, which faces the east wing of the National Gallery on Trafalgar Square.

The Strand in the seventeenth century was not yet lined with tall buildings; the steeples of St. Clement Danes and St. Mary-le-Strand would have been dramatically visible above the low dwellings of the City. Now they form modest eminences on either end of a small island around which motor traffic flows. Slim-hipped and elegant, the tall, double-decker shape of Gibbs's building has a rounded nave reminiscent, though perhaps only to me, of the nave of Notre Dame de Paris, which adapts itself well, *mutatis mutandis,* to its position in the modern city.

>>>>>>>>

At the junction of Lombard Street, Cornhill, and King William Street stands one of the strangest buildings in London: St. Mary Woolnoth, the only church Nicholas Hawksmoor built in the City. Strange because this 1727 structure looks so little like a church. A colonnade rises above the two semicircular arches of the entrance and a shell-like window above the door. Atop the corniced colonnade are two tiny pavilion-like turrets topped with balustrades, where bells hang. These twin turrets pay only the most austere homage to the idea of a steeple. The interior of the church is a cube with a square ceiling that seems to want to be topped with a dome, supported by massive fluted Corinthian columns. The windows are glazed with clear glass. It is very much an Enlightenment building, and its geometrical starkness makes an odd and powerful impression.

When I visited, the place was empty, as were the surrounding streets. It was a bank holiday, and the silence inside the church was accented by the ticking of an ancient clock. On a work day this quarter, the center of London's financial district, would have been filled with clerks, secretaries, and executives. T. S. Eliot worked as a bank clerk at Lloyds Bank, 17 Cornhill.

Bob Cratchit in Dickens's story "went down a slide on Cornhill, at the end of a lane of boys, twenty times, in honour of its being Christmas Eve, and then ran home to Camden Town as hard as he could pelt." It's impossible to imagine T. S. Eliot running to Camden Town, or anywhere else, for that matter. His office was in the bank just a few steps from the church, and this quarter was the London of *The Waste Land*:

> Unreal City,
> Under the brown fog of a winter dawn,

A crowd flowed under London Bridge, so many,
I had not thought death had undone so many.
Sighs, short and infrequent, were exhaled,
And each man fixed his eyes before his feet.
Flowed up the hill and down King William Street,
To where Saint Mary Woolnoth kept the hours
With a dead sound on the final stroke of nine.

Just as St. Clement Danes and St. Mary-le-Strand would have looked different before motor traffic came to the Strand and tall buildings were erected along it, so would St. Mary Woolnoth. When this church was built, there was no open space in front of it. Wide thoroughfares like King William Street, built in 1835, were an idea belonging to the future.

Instead of the broad streets of today, menacing with traffic, the church was hemmed in by a warren of noisome alleys and lanes— Poultry Lane and Scalding Alley, where the feathers were burned off geese, chickens, ducks, and turkeys brought in from the countryside. A thousand head of cattle were driven through the neighborhood two or three times a week on the way to nearby Smithfield Market. In rainy weather the potholes were so bad that children drowned in them. Light was provided at night by setting fire to huge frying pans filled with animal fat. The heat would have been welcome last December.

Enthusiasms of a Colonial

My enthusiasm for England, its history and culture, began when I was twelve. In 1952 our teacher shepherded my sixth-grade class across South Cox Street in Memphis to the Baptist Church, where they had something new, a television set. Here we children watched, on the tiny screen of that novel device, through snow and static, the coronation of Queen Elizabeth II, taking place on a rainy day in London, far across the sea. The route of the coronation procession was lined, I remember, with people sheltering under black umbrellas, slick with rain. My ancestors had left East Anglia in 1640 to settle in Rhode Island, but in a sense we were still colonials.

While I still lived in Ireland I visited London regularly. There I stayed in Putney, on the south bank of the Thames. It was a happy occasion to board the red Number 22 double-decker bus on Putney High Street and begin the journey into central London. I would spend the day prowling through neighborhoods like St. James, where the indefatigable diarist James Lees-Milne did his research at the London Library and his writing in the library of his club, Brooks's, across the street from John Lock at number six St. James's, where I bought my hats. Discovering obscure churches by Hawksmoor, like St. Anne's Limehouse, and my favorite, St. Mary Woolnoth in the banking district, was a clandestine pleasure.

And then there were literary pilgrimages to places like Keats's house in Hampstead and Coleridge's in Highgate. For a William Morris enthusiast, the Victoria and Albert Museum in South Kensington felt like a temple to this energetic, greatly gifted Victorian. And then there is the house in what is now the dreary suburb of Walthamstow—now all turbans and saris—where Morris grew up, and his later residence, Kelmscott House in Hammersmith, looking out on the River Thames.

The fashion for all things medieval that surfaced in the Victorian age did not appear out of nowhere. The English countryside was dotted with medieval churches, and many country houses began life as cuckoo's nests for Tudor grandees whom Henry VIII rewarded for their services to the Crown by granting them confiscated monastic lands and buildings. The names of estates like Forde Abbey and Woburn Abbey reflect their provenance. And when the Gothic Revival began with Horace Walpole's mansion, Strawberry Hill in Richmond, just west of my perch in Putney, many Georgian big houses were "Gothicized" by the addition of turrets, battlements, and castellations.

The Gothic Revival earned the imprimatur of John Ruskin, an arbiter of taste in the late nineteenth century. Ruskin was reacting against bastardized versions of Renaissance architectural styles he saw on high streets throughout Britain. Fresh and exhilarating buildings from the seventeenth century like Inigo Jones's Banqueting House in Whitehall and the Queen's House that Jones built in Greenwich—commissioned by Queen Anne, wife of James I— have the sparkle of newness and invention about them. Anyone can see that. It is hard to put one's finger on exactly why the neoclassical impulse lost its vitality. But as I rode through London on top of a double-decker bus, it was clear to me how perfunctory many of the government buildings and commercial establishments in Westminster look. This was the style Ruskin hated.

Ruskin as an author, lecturer, and critic and the architect A. W. N. Pugin were quickened by similar motivations: a reaction against what they saw as the trivialization of the neoclassical style, particularly as expressed in the Regency designs of John Nash, who favored gracefully curving facades like the terraces of Regent's Park, wrought iron balconies, striped wallpaper, bow windows, stucco facades.

Both Ruskin and Pugin felt the integrity and sincerity of older English buildings had been lost, and both preached a return to the older, Gothic style—Ruskin with his pen and Pugin through his many ecclesiastical commissions. Pugin's influence found its way even to remote and rainy Ireland. I used to drive around the countryside seeking out buildings like St. Aidan's, the Roman Catholic cathedral in Enniscorthy, the exquisite little chapel at Borris House in County Carlow, the chapel of the former Presentation Convent in Waterford, and the rooms Pugin decorated and the furniture he built for Lismore Castle, the Duke of Devonshire's estate in Waterford, only twenty-five miles from where I lived in Tipperary.

Why would the Gothic Revival and the Victorian age in Britain speak to a transplanted boy from Memphis, Tennessee? Well, Southern culture during the era I was born into loved nostalgia, romanticized death in a Dickensian way, and was as thoroughly Victorian in its sentiments as it was in its architecture. "The Letter Edged in Black" played on country music radio stations when I was a boy, as did "The Little Rosewood Casket," which begins:

There's a little rosewood casket
Lying on a marble stand,
And a packet of old letters
Written by a cherished hand.

Won't you take them down, dear sister,
And read them over to me?
For at times I try to read them,
But for tears I cannot see.

Both songs date from the 1890s but were still popular throughout the South in the 1940s.

‹‹‹‹‹‹‹‹‹

The family party my parents hosted at our house in Memphis every Christmas Eve was not complete without a reading from Dickens's *Christmas Carol*, a copy of which my mother's Aunt Blanche gave her in 1912, with superb hand-tinted etchings that afforded me my first glimpses of how London might have looked in the nineteenth century.

We even had a few old children's books around the house like *The Birds' Christmas Carol*, a tear-jerker from 1887, and *Why the Chimes Rang*, the 1909 classic by Raymond MacDonald Alden, which begins, "There was once, in a faraway country where few people have ever travelled, a wonderful church. It stood on a high hill in the midst of a great city; and every Sunday, as well as on sacred days like Christmas, thousands of people climbed the hill to its great archways . . ." These archways were, naturally, Gothic.

>>>>>>>>

William Morris's work grew out of a fantasy version of the Middle Ages, and his utopian novel, *Erewhon,* posits a future society imagined in terms of how Morris dreamed people had lived in medieval England. Morris even wrote a few carols of his own. His work reflected the widespread Victorian love affair with the Middle Ages. It is no accident that the words for "Good King Wenceslas," that most medieval of traditional carols, were written in the 1850s and set to the tune of a thirteenth-century melody:

> Good King Wenceslas looked out,
>   on the Feast of Stephen,
> When the snow lay round about,
>   deep and crisp and even;
> Brightly shone the moon that night,
>   tho' the frost was cruel,
> When a poor man came in sight,
>   gath'ring winter fuel.

The words may look like doggerel when written out on the page, but they are anything but that when sung on a frosty December night, particularly if you are out caroling. You might even find yourself trudging, in your imagination, through the snowy streets of London.

Looking at English
Art and Architecture

Sir John Soane was the most illustrious architect of his day and a close friend to J. M. W. Turner, who was himself the greatest of English painters. Sir John Soane's Museum, one of the most exquisite of London's many small museums, stands at number 13 Lincoln's Inn Fields in Holborn. Soane first saw the light of day in 1753 and died in 1837—the year of Queen Victoria's accession to the throne. In addition to his work as an architect, Sir John was a tireless collector of both antiquities and the art of his contemporaries. He bought William Hogarth's *Rake's Progress* from Christie's in 1802.

The name Hogarth calls up images of time-darkened prints in antiquarian bookshops and foxed engravings on the walls of senior common rooms from Oxford to Harvard and beyond. Slatternly maids-of-all-work empty chamber pots onto the heads of drunken louts in the street below; grotesque fat gentlemen leer at the pillowy bosoms of serving girls in seedy London taverns along Gin Lane and Beer Street. Hogarth does many things well, but his paintings allow little room for the experience of sublimity that Turner brings.

Hogarth, unlike Turner, is an "impure" artist squarely in the English tradition, and this is exactly what makes him so engrossing.

Hogarth's work typifies the empirical British disinclination to go overboard—unlike Britain's traditional rivals, the *pensée*-driven French. Shakespeare's mixtures of high and low life, comedy and tragedy, come to mind. This quintessentially English artist succeeded in defining his milieu and his era, the eighteenth century London of Dr. Johnson and Boswell, just as surely as Dickens serves up Victorian London and Martin Amis gives us the chilling vulgarity of 1980s London with its City stockbrokers, pub louts, and spiritual emptiness.

A Londoner from a poor but educated family, Hogarth knew his city well. He turned his merciless gaze toward London's cast of fools and buffoons, ripe targets for thieves, pimps, shyster lawyers, and fawning flatterers ready to empty pockets and exploit every weakness. Hogarth excelled at painting as a form of journalism. In some of his series he is as much cartoonist as artist. Just as English theatre leans more toward language than toward spectacle, Hogarth is an artist for whom the stage resonated powerfully. His engravings can be viewed as scenes from plays. *Marriage à la Mode* and *The Rake's Progress* detail, scene by scene, his hapless characters' headlong plunge into vice and ruination. He did a charming group portrait of his servants, five of them circling the kindly but self-important butler, reminiscent of Mr. Hudson in *Upstairs, Downstairs*.

>>>>>>>

Though there was over twenty years' difference in their ages, John Soane and J. M. W. Turner had much in common. Both, like Hogarth, were self-made men—Turner the son of a barber, Soane the son of a bricklayer. Architecture exercised a strong appeal for both of them. They steeped themselves in the buildings of ancient Rome and Palladio's re-imaginings of classical architecture. The older man, Soane, was Architect to the Bank of England, while Turner began his career as a watercolorist employed by architects and landowners to do impressions of their houses.

While the ruins of medieval abbeys and churches most certainly helped form the Romantic imagination, so did places like the Roman Forum, which English travelers saw on their Grand Tours. The circle of neoclassical painters and architects of which Soane and Turner were leading lights would have counted Piranesi's fanciful etchings of the ruins of Rome as an important influence. Soane employed the gifted but tragically unstable J. M. Gandy to do architectural renderings of the buildings he designed.

The moody palette Gandy employed when painting Tyringham Hall in Buckinghamshire, which Soane designed, with dark clouds blowing across the sky at sunset, is reminiscent of Turner. Soane had recently built the Bank of England, and it says something about these men's complexity and historical pessimism that Soane asked Gandy to paint the Bank as a ruin, its neoclassical lines giving it a close resemblance to the Roman structures whose ruins haunted Piranesi and, later, Turner and Soane. With a splendid sense of irony, Gandy even pictures archeologists at work excavating the ruins. Gandy's eerily prophetic *Bird's Eye View of the Bank of England*, 1830, which "deconstructs" the Bank and its environs, could be a scene from London after the Blitz.

When Turner painted a scene, a sunset or sunrise would often be lighting up the sky, and clouds would pass diaphanously over the moon. Indeed, effects of light and dark make up a large part of the charm of a visit to the Soane Museum. The space is carefully articulated: Soane placed alcoves and arches strategically, and convex mirrors make rooms seem larger than they are. He was as skilled an interior decorator as he was an architect, employing striking colors such as Pompeian red, probably based on a fragment of wall plaster he stuck in his pocket on a visit to the ancient Roman city and brought home with him, and Turner's Patent Yellow (no connection to J. M. W. Turner), which is used to great effect in the drawing room.

As for Turner, he was in love with light. The Tate Britain on Millbank has large holdings of Turner's work both in oils and watercolors. The painter's obsession with the mysterious essential of our existence called light can be seen in paintings like *Shade and Darkness, the*

Evening of the Deluge, 1843. Here Noah's flood becomes the occasion for a study in the gloomier shades of his palette, as does the companion canvas called *The Morning after the Deluge*.

Turner's interest in atmospheric effects, filtered sunlight, mist, and cloud would suggest he was an important precursor for the French Impressionists. Those artists must have studied paintings of his like *The Evening Star*, ca. 1830, and the well-known *Rain, Steam and Cloud*, 1844, in which a steam engine crossing the railway bridge over the Thames at Maidenhead provided a symbol for the Age of Steam. French Impressionism comes off looking rather *petit bourgeois* when set beside Turner's encounters with the sublime.

To define Turner's most characteristic palette would be impossible, because he had several palettes to suit various moods. Some of his more Beethovenesque canvases are dominated by grays, whites, and brooding earth-colors. But he is also partial to the brilliant chromium yellow that announces the sun's emergence over the horizon. He has a touch with blues as well: his *Harbour of Brest* from the mid 1820s is a celebration of sublime cerulean—*cobaltous stannate*, most likely, a compound of cobalt and tin oxides. His paint box is on display in the Turner wing at the National Gallery in London, and while there are blocks of dry pigment there, he used nothing that came ready-made out of a tube.

Turner liked to be up at dawn to catch the first glimpses of light and the subtle modulations of color that can be seen before the sun dominates. Anyone who has attempted watercolors will be astonished that such diverse effects could be achieved in the medium. *The Blue Rigi* is one of a series of watercolors the artist did in 1842. The Swiss peak he painted was a must-see for British tourists in the Victorian age. Sketchbooks and journals—memorabilia of Turner's trip to Switzerland—survive, as do preliminary studies. A guidebook from the nineteenth century tells us that "Before traveling into Switzerland, or, at all events, soon after arriving in it, every one hears of the Rigi. 'Have you been up the Rigi?' is the universal question; 'You must be sure to ascend the Rigi' is the universal injunction."

Turner did not ascend the Rigi with the crowds, choosing rather to paint it from across the lake during the summer months. He painstakingly built up the scene in stages, with successive washes of color overlapping each other. Layers of gauzy mist rise from the surface of the lake, creating tilted horizontals poised between the painter's vantage point and the mountain. Turner is not painting just the mountain, but the space between the viewer and the blue peak in the distance. Painting that space, that air, between viewer and viewed would become the Impressionists' trademark.

The sun announces itself as a white glow behind the late sunrise. The morning star floats above a wash of chromium yellow. You can see its reflection on the waters of the lake. John Ruskin, the most insightful critic of Turner's genius, perceived that his aim was to give us dynamic pictures of a scene just as it was manifesting itself. In *The Blue Rigi*, if you stand as close to the painting as the museum guard will allow and look carefully, you can see the flash of a fowling piece coming from a floating duck blind in the foreground. Birds rise off the surface in response to it.

‹‹‹‹‹‹‹‹‹‹

Can happiness be expressed in a painting? Yes. Turner likes to focus, as he does in *The Blue Rigi*, on a light source, usually the sun—the equivalent in photography of shooting into the light rather than putting the light source behind you—which expands to fill the painting. In *Lichfield Cathedral, preparatory study*, ca. 1832, the sun coming out from behind the cathedral towers seems to appear and grow during the time one spends in front of the painting.

My favorite room in the Turner Wing at the Tate Britain is called "Interrupted Visions" and contains sketches in oil that have much in common with the watercolors. The unfinished paintings are among Turner's greatest because here the human details—the soldiers, elephants, and so on that struggle across the canvas in paintings like *Snow Storm: Hannibal and His Army Crossing the Alps*—do not appear. In his dynamic use of color, the twentieth-century painter who most reminds me of Turner is Rothko, someone who also has a way of making light rise and radiate toward the viewer, particularly in his use of yellows and oranges. But there are so many more varying moods, so much more fresh air, and so much more movement in Turner's works than Rothko was capable of.

>>>>>>>>

The skills Soane employed in building his own house-cum-museum served him well when he designed the Dulwich Picture Gallery in that London suburb. The Picture Gallery, built from 1811 to 1814, is one of Soane's most winning buildings, its charm enhanced by the anticipation that builds during the long train ride from the center of town and the walk through leafy Dulwich—a relief from the urban grit and noise of London. Soane's building at Dulwich is a great place to look at art. Its arches, high windows, and pleasing articulation of interior space make it a place one wants to linger.

I went to Dulwich some years ago to see an exhibition called "Canaletto in England: a Venetian Abroad." Canaletto, who lived in London from 1746 until 1755, painted his London scenes over canvases primed with gray in deference to the subdued English light, as opposed to the vermilion undercoating he used for his Italian scenes. And yet I feel that Canaletto's English scenes look too much like Venice. It is as if he simply cannot stop painting it.

Can the river Thames ever have been the jade green of the Grand Canal? Can London skies ever have been that clear, that susceptible to being rendered with the Pozzuoli blue or Egyptian blue the artist used in views of Venice that attracted British patrons to commission Canaletto to paint their own country houses and views of London in the first place? Who knows; perhaps the British would have liked their Canalettos less had the Italian artist made the skies and waters look less like Venice.

In any case, his nine-year stay in London was a success. His *capricci*, imaginary scenes bringing together buildings, monuments, and scenes of the countryside from diverse sources, were the best part of this exhibition. One amazing London scene is *The City Seen Through One of the Arches of Westminster Bridge*. The view of the Thames is framed by a wooden arch of scaffolding from Westminster Bridge, in construction at that time. A bucket hanging from the bridge gives the scene a sense of scale—St. Paul's and other London buildings on the horizon, the huge arch of the bridge in the foreground.

〈〈〈〈〈〈〈〈〈

E. M. Forster is famous for his maxim, "Only connect." The history of the arts in England is a study in how tradition works: a history of imitation, mutual influence, parody, pastiche, from Shakespeare's voracious borrowings to Gilbert and Sullivan's parodies of Handel and beyond. Hogarth's work was enriched by his connection to English theatre as well as to journalism. Turner and Soane were stimulated both by each other's creative energies and by their shared excitement over what could be learned from the art and architecture of the past. Tradition is about not only our debt to the past but how a sense of continuity can inform the creation of new work.

"Only connect." It sounds simple enough.

Pugin and the
Gothic Revival

Tourist, when you look up at the clock tower that rises above the Houses of Parliament in Westminster, spare a thought for A. W. N. Pugin. Make that *Augustus Welby Northmore Pugin*—a grandiose name for a man with grand ambitions and grand achievements. Not only did Pugin design Big Ben, one of the world's most instantly recognizable landmarks, he also handled the detailing and interior decoration of the Houses of Parliament. This was Victorian England's dream of the Middle Ages realized in vivid wall paintings, hand-worked brass fixtures, lamps, and throne-like chairs of hand-carved mahogany.

In the opening years of the nineteenth century, taste was shifting in the British Isles. Neoclassical architecture had gone stale, while the Middle Ages no longer seemed so dark and primitive. The "Dark Ages" were beginning to look positively picturesque and romantic. A building like Castle Ward in County Down, Northern Ireland, reflected the craze for all things Gothic. Castle Ward was built in about 1760 with an unusual, perhaps even unique feature: one façade in the accepted Palladian style, the other in the newly fashionable Gothic—the result of aesthetic differences between a husband and wife. The poet John Betjeman, visiting there in the 1930s, wrote: "Spent some time in Lady Ward's boudoir," a room famous for its fabulous swagged ceiling—"Like sitting under a cow's udder."

In this changing climate Pugin, the son of an *émigré* Frenchman and a patrician Englishwoman, almost singlehandedly transformed the face of architecture across the British Isles. If ever in the history of architecture someone appeared in the right place at the right time with the right vision and skills, it was Pugin. His buildings can be seen throughout England, Scotland, and Ireland, and from there his influence spread to church buildings throughout the world.

Pugin's father Auguste, son of a French soldier, had been a commercial artist in Paris, producing drawings and engravings for periodicals catering to the trade in luxury goods. In the 1820s, after emigrating to London, he ran a drawing school on Great Russell Street near the British Museum where he let it be known that he had been a person of importance in pre-Revolutionary France—a count, no less! He wandered the streets of London wearing a tricorn hat and a cape, sporting a gold-topped cane. Auguste worked as a draftsman for the Regency architect John Nash, designer of Regent Street and Regent's Park in London, as well as of the Royal Pavilion in Brighton and Lough Cutra Castle just outside Gort, County Galway, Ireland, a few miles up the road from Kinvara, where I used to live.

For someone who would go on to revolutionize church building throughout the British Isles, the work and study with which Pugin prepared himself was remarkably secular. From an early age he was enthralled by the theatre. As a boy he persuaded his parents to let him build a little theatre in the attic so he could design stage sets and produce his own plays.

Like many other gifted only children, starved for company when young and thrown back on his own resources, Pugin sowed, through what we would call creative play, the seeds of what would become his profession. Impatient with life in the confines of his father's drawing school, he found work for himself in the theatre, working as a set designer in the louche precincts of Drury Lane in London. His parents were alarmed by what they saw as a descent into a highly disreputable world, but they were powerless to stop the headstrong young man. Augustus was good at getting his own way.

The nineteenth century was an age of spectacle, extravaganza, special effects, paving the way for Italian grand opera and the operettas of Gilbert and Sullivan, which were such a feature of cultural life in the latter part of the century. Victorian enthusiasm for grand theatrical gestures no doubt even laid the groundwork for our passion for cinema, even for the Hollywood blockbuster. The fifteen-year-old Pugin was a stage-struck young man who hung around the theatres in Covent Garden. This early enthusiasm of his gives us a glimpse into the theatrical nature of architecture, a sense of how important illusion, atmosphere, and modulation of space are to the success of a building.

Nowhere are these qualities more important than in the Gothic church or cathedral. It is worth quoting Pugin's biographer, Rosemary Hill, on the connection between stage design and architecture:

> Pugin learned a great deal from the theatre that he would apply and develop in architecture. . . . By the time he was working at Covent Garden the stage was . . . the size, if not the shape, of a substantial church. . . . A three-arched structure divided the stage half-way down to define an interior playing area. It might represent doors or windows; in one case at least, it was actually a Gothic rood screen.

When Queen Victoria came to the throne in 1837, this energetic, passionate, and opinionated young man was well positioned to design works that would come to embody the Victorian style. As an interior decorator Pugin started early, making furniture for Windsor Castle when he was only fifteen. He was responsible for the Medieval Court, one of the most striking parts of the Great Exhibition at the Crystal Palace, and the gorgeous marble fireplace in the banqueting hall at Lismore Castle in County Waterford, which was brought there from the Crystal Palace. Though not all of Pugin's commissions were for Catholic churches, many of them were. Pugin converted at the age of twenty-three, becoming associated with a group called the Romantic Catholics. In his vision of a unified culture, religion, the community, and architecture each played a role.

Catholic Emancipation in 1829 opened the door for Roman Catholic places of worship to be constructed, and they were especially needed in predominantly Catholic Ireland. Catholicism had stepped out of the shadows, and wealthy laymen came forward to pay for the construction of new churches. Perhaps the best known of Pugin's Irish buildings is St. Aidan's Cathedral in Enniscorthy, County Wexford. Equally magnificent but with limited public access is the banqueting hall at Lismore Castle, County Waterford. I visited St. Aidan's on a bitterly cold afternoon in February and was also able to finagle a closer look both at the banqueting hall and at the extraordinary collection of furniture designed by Pugin that has been gathered at Lismore Castle. Both spaces make it clear that Pugin's genius lay in his thorough control of every aspect of interior decoration.

Entering St. Aidan's, which was meticulously and faithfully restored in 1994, visitors find themselves enveloped in an atmosphere of sacral mystery. The light is artfully controlled, and the delighted eye moves from one part of the church to another, never losing a sense of the whole. Pointed arches rising from pillars that divide the soaring nave from the low aisles unite the peripheral spaces with the church's core. The ensemble effect gives a sense of vertical lift—the way Gothic church design expresses spiritual realities. The low-ceilinged aisles serve the whole in at least two ways: their intimate scale, the windows admitting muted light through stained glass, allows for clerestory windows along the top of the nave. Glass in the clerestory has been kept clear to introduce soft daylight into the building.

Between the bold crossing supports of the wooden ceiling, the surface has been painted sky blue and dotted with gold stars that reflect the church's interior light. Round light fixtures suspended from the apex of each pointed arch are painted a dramatic crimson that counterpoints the gold-starred cool blue of the ceiling. The individual fittings are just as important as the overall shape of the church.

The crossing, that point in a Gothic church where the transepts perpendicularly bisect the nave, is brilliantly decorated with a cluster of features both beautiful in themselves and filled with ritual significance. Vatican II eliminated the separation between people and clergy that lies at the heart of traditionally constructed churches, but that distinction can still be seen in St. Aidan's as in other Gothic churches. The crossing is where the people's nave meets the chancel, set aside for choir and clergy. And this is where the horizontality of the floor plan intersects the verticality of the steeple, supported here by four powerful pointed arches, all of equal height, with meticulous stenciling applied along the wall spaces between each pair of arches.

In this space are situated a carved oak pulpit and a patterned rug designed by Pugin to lie underneath the altar (I cringed to see it being so vigorously hoovered the Saturday afternoon I visited) and the exaggeratedly vertical bishop's throne, reminiscent of Sir Gilbert Street's Albert Memorial in Hyde Park, London, with its elaborate Gothic canopy. Pugin in this space proclaims the power of church hierarchy; in Hyde Park, Street's memorial celebrates the power of the monarchy. Both thrones are awesome proclamations of authority, temporal and spiritual.

Painted on massive pillars that support the spire are the names of all the bishops of the diocese from St. Aidan to the present. Their names are flanked by the patterned stenciling that in Pugin's work prefigures much that flowed from him, such as Pre-Raphaelitism and the Arts and Crafts Movement. All these things provide the interior of the church with a medley of colors, materials, and surfaces at once various and harmonious. Without details like these, a Pugin church would not be what it is—a space where, on every surface, color and pattern proliferate—almost as if they were growing organically, but in colors of vermilion, crimson, and gold. It is a vision of heaven on earth, and, I believe, a vision such as churches offered the faithful before the Reformation.

‹‹‹‹‹‹‹‹‹‹

Pugin enjoyed the position of celebrity architect that has become a fixture of cultural life in modern times. In Britain perhaps Christopher Wren was the first of these, though architects in his day were just beginning to rise, in the eyes of their patrons, above the level of the builder or the engineer. Or perhaps John Nash, with his scandalous divorce and his access to the Prince Regent, who would ascend to the throne as George IV, qualifies as the first in a line that would include modern-day stars like Frank Lloyd Wright, Norman Foster, and Frank Gehry.

Unlike his follower Richard Norman Shaw, who had his shirt cuffs cut wide so that he could sketch out plans for potential patrons seated beside him at dinner parties, Pugin was temperamentally unsuited both to mix in society and to run a professional architectural firm. His tactlessness and loquacity, his tendency to lecture his patrons and bully his employees meant that this great artist and visionary never quite succeeded as a professional architect. Never knighted, never awarded an MBE or OBE or other honorary title that might have been expected by someone so prominent in his profession, Pugin joked that the only initials that would ever appear after his name would be VP, "Very Pointed."

William Morris, Maker

When you hear the name William Morris, probably the first thing that comes to mind is William Morris wallpaper. And why not? Windrush, Cherry Thief, African Marigold, Willow, and other designs of Morris & Co. that one knows by sight if not by name are among the glories of interior decoration, ranking with Iznik tiles of the sixteenth century for their combination of sumptuousness and restraint. Most of them are still commercially available. But beyond these, Morris had a mind-boggling range of interests and talents, and a level of energy to match.

Yeats might have been alluding to him when he wrote: "Some burn damp faggots, others may consume / The entire combustible world in one small room." Since Morris was a prominent figure on the artistic and literary scene in London during the last quarter of the nineteenth century when Yeats was getting his start, there is every likelihood that he did have Morris in mind. Another great Victorian, Thomas Carlyle, might also have been thinking of Morris when he wrote, "Blessed is the man who has found his work." As Fiona

MacCarthy writes in her 1995 biography, "When Morris was dying, at age 62, one of his physicians diagnosed his disease as 'simply being William Morris, and having done more work than most ten men.'"

Morris was a maker. In him, the knowledge of the connoisseur combined with the craftsman's practical urge to learn how things are made. Whenever any art or craft attracted his enormous curiosity, he found out how it was done—from weaving to mixing dyes for his tapestries to learning how medieval stained glass was fashioned to reviving the art of hand printing, as he did with the Kelmscott Press in his later years. When he wrote poetry, he composed as many as a thousand lines a day.

As an adviser to the South Kensington Museum, which became the Victoria and Albert (V&A), one of his most notable recommendations led the museum to acquire the Ardabil Carpet, probably the world's most famous Persian rug, and certainly one of the largest. The Ardabil is now magnificently displayed in the V&A's Jameel Gallery of Islamic Art. Morris mounted a public campaign to acquire it in 1893 for what was at that time the princely sum of two thousand pounds.

I never go into the Victoria and Albert Museum in South Kensington without thinking of William Morris. In important ways the V&A, which justly styles itself "the world's greatest museum of art and design," could not have come into being had Morris never existed. More than anyone else I can think of, he elevated craftsmanship to the level of art. You can see his designs for wallpaper, tiles, fabrics, carpets, embroideries, and stained glass in the museum, and of course you can also see the famous Morris chair. The Morris Room, originally called the Green Dining Room, shows the rich eclecticism he brought to an entire ensemble.

>>>>>>>

In the 1880s William Butler Yeats's impecunious artist of a father, John B. Yeats, moved his family from a dreary flat in Earls Court to a modest Queen Anne house on a pleasantly winding street in the Bedford Park estate that Norman Shaw built in west London, with its pub, The Tabard, and its Gothic Revival church, St. Michael and All Angels, decorated in the Arts & Crafts manner. The estate was built with artists in mind, and many of the houses came with large, light-filled studios. Here, Yeats wrote in his *Autobiographies,*

> We were to see De Morgan tiles, peacock-blue doors and the pomegranate pattern and the tulip pattern of Morris, and to discover that we had always hated doors painted with imitation grain, the roses of mid-Victoria, and tiles covered with geometrical patterns that seemed to have been shaken out of a muddy kaleidoscope. We went to live in a house like those we had seen in pictures and even meet people dressed like people in story-books.

The Yeats family was not alone in falling under the spell of Morris's designs. He summed up his aesthetic this way: "Have nothing in your houses that you do not know to be useful or believe to be beautiful." William Morris patterns were as integral to late Victorian taste as were churches like St. Michael and All Angels, Pre-Raphaelite paintings, the Albert Memorial, the poems of Tennyson, John Ruskin's art criticism, Matthew Arnold's Hebraism and Hellenism and "sweetness and light." Morris wallpapers were as much a part of this world as were Kipling's and Robert Louis Stevenson's books and the operettas of Gilbert and Sullivan, with their Pirate King, Ruler of the Queen's Navee, Lord High Executioner, and "Three Little Maids from School."

When the *Daily Telegraph* ran its obituary of Morris, it noted that "when married tutors dawned upon the academic world, all their wives religiously clothed their walls . . . with Morrisian designs of clustering pomegranates." Oscar Wilde furnished the smoking room of his house on Tite Street in London with an embossed paper from Morris's firm. Beatrice Webb, the Fabian Socialist, pleading "limited cash and still more limited taste," chose Morris furnishings, and Aldous Huxley grew up in a house with "chintzy rooms, modern with William Morris." Morris wallpapers were also the choice of later luminaries such as Kenneth Clark. John Betjeman, who began his career as a writer in the 1930s for the *Architectural Review,* champion of a Modernist aesthetic, papered his office with Morris wallpaper as a form of rebellion against the periodical's prevailing taste.

Betjeman's choice of Morris wallpaper for his office made sense as a protest against the Modernist aesthetic sweeping the world in the years following the First World War. It didn't take long for British designers, writers, architects, and musicians to discover that the impulse in favor of radical deracination coming from the Continent and from America did not suit their sense that art is at its most pleasing and effective when rooted in the national traditions out of which it grows.

>>>>>>>>

Norman Shaw's way of modeling his buildings on vernacular architecture caught on with his clients perhaps because he took a familiar look and improved upon it, as opposed to the architecture of Modernist architects like Le Corbusier, who set out to confront rather than please his patrons. Ralph Vaughan Williams's fantasias found their audience because his method was to elaborate on familiar folk melodies. The Gothic Revival was so easily accepted because it appealed to a sense of medieval nostalgia where the British national identity felt most rooted.

The rediscovery and affirmation of Englishness that Norman Shaw, Vaughan Williams, and writers ranging from Virginia Woolf, Siegfried Sassoon, Vita Sackville-West, and E. M. Forster to the T. S. Eliot of *Four Quartets* were to promulgate later on was powerfully prefigured by Morris, whose role as a champion of the native English genius had in turn been prefigured by the Romantics—painters like Samuel Palmer and William Blake, who saw the "dark Satanic Mills" of the Industrial Revolution threatening "England's green and pleasant land."

Morris was a utopian socialist who preached against the soul-deadening effects of industrialization. He showed by example how beautiful things to enrich people's lives could be made by hand if one were willing to apprentice oneself to the rediscovery of ancient crafts and their techniques. His vision of a medievalism that could serve contemporary lives is stated emphatically in his long poem, *The Earthly Paradise*:

Forget the counties overhung with smoke,
Forget the snorting steam and piston stroke,

Forget the spreading of the hideous town;
Think rather of the pack-horse on the down,
And dream of London, small, and white, and clean.

Dante Gabriel Rossetti and the Pre-Raphaelite painter Edward Burne-Jones were Morris's friends and business partners. Many Gothic Revival churches throughout England have stained-glass windows designed by Morris & Co. But it was through Rossetti that the serpent crept into Morris's earthly paradise. In the picture gallery of the V&A hangs one of Rossetti's paintings of Morris's wife Janey, a Pre-Raphaelite "stunner" surrounded by the gloom of Hades, holding an emblematic pomegranate. Rossetti, who became Janey's lover, pictured her as Persephone, Queen of Hades, sultry and brooding because of her unhappy marriage to Morris. Rossetti saw himself as her redeemer, the bringer of light into her dark world.

William Morris had an unruly mop of hair that reminded Burne-Jones of Topsy in *Uncle Tom's Cabin*, so Topsy became Morris's nickname. He was by all accounts a loud, exuberant man. His Oxford scout is said to have admonished him at one point, "A little more *piano*, sir, if I might suggest it." He had a vile temper and would sometimes beat his head against a wall hard enough to make a dent in it (the wall, not his head). Displeased on one particular occasion with the Christmas pudding that was served at his lodgings in Red Lion Square in London, he hurled the offending dish down the stairs.

Rossetti's life was as chaotic and dissolute as Morris's was ordered, purposeful, and wholesome. In the familiar story of artists and models, while Morris fell in love with and married Janey Burden, Rossetti married Elizabeth Siddal, whose image appears in many of his paintings, most famously his *Beata Beatrix*, which depicts Beatrice on the Ponte Vecchio in Florence at the moment Dante first laid eyes on her, an encounter made famous in the great Italian poet's *Vita Nuova*. Both women came from working-class backgrounds. Janey's father was a stable hand in Oxford.

Rossetti's and Siddal's conjoined lives descended into chronic illness, depression, madness, and addiction to alcohol and laudanum. When Elizabeth died, perhaps by suicide, Rossetti melodramatically placed a journal containing his only copies of poems he had written to her in her coffin, thrusting the journal into her luxuriant red hair. Seven years later, in a macabre footnote, he obtained permission to have her body exhumed so that he could retrieve the poems. Regrettably, worms had damaged the manuscript, so that some of them had become illegible.

›››››››

The phases of Morris's work can be tied to the various places where he lived and worked: first Kelmscott Manor in rural Oxfordshire, then the Red House in Kent, followed by his London ateliers in Red Lion Square and Queen Square. Kelmscott Manor, a largely Elizabethan manor house that Morris and Rossetti rented for five years in the early 1870s, became Morris's model for a habitation where ordered domestic beauty was rooted in tradition. The very opposite of all that is logical in Bauhaus architecture, Kelmscott is a jumble of odd angles, arches, battered walls, yew hedges, and old roses in its garden.

The Thames is a small river here, and Morris loved to get out on it in a punt—fishing was a favorite pastime. Windrush, one of Morris's most familiar and successful wallpaper patterns, takes its name from the Windrush River in Oxfordshire. His socialism and the future he imagined after writing *Erewhon*, one of the first utopian novels (note the anagram in its title), were rooted in medieval ideas of equality among men. Later in his life, writing for the Socialist newspaper *Commonweal*, he evokes a vision of traditional life and work in the English countryside:

> Midsummer in the country: here you may walk between the fields and hedges that are as it were one huge nosegay for you, redolent of bean-flowers and clover and sweet hay and elder-blossom. The cottage-gardens are bright with flowers, the cottages themselves mostly models of architecture in their way. Above them towers here and there the architecture proper of days bygone, when every craftsman was an artist and brought definite intelligence to bear upon his work.

I don't recall Marx ever writing about flowers.

›››››››

The Oxfordshire idyll, however much it refreshed the springs of Morris's inspiration, was too far from London for business. And Morris, whose father was a successful financier in the City, was equal parts artist and businessman. When he and Janey married, Morris hit on a compromise between business and domestic life by having Philip Webb build them a house that he called the Red House, in Bexleyheath, Kent, ten miles out of London. Burne-Jones painted murals, and Janey and her husband worked together on tapestries to hang on the walls. Morris turned his hand to embroidery as easily as to decorating furniture, making tiles and designing stained glass. At the Red House each part contributes to the whole, from the orchard and garden surrounding the place to the windows, walls, and carpets within.

Perhaps the Red House and the life that Morris led there were the closest he came to his ideal of a wholeness that incorporated life and work, beauty and utility. This hardworking but genial man liked to combine business with pleasure, and the series of lectures he gave in the 1880s is aptly called "How We Live and How We Might Live." Philip Webb wrote that business decisions were made and carried out in an atmosphere "like a picnic." This was of a piece with Morris's view of work as play. In *News from Nowhere*, a crew of men out working on the roads look like "a boating party at Oxford," refreshing themselves at lunch with a picnic basket stocked with cold pie and bottles of wine. Morris was a great wine drinker, and Fiona MacCarthy paints a pleasant picture of him at the Red House:

> . . . Morris coming up from the cellar before dinner, beaming with joy, with his hands full of bottles of wine and more bottles tucked under his arms. At Red House, aged twenty-six, Morris was in his element, the reincarnation of the medieval host. The house swarmed with his friends, who were collected from the station in a horse-drawn wagon with curtains made of leather.

The Red House was succeeded by studios in London that Morris, Burne-Jones, Rossetti, and their partners, in what would be known simply as "The Firm," established for the manufacture and sale of tapestries, metal work, stained glass, wood carving, and furniture painted with medieval designs. A visitor described Morris wearing a blue smock, attending to clients in person, writing out the bills himself. Rossetti, whose merciless and relentless caricatures of Morris border on the sadistic, did one called "The Bard and Petty Tradesman," where two bearded, roly-poly William Morrises stand back to back, one playing the harp of the poet, one hunched behind the shop counter determinedly ready to close a sale.

Rossetti mocked him for sullying the purity of his artistic mission, but Morris's happy ability to happily include many capabilities within his capacious personality represents the essence of his being. When William De Morgan first visited the ateliers at Red Lion Square, he found Morris "dressed in vestments and posed as if playing on a regal, a small portable organ, 'to illustrate points in connection with stained glass.' Somehow he stayed dignified."

Later still, Morris moved to a house he dubbed Kelmscott House, on the banks of the Thames in Hammersmith. Bernard Shaw celebrated the house in these terms:

> There was an extraordinary discrimination at work in this magical house. Nothing in it was there because it was interesting or quaint or rare or hereditary, like grandmother's or uncle's portrait. Everything that was necessary was clean and handsome: everything else was beautiful and beautifully presented. There was an oriental carpet so lovely that it would have been a sin to walk on it; consequently it was not on the floor but on the wall and halfway across the ceiling.

Kelmscott House is now privately owned, but the basement and coach house are home to the William Morris Society, and the place is well worth a visit. I was thrilled, when I went there, to find myself in the space where this extraordinary man lived and worked. One of the presses that were used to print Morris's handset books is there, along with racks of lead typefaces. Nearby on the banks of the Thames stands the Dove, one of the pleasantest and most old-fashioned pubs left in London. At the museum itself a plaque has been erected, quoting from *News from Nowhere*: "Guests and neighbours, on the site of this Guest-hall once stood the lecture-room of the Hammersmith Socialists. Drink a glass to the memory!"

Max Beerbohm: Taking the Starch out of Eminent Victorians

Much of what we know about the milieu, the personalities, the subtleties of life in late Victorian and Edwardian England we owe to caricatures drawn by Max Beerbohm and the witty commentaries he wrote to accompany them. "So many dead people," his friend and biographer S. N. Behrman wrote, "depend for their lives on Max." My favorite caricature, I suppose, is "Mr. W. B. Yeats presenting Mr. George Moore to the Queen of the Fairies." The willowy, effeminate young Yeats, with his lank hair, pince-nez, and flowing bow tie introduces the dumpy, saturnine Moore, blank and clueless, to little Tinker Bell.

Max's was an age of great pretentiousness. People took themselves very seriously—Yeats certainly did!—but that became impossible once Max's pen went to work on them. Not even the royals could claim an exemption. "Queen Victoria and the Prince of Wales" shows a very fat Queen Victoria seated like a Buddha (supposing Buddha to have been fond of sausages) with her hands in her lap, every inch of her amplitude oozing self-righteousness, while her playboy son, chastened, also very fat, stands in the corner, penitently facing the wall.

If we did not have caricatures like "The small hours at 16, Cheyne Walk—Algernon reading 'Anactoria' to Gabriel and William," we would be robbed of a way of imagining some of the leading figures of the late Victorian age: the tiny, strange-looking, chinless Swinburne reading to a morose William Michael Rossetti and his brother, the poet and painter Dante Gabriel Rossetti, as fat as Queen Victoria herself, sprawled on a chaise longue, looking like Jabba the Hut in a three-piece suit.

In addition to his renown as a caricaturist and the author of a cult novel, *Zuleika Dobson*, which gives perhaps the best picture of Oxford ever committed to print, Beerbohm's most enduring legacy is his essays. One must stretch one's idea of what is meant by an essay, however, because like Charles Lamb, Beerbohm was as much memoirist and social historian as he was author of the classic, unified composition we think of as the English essay. His writings are filled with retrospective evocations of places like the domino room in the legendary Café Royal in Piccadilly in "Enoch Soames: A Memory of the Eighteen-Nineties":

> There, in that exuberant vista of gilding and crimson velvet set amidst all those opposing mirrors and upholding caryatids, with fumes of tobacco ever rising to the painted and pagan ceiling, and with the hum of presumably cynical conversation broken into so sharply now and again by the clatter of dominoes shuffled on marble tables, I drew a deep breath and, "This indeed," said I to myself, "is life!"

Readers would hardly guess that Enoch Soames was a made-up character, so true to type is he, so real are his surroundings. To borrow Marianne Moore's words, he is an imaginary toad in a real garden. The gilded and mirrored room where Soames is standing—crimson velvet curtains, faux classical decor and all the rest of it—can be found under the heading DINING AND LUNCHEON ROOMS—WESTWARD OF TEMPLE BAR in *Murray's Handbook to London As It Is*, 1879, with this description: "*Café Royal*, 68, Regent-street—good foreign cookery and French wines."

"Already I feel myself a trifle outmoded," this twenty-year-old roué wrote back in Queen Victoria's century. "I belong to the Beardsley period." Max Beerbohm was born in 1870, just nine years before the date of *Murray's Handbook,* and he flourished from the last decade of Queen Victoria's reign through the First World War and on into the reign of George V. He lived, astonishingly, until 1956, the year Elvis Presley topped the charts in America with "Hound Dog." He died in Rapallo, where he had lived for almost fifty years.

Virginia Woolf wrote of Beerbohm's contribution to the English essay in her *Common Reader:*

> What Mr. Beerbohm gave was, of course, himself. This presence, which has haunted the essay fitfully from the time of Montaigne, had been in exile since the death of Charles Lamb. . . . Thus, some time in the nineties, it must have surprised readers accustomed to exhortation, information, and denunciation to find themselves familiarly addressed by a voice which seemed to belong to a man no larger than themselves. . . . He was himself, simply and directly, and himself he has remained. . . . He has brought personality into literature, not unconsciously and impurely, but so consciously and purely that we do not know whether there is any relation between Max the essayist and Mr. Beerbohm the man.

Virginia Woolf calls Beerbohm "the prince of his profession," and Philip Lopate echoes her words in his selection of Beerbohm's work called *The Prince of Minor Writers.* Max never, I think, aspired to be anything *but* minor.

‹‹‹‹‹‹‹‹

The reader will forgive me for referring to Sir Henry Maximilian Beerbohm as Max. Everyone called him that, and there is something about the persona he projects that makes it seem wrong to call him anything else. He was known not only as Max but as "the incomparable Max," an epithet bestowed by George Bernard Shaw. Max was having none of it: "Note that I am *not* incomparable. Compare me. Compare me as essayist (for instance) with other essayists. Point out how much less human I am than Lamb, how much less intellectual than

Hazlitt, and what an ignoramus beside Belloc; and how Chesterton's high spirits and abundance shame me."

The juxtaposition puts Max in choice company. But if we are going to make the comparisons he suggests, it must be admitted that Max never wrote an essay so daringly imaginative, strangely moving, and just flat-out brilliant as Charles Lamb's "Dream Children," which goes, almost frighteningly, to the very edge of human existence, probing the porous membrane that separates the living from the dead. Nor did Max ever write anything that reveals the oneness of existence as G. K. Chesterton's *A Piece of Chalk* does.

Having acquired the reputation at Oxford as a force to be reckoned with, young Max was introduced into the theatrical world by his half-brother, the actor and impresario Sir Herbert Beerbohm Tree, owner of His Majesty's Theatre in London. His brother enlisted the young man as his press agent, but Max spent too much time polishing his lapidary prose ever to be a success at the job. Despite this, the theatrical world was forever Max's milieu. The heroine of *Zuleika Dobson* is an actress. In 1898 Shaw chose him to be his successor as drama critic for the *Saturday Review*, and though he claimed not to like the theatre, he continued in that job for twelve years before moving to Italy in 1910. His first contribution was an essay called "Why I Ought Not to Have Become a Dramatic Critic."

Max had a habit of falling in love with actresses, one of whom described her first impression of him at a supper party given by Tree, "smiling that insidious smile of his, bowing gently to his partner while his great eyes stared dreamily ahead." Finally he married the American actress Florence Kahn from Memphis, Tennessee, who had starred in the role of Rebecca West in a London production of Ibsen's *Rosmersholm*. "Miss Kahn's acting," Max wrote in a rave review, "is not more remarkable than in its appeal to the sense of beauty. Throughout the play, not a tone is inharmonious, not a movement without grace." For this dandy, this self-described holdover from the Nineties, with its gospel of aestheticism, there was no art without beauty. The new theatre of Ibsen and Shaw could never please him, because it dealt in ideas rather than human emotions, and beauty was not its aim. "G.B.S. has no aesthetic sense," he once remarked. "He is not an artist."

This was also Yeats's view. After seeing a performance of *Arms and the Man*, the great Irish poet wrote, "I had a nightmare that I was haunted by a sewing-machine, that clicked and shone, but the incredible thing was that the machine smiled, smiled perpetually." The sewing machine, of course, was Shaw. Of the playwright's audience, Max asked, "Do they remember what G.B.S. said to them? Has it clarified their minds? Are they kinder, more thoughtful, more civilized, happier?"

Max by contrast never tries to improve or reform his readers. He is always himself—frank, not shy about coming across as lazy or unintellectual, always sublimely unimproved. His commonsensical attitude undercuts the posturing of figures like Shaw, Kipling, and Yeats. His wonderful essay, "Laughter," begins: "M. Bergson, in his well-known essay on this theme, says . . . well, he says many things; but none of these, though I have just read them, do I clearly remember, nor am I sure that in the act of reading I understood any of them."

Ever the empirically minded, plain-spoken Englishman, he also delighted in taking exception to the improving habits of the Victorians. His essay "Going Out for a Walk" begins, "It is a fact that not once in all my life have I gone out for a walk. I have been taken out for walks; but that is another matter. Even while I trotted prattling by my nurse's side I regretted the good old days when I had, and wasn't, a perambulator."

Among the most winning of his taking-the-starch-out-of-stuffy-people essays is "A Point To Be Remembered by Very Eminent Men." The essay is hard to quote from because the humor builds up in waves, as Max, with a straight face, gives helpful hints for the best ways a "Very Eminent Man" should set up an acolyte's first meeting with him. The meeting, for starters, should not be outdoors, but in a room. "The open air is not really a good setting for a hero. It is too diffuse. It is too impersonal. Four walls, a ceiling, and a floor—these things are needed to concentrate for the worshipper the vision vouchsafed."

‹‹‹‹‹‹‹

Dividing mankind into two categories is something every essayist must, it seems, try at least once. Charles Lamb's "The Two Races of

Men" (borrowers and lenders) is perhaps the locus classicus. In our own day there is Isaiah Berlin's "The Fox and the Hedgehog." Max probably modeled his essay, "Hosts and Guests," after Lamb's. Discoursing on the uniquely human custom of hospitality, Max reminds us that "Lions do not ask one another to their lairs, nor do birds keep open nests. . . . when you give a bone to your dog, does he run out and invite another dog to share it with him?—and does your cat insist on having a circle of other cats around her saucer of milk?"

Surveying the annals of history for outstanding examples of hospitality violated, he says, "I maintain that though you would often in the fifteenth century have heard the snobbish Roman say, in a would-be off-hand tone 'I am dining with the Borgias tonight,' no Roman ever was able to say 'I dined last night with the Borgias.'" To cap the succession of drolleries from history, Max deadpans it: "To mankind in general Macbeth and Lady Macbeth stand out as the supreme type of all a host and hostess should not be. Hence the marked coolness of Scotsmen toward Shakespeare."

Belying somewhat his early pose as a dandy, Beerbohm had been, at Charterhouse and Merton College, a more than passable Latinist. Ronald Searle was on target when he drew, for a *Festschrift* celebrating Max's eightieth birthday, the frail old man wearing a toga, smoking a cigarette through a long holder, world-weary, his heavy-lidded eyes drooping, a laurel wreath set rakishly, in S. N. Behrman's words, at "the same angle at which he habitually set his straw hat." The caption is, "Max accepting with resignation his place among the classics."

My favorite Beerbohm of all is "No. 2. The Pines," a hilarious and at the same time affectionate and touching account of the young Max's visits to the aging former *enfant terrible* of English poetry, Charles Algernon Swinburne, and his companion, Theodore Watts-Dunton, at Watts-Dunton's modest home in Putney—a London suburb in those days, now absorbed by the metropolis. To appreciate Max's sense of wonder that Swinburne should still be living, and living in Putney, one has to see the poet as Max's generation saw him: "The essential Swinburne was still the earliest. He was and would always be the flammiferous boy of the dim past—a legendary creature, sole kin to the phoenix." Now, in 1914, when the young Beerbohm goes timorously to pay a call, he casts himself as the very type of the acolyte going to meet A Very Eminent Man.

> You do not usually associate a man of genius, when you see one, with any social class; and, Swinburne being of an aspect so unrelated as it was to any species of human kind, I wondered the more that almost the first impression he made on me, or would make on any one, was that of a very great gentleman indeed. Not of an old gentleman, either. Sparse and straggling though the grey hair was that fringed the immense pale dome of his head, and venerably haloed though he was for me by his greatness, there was yet about him something— boyish? girlish? Childish, rather; something of a beautifully well-bred child. But he had the eyes of a god, and the smile of an elf.

In describing Swinburne's way of talking, "The whole manner and method had certainly a strong element of oddness; but no one incapable of condemning as unmanly the song of a lark would have called it affected."

It is true that Max Beerbohm as a satirist, caricaturist, and student of human nature could pull the pedestal out from under any eminent person and enjoy it immensely, and yet at the same time his work is suffused with kindness. Who else could have resisted the temptation to make sport of so singular a character as poor old Swinburne? Montaigne famously had Terence's words, *Homo sum, humani nihil a me alienum puto*, "I am a man, nothing human is alien to me," carved into the roof beam of his tower in the Dordogne. Max would have found a way to poke fun at this saying, too, and yet it suits him right down to his spats.

John Betjeman
in His Element

J ohn Betjeman was a High-Church Anglican whose passions included trains, off-the-beaten-track English villages, church bells, tea rooms, Victorian pubs, amateur theatricals, and champagne at breakfast. *Summoned by Bells* is his autobiography, written in blank verse. After working as a journalist and film critic when he first came down from Oxford, he edited the Shell series of travel guides to the English counties, wrote poetry that was immensely popular in Britain, and became a television personality during the late sixties and seventies. He was knighted by Queen Elizabeth in 1969, becoming Sir John Betjeman. In 1972 he was named Poet Laureate.

Betjeman's love for old architecture extended to train stations and to unfashionable Victorian churches like William Butterfield's polychromatic All Saints' Margaret Street in London. Without his efforts and those of like-minded friends, London landmarks like Liverpool Street Station would have been torn down and replaced with hideous, second-rate modern structures. It's hard to look without a shudder at drawings of the replacement proposed by supposedly reputable architects in 1971 for the magnificent old station at Liverpool Street, with its soaring cast-iron Gothic arches and its airy roof. Too bad there was no John Betjeman in the United States when New York's Penn Station was demolished and replaced by the shadowy and shoddy grotto that now goes by the same name, with water dripping from the ceiling and homeless people sleeping on cardboard in shadowy corners.

Perhaps the greatest debt that lovers of trains and Victorian architecture owe to Betjeman is for the support he marshaled to save St. Pancras Station, a stunning Gothic Revival extravaganza that now serves as the British terminal for the Eurostar express to Paris. British Rail named an engine after him, the Sir John Betjeman. A statue of Betjeman was erected on one of the platforms at St. Pancras. There he stands in bronze—distracted, untidy, his overbite noticeable, the buttons of his waistcoat under strain, looking like the White Rabbit from *Alice in Wonderland*, his jacket pockets stuffed with papers, craning up at Arrivals and Departures.

>>>>>>>>>

As a man, Betjeman has an honorable place in a long tradition of British aesthetes and eccentrics. Evelyn Waugh modeled Sebastian Flyte's teddy bear affectation—if affectation is what it was—after Betjeman's. Lord Sebastian's stuffed animal was called Aloysius, Betjeman's was Archibald Ormsby-Gore, Archie for short. Like many gifted people before and since, Betjeman was bisexual—schoolboy crushes and locker-room intimacies followed by marriage and family.

Waugh and Betjeman had a brief fling at Oxford, difficult as that is to imagine when one sees pictures from later in life of the portly cherubic poet and the apoplectic novelist in his checkered tweed suits. Waugh's story and Betjeman's are intertwined in many ways. Both grew up in middle-class Highgate, North London, both were briefly schoolmasters after undistinguished careers at university, both became writers who indelibly recorded choice aspects of British life.

The poet's father, Ernest, prospered as a manufacturer of luxury items for the rich. Here is an employee's account of one commission the firm garnered:

The Maharajah of Patiala was in the Haymarket Hotel. Through Asprey's we were given the commission to make five huge teak trunks, one for each of his five wives. Each trunk was fully fitted with solid silver washing and bathing utensils—bowls, wash-basins, hand-basins, soap-boxes, toothbrush holders. The bottles for pouring hot water had spouts with tigers' heads.

The family later moved to the posher confines of Cheyne Walk in Chelsea, one of the best addresses in London, and the home for many years of Dante Gabriel Rossetti, whom we encountered in the previous chapter. But Betjeman's early years were spent in his family's villa in Highgate. Social distinctions are the bread and butter of English life, the secret vice of many an Englishman, and the young Betjeman was acutely conscious of living betwixt and between, as he writes in *Summoned by Bells*:

> We were a lower, lesser world
> Than that remote one of the carriage folk
> Who left their cedars and brown garden walls
> In care of servants.

After Highgate Junior School, Betjeman was enrolled at the Dragon Preparatory School in Oxford, and in these surroundings he taught himself the varying styles of English architecture, cycling with other boys to see churches in the town and the surrounding countryside. In *Summoned by Bells* he recounts the excitement that accompanied this learning experience, humorously quoting a phrase from some old guidebook and using the common abbreviations for Norman, Early English, Decorated, and Perpendicular, architectural nomenclature for the four periods of English Gothic:

> Can words express the unexampled thrill
> I first enjoyed in Norm., E.E., and Dec.?
> Norm., so crude and round and strong and primitive,
> E.E., so lofty, pointed, fine and pure,
> And Dec. the high perfection of it all,
> Flowingly curvilinear, from which
> The Perp. showed such a 'lamentable decline'.

Betjeman's love for old buildings extended, of course, to secular architecture, and when, after matriculating at Oxford following boarding school at Marlborough, he met, among the toffs and aesthetes, other undergraduates with similar tastes to his own. Betjeman had hated Marlborough, where like many another schoolboy before and since, he was bullied by the "hearties." His tutor at Magdalen College was C. S. Lewis, for whom Betjeman developed a life-long antipathy.

Among his friends was Robert Byron, author of several incomparable travel books including his masterpiece, *The Road to Oxiana,* which narrates a trip through Iran and Afghanistan in search of rare examples of Timurid and Sassanian architecture, and *The Station,* the story of an excursion to Mount Athos with a group of friends that included David Talbot Rice, whose little book, *Byzantine Art,* is still one of the best introductions to the subject. Bevis Hillier remarks of Robert Byron that "He looked remarkably like Queen Victoria, and he made full use of the resemblance whenever he went to fancy-dress parties." Byron was tragically killed in 1941 when the ship he was on, bound for Cairo, was torpedoed by the Germans.

Betjeman had altogether too much fun at Oxford, did poorly on his exams, and was eventually sent down. Some of his circle there came from the landed aristocracy, and through friendships with them, he got inside some magnificent houses. One such chum was John Dugdale, whose family seat was the remarkable Sezincote, an eclectic masterpiece built in the Neo-Mughal style for a nabob, one of those eighteenth-century grandees who got rich in India, brought their wealth home, and built impressive country houses for themselves in England. Here the young poet took his "First steps in learning how to be a guest, / First wood-smoke-scented luxury of life / In the large ambience of a country house."

>>>>>>>>

The story of Charles Ryder's romance with the Marchmain family in Evelyn Waugh's *Brideshead Revisited* reflects the give-and-take between the upper middle class and the landed aristocracy that has quietly gone on for centuries. Both groups have always had something the other wanted. In some cases it has simply been money. Many a well-heeled middleclass parvenu has married the daughter of an earl or duke and thus provided his son with a title. Many a rich heiress, often from the western side of the Atlantic, has brought to her marriage with a member of the aristocracy the money needed to save an ancient family and their country seat from ruin. Waugh himself, once he had made a small fortune as a novelist, married the daughter of an Old Catholic family and bought an estate in Gloucestershire called Piers Court, where he set himself up as a country squire.

But it is not always simply money that attracts aristos to those outside their circle. Often they just want an escape from the boredom of conventional lives. The interplay continues, in rock'n'roll as in literature. Keith Richards writes in his memoir, *Life*:

> Suddenly we [the Rolling Stones] were being courted by half the aristocracy, the younger scions, the heir to some ancient pile, the Ormsby-Gores, the Tennants, the whole lot. I've never known if they were slumming or we were snobbing. They were very nice people. I decided it was no skin off my nose. If somebody's interested, they're welcome. You want to hang, you want to hang.

Everyone, seemingly, wanted to hang with John Betjeman. And he was glad to play court jester in the homes of friends with titles and country seats to match.

Later in life, his own marriage disintegrating, Betjeman fell in love with Lady Elizabeth Cavendish, sister to the Duke of Devonshire, who was to be his companion for the rest of his life. She was lady-in-waiting to Princess Margaret, the Queen's unconventional younger sister, with whom Betjeman shared a taste for outrageous jokes and large whiskeys. Through her he ended up meeting other members of the royal family, including Prince Charles, who shared Sir John's conservative taste in architecture. The new Poet Laureate had a way of making the Prince laugh, and judging from the Prince of Wales's public demeanor, that would seem to be no small accomplishment.

Saving England

From the late Middle Ages up to the Second World War, country houses were where Britain's greatest concentrations of art and architecture were to be found. These establishments were a focal point for the patronage and collecting of art. The gentleman's "cabinet of curiosities" and the paintings he hung in his drawing room were the first British museums and galleries.

And just think what a lovely gallery space a country house drawing room makes. When you look at Velasquez's *Rokeby Venus* in the National Gallery in London, spare a thought for the painting's nineteenth-century owner, J. B. S. Morritt, owner of Rokeby Park in County Durham. Mr. Morritt referred once to the painting as "my fine picture of Venus's backside which I have at length exalted over my chimney piece in the library."

Britain's great architects—Inigo Jones, Christopher Wren, Vanbrugh, Hawksmoor, William Kent, the Adams, Nash, Sir John Soane, Charles Barry, even the arch-Gothick Pugin, up through the great purveyors of Arts & Crafts, Norman Shaw, Voysey, and Lutyens—not to mention dozens of unknowns—made their mark on these houses.

As a sub-plot to the tragedy of the Great War and Britain's stubborn refusal to surrender to tyranny during World War II, a half-millennium of aristocratic civilization came to an end in the twentieth century. During this period the National Trust was founded in the hope of preserving at least some of the nation's most distinctive great houses. The young James Lees-Milne got a job there when the Trust was first established, and he was assigned the task of drawing up a list of houses to be saved.

>>>>>>>>>

Lees-Milne is known as a biographer of aristocratic subjects and a prolific author on architecture and interior design, but chiefly he is celebrated for his diaries, which chronicle the world of upper-crust life in England from his schooldays at Eton in the early 1920s through his pioneering work with the Trust, beginning in the 1940s and lasting for thirty years. By the time of his death at the age of eighty-nine in 1997, he had become recognized as "a national treasure" like the country houses he helped save from destruction.

Lees-Milne was refreshingly self-effacing, sometimes embarrassingly so. He wrote the following self-assessment two years before his death: "I suppose an intellectual is someone who thinks thoughts and pursues them. I haven't really thought a thought in fifty-five years." In common with his friend, fellow aesthete, and hero of architectural preservation John Betjeman, Lees-Milne emerged from an undistinguished undergraduate career at Oxford with few prospects. His bewildered father, the very model of a country squire (though the family fortune was made in the cotton mills of Lancashire), told the young man to put on his only decent suit and pack a bag, then drove him up to London and enrolled his son in Miss Blakeney's Stenography School for Young Ladies in Chelsea, paying a year's tuition in advance.

But Oxford had provided Jim (as everyone seems to have called him) with an education that would be the making of him. He writes in his autobiography, *Another Self*:

The university city is unsurpassed in the variety of distinguished buildings. I learnt at Oxford how of all the arts architecture is the only one which cannot be ignored by the philistine or the indifferent. ... I also realised the terrible fragility of architecture. It is vulnerable to every insult, whether from mutilation or indirect neglect, ignorant improvement, or environmental change.

Lees-Milne was dirt-poor in London—even though his wealthy parents spent money like it was going out of style—and he had to walk everywhere, which meant that he came to know London and its architecture from the ground up. Being penniless, but well-connected as an Old Etonian, the young man also depended on the patronage of the great and the good. After a few years in the capital he became a protégé of the bisexual Harold Nicolson, husband of Vita Sackville-West. His biographer, Michael Bloch, describes how he came to work for the newly formed National Trust, and Bloch's description sums up how things were done in the circles the young Lees-Milne had come to move in.

> Jim heard about the vacancy from the Nicolsons. Through Harold he had got to know Vita, to whom he had confided his desire to help save country houses. Hilda Matheson, a formidable lesbian who had worked for the secret service and the BBC, learned about the job from her brother Donald MacLeod Matheson, the Trust's Secretary since 1934; she mentioned it to Vita (her former lover), who mentioned it to Harold, who mentioned it to Jim.

Lees-Milne's marriage, when he was forty, to Alvilde Bridges (Viscountess Chaplin) mirrored that of Harold Nicolson and Vita Sackville-West. When they moved into a house on the Badminton estate called Essex House, some of their friends found it amusing to refer to the place as "Bi-sex House." Jim's long-running involvement with Harold Nicolson was matched by Alvilde's torrid affair with Vita Sackville-West.

Lees-Milne's modesty, combined with his immense knowledge of the subjects he most cared about, served him well when meeting and gaining the confidence of the owners of great houses which could be saved only if the National Trust stepped in. As Michael Bloch observes, "He admitted to an ability 'to adjust myself to different sorts of people . . . from the sophisticated to the simple, the rich to the poor, the clever to the stupid. . . . Which means of course that I am a chameleon . . . a mirror of other people's moods, opinions and prejudices.'" When these down-at-heel landowners met Lees-Milne, they knew they were in the presence of one of their own, not some presumptuous bureaucrat—a self-effacing, unassuming young man who often cycled to the houses he visited.

The early diaries constitute Lees-Milne's masterpiece. He was a Londoner when Hitler tried to bomb the British into submission, and he came close to being killed more than once during the Blitz. Discharged from the army because of nerve damage, blackouts, and spells of amnesia, he was later diagnosed with a rare form of epilepsy brought on by traumas caused by the several bombs that exploded close to him. Lees-Milne's accounts of country houses and their owners are priceless both as historical record and as brilliant vignettes in their own right. Here is one from 1943:

> Arrived at Elsing Hall late. It is a 1740s house built in square knapped flints; and has square gables typical of these parts with heraldic flints. . . . It has been unfortunately restored in the 1850s. . . . Mrs Thackerary and her sister Miss Clarendon Hyde are the owners, and the last of their line since the reign of Egbert. . . . They are impoverished. . . . The house is incredibly shabby, dirty and primitive. . . . In spite of the terrible *délabrement* among which they live, these ladies with their long Plantagenet pedigree, their courtesy and ease of manner, were enchanting.

The later *Diaries, 1984–1997* provides an unparalleled social history of the time. They show the *dramatis personae* of the author's early years as those characters decline and die. Funerals fill these pages, some of them very grand, such as that of the old Duke of Beaufort, on whose estate the Lees-Milnes lived during their last years. Because of the part he played in saving something of its heritage, it is appropriate that Lees-Milne should have lived long enough to chronicle the last years of Britain's remarkable tradition of great architecture and artistic patronage.

Given the circles in which he moved, who else could have given us sketches of notable Englishmen of the twentieth century ranging from Sir Winston Churchill to Prince Charles to Sir Mick Jagger? Here is his unflattering sketch of the great statesman and national hero at a small luncheon party in 1954:

> Sir W. looks like a small, fat and frail doll or baby, with a white and pink face, most unnatural in an adult, and no lines at all. There is a celluloid quality about the skin which is alarming. He shuffles. His back view is funny. He was wearing too short a black jacket exposing a shiny striped seat. The front part of him is different in that it is smartly dressed—an expanse of white, semi-starched shirt and cuffs with links, the habitual white winged collar and spotted bow-tie.

As for HRH Charles, Prince of Wales, Lees-Milne agreed with the Prince's conservative views of architecture:

> sat up watching the Prince of Wales talking about modern architecture. I agreed with every word. . . . He spoke well and confidently, never tripping up. Very outspoken on how during the Sixties the landscape was blighted by tower blocks etc. . . . The modernist architects build for themselves without considering either the public at large or the wretched victims obliged to live in their terrible cages of torture.

> Upon meeting him, we have a jolly talk. I feel this very sweet man is deadly serious and worries more about the devastation caused to the world's face than any other problem. He says he feels John Betjeman's mantle has fallen on his shoulders. This is rather touching, but alas he is too ignorant, groping for something which eludes.

Alvilde Lees-Milne, his wife, was a celebrated designer of gardens who was asked by Mick Jagger to design the garden at his chateau in France, and thus she and her husband got to know him. Here is Mick thirty years ago:

> A nice little man, unassuming. He had been looking at schools for his daughter. Dressed very soberly, as a parent should. He is tiny. Fresh, youthful face. Figure not good. Too thin and chest hollow. Proffers the fingers to shake hand. No firm grip.

Poor Mick.

Questions of Travel

The term "travel writing" is badly in need of an overhaul. A workhorse and a thoroughbred share ſtable room within the capacious barn of this genre. The workaday version directs you to the moſt priſtine beaches, tells you which reſtaurants to eat at, which hotels to ſtay in. On the other side of the ſtable ſtands the more elegant mount: literary travel writing, a form of imaginative literature sharing with poetry and fiction a deployment of imagery, characterization, and memorable evocations of local color, drawing its subject matter from the places you travel to when you are not ſtaying at home—"wherever," in Elizabeth Bishop's equivocal words, "that may be." Patrick Leigh Fermor rode the thoroughbred.

"Criticism has never quite known what to call books like these," Paul Fussell wrote in his classic ſtudy, *Abroad: British Literary Traveling between the Wars*. "A travel book, at its pureſt, is addressed to those who do not plan to follow the traveler at all, but who require the exotic or comic anomalies, wonders, and scandals of the literary form *romance* which their own place or time cannot entirely supply."

The British own the franchise. From Lady Mary Wortley Montagu in the eighteenth century on, restless curiosity and a sense of adventure have impelled travelers from those islands on the northwestern edge of Europe to escape the insularity of home and wander freely through the world, large chunks of which were once occupied by an empire on which the sun never set—until it finally did. Lady Mary chronicled life among the Ottoman elite in Constantinople; Arabists like Sir Richard Burton, Freya Stark, Gertrude Bell, Wilfred Thesiger, and Charles Montagu Doughty prefigured Lawrence of Arabia, living and traveling among the Bedouin. Doughty's 1888 *Travels in Arabia Deserta* is a classic of the genre. The young Evelyn Waugh also excelled at literary travel writing; some of his best efforts have been collected in a volume called *When the Going Was Good*. The gold standard is Robert Byron's 1937 book, *The Road to Oxiana*.

Leigh Fermor holds his own with the best of them. His life as a traveler began when he was eighteen. At loose ends, living a louche life in London since being expelled from boarding school for his attentions to the daughter of a local greengrocer, he set out to walk across Europe from the Hook of Holland to Constantinople (a lifelong Hellenophile, he refused to call the city by its Turkish name, Istanbul). Ahead of him, "the Rhine uncoiled . . . the Alps rose up and then the wolf-harbouring Carpathian watersheds and the cordilleras of the Balkans," and at journey's end, the "levitating skyline of Constantinople pricked its sheaves of thin cylinders and its hemispheres out of the sea-mist." The year was 1933, and the young adventurer couldn't have picked a more momentous or pivotal year to traverse the continent. European civilization, shaken by the tragedy of the Great War, would soon be radically altered by the evil forces conjured up by Nazism and Soviet Communism.

Out of this epic journey emerged Leigh Fermor's two best books, *A Time of Gifts*, 1977, and *Between the Woods and the Water*, 1986. The attentive reader will notice how many decades elapsed between making the journey and writing the books. The middle-aged writer managed to slip back into the skin of the young traveler, remembering his adventures, and no doubt inventing what he could not remember. His excitement in reliving youthful adventures adds relish to the telling of the tale.

During World War II, Leigh Fermor fought with the Greek resistance on Crete and became a legendary hero for the daring stunt he and a few comrades pulled off. They kidnapped a German general right under the guns of the occupying army and spirited him away across rugged mountains and finally to captivity in Cairo, giving a huge boost to Greek self-confidence in a very dark time. By the time he got around to writing *A Time of Gifts* and *Between the Woods and the Water*, Paddy had settled in the Mani district of southern Greece and published two books about his adopted country: *Mani: Travels in the Southern Peloponnese*, 1958, and *Roumeli: Travels in Northern Greece*, 1966.

During his sojourn in Germany in 1933, Paddy instantly saw Nazism for what it was. He recognized from the very beginning its swaggering brutality, the easy way its ideology—equal parts paranoia and *folie de grandeur*—won the allegiance of German burghers and prosperous peasants. Among the beer guzzlers in "The Munich Hofbräuhaus" from *A Time of Gifts*, the young backpacker finds that he has "strayed by mistake into a room full of SS officers, Gruppen- and Sturmbannführers, black from their lightning-flash collars to the forest of tall boots underneath the table. The window embrasure was piled high with their skull-and-crossbones caps." It's an unsettling image, and the sense of foreboding is eerie.

The walk across Europe turned out to be something less rigorous and more fantastic than Leigh could have anticipated. The magnetic young Englishman finds himself on an island in the Danube drinking *raki* with descendants of soldiers from the old Turkish occupation, being adopted by members of the aristocracy from the former Austro-Hungarian Empire and passed from *schloss* to chateau to book-crammed manor house. In "Bicycle Polo" Paddy bangs around the courtyard of a fabulous chateau with his host and their guests, who play the sport of kings while mounted on rusty old bicycles in lieu of polo ponies.

This gregarious traveler is as much at home sharing a supper of lentils and mackerel with Bulgarian fishermen in a cave on the Black Sea coast; accepting the hospitality of gypsies in their camp and sleeping with one eye open, lest his horse (borrowed) be stolen during the night; having dinner on the roof of a tower in the Mani district of Greece; and playing billiards and drinking whisky-and-soda with Lady Wentworth, a descendant of Lord Byron, in an English country house, where "All was quiet, except for the occasional squeak of French chalk, the fall of a log, a splutter of raindrops down the chimney, the occasional hiss of the syphon."

>>>>>>>>

Paddy is a master of prose fantasies in which he uncorks some elaborate conceit where the author's imagination leaves the limitations of time and space far behind. In "The Polymath" from *A Time of Gifts,* a *Mitteleuropean* aristocrat with seemingly encyclopedic knowledge recounts the story of Western civilization in a sweepingly brilliant telescoping of centuries into minutes. In "The Last Emperor of Byzantium," during an *ouzo*-powered session in a Greek fisherman's hut, Paddy spins out a glorious fantasy of the restoration of Byzantine civilization to Constantinople.

Though he lived most of his later life in Greece, Leigh Fermor was also back home in England from time to time, and his portraits of eccentric aristocrats like Lady Wentworth, Iain Moncreiffe, and Auberon Herbert make for choice reading. The piece on Auberon Herbert begins on Jermyn Street in the heart of London's clubland:

> It was twelve o'clock on a dirty and rainy morning toward the end of the war, but inside the old Wilton's just off St James's Square everything was lamplit and snug. The only other customer was a spectacular young Polish officer who was ordering a double vodka at the bar in such a way that I had to cast a second glance at the white eagles on the collar, the coloured flashes and the blue and white decorations and medal ribbons.

We are in the hands of a virtuoso storyteller. Leigh Fermor sketches out character, creates atmosphere, and effortlessly seizes our attention. Travel writer, memoirist, elegist of a vanishing past—describe him how you will—Patrick Leigh Fermor is one of the masters of English prose, someone whose work bears comparison to Gibbon, Waugh, and the author of *The Anatomy of Melancholy.*

TENNESSEE

River Town

A JOY AND A SADNESS

The Mississippi Delta, I told my companion, repeating a well-known local saying, begins in the lobby of the Peabody Hotel. When I passed on this bit of Memphis lore, Suzy and I were sitting in that commodious lobby underneath the elaborately carved ceiling beams, drinking our mint julep and gin-and-tonic beside the fountain where the famous ducks swim. We were back for a brief visit in Memphis, where I grew up.

"There is a joy, and a sadness in coming back," the Memphis painter Carroll Cloar wrote. "There is a joy in the sense of belonging, of possessing and being possessed by the land where you were born. There is a mixed emotion in remembering, places altered, people long passed." As I look into my native city's past, it occurs to me that some of my own memories may help illuminate aspects of its mixed and sometimes troubled and troubling history.

Upon returning, I found myself rediscovering many things that were once so familiar I didn't even think about them. Summer heat so overpowering that one instinctively looked for the shady side of the street took me by surprise on this visit, but after a day or so I wondered how I could have forgotten about it. I had even forgotten how Memphians pronounce the name of their city. Not MEM-fiss, the first syllable fully pronounced and ending with a rounded labial "m," but more like MEN-fiss, which you say quicker and just touch, in passing, on the final letter of the first syllable.

So many tourists—well-dressed tourists, some of them British, some Australian, some German and French, some with Midwestern accents—surrounded us at the Peabody that it took some effort to reimagine the fabled lobby as the gathering place of Delta planters and Memphis society people that it once was. It took an act of the imagination to summon up those old Memphis and Mississippi accents with which that older generation spoke—a cross between plummy and countrified. Part of me asked: What are tourists doing in my old hometown, the place I couldn't wait to get out of when I was twenty? I was forgetting that Memphis and the Mississippi Delta have now become mythic, legendary places.

THE DELTA

The rich and storied kingdom of the Delta, home of the blues and staging ground for some of America's most enduring literature, is a broad alluvial plain in the northwest sector of Mississippi. One of our great historians, Shelby Foote, author of a magisterial three-volume narrative history of the Civil War, was a son of the Delta, and this is how Mr. Foote characterized the land between the Mississippi and Yazoo Rivers in its early days:

> This incredibly fertile, magnolia-leaf-shaped region, 200 miles in length and 50 miles in average width, bounded east and west by the two rivers that gave it its compound name, and north and south by the hills that rose below and above Memphis and Vicksburg, was nearly roadless through its flat and swampy expanse, was subject to floods in all but the driest seasons, and—except for the presence of a scattering of pioneers who risked its malarial and intestinal disorders for the sake of the richness of its forty-foot topsoil, which in

time, after the felling of its big trees and the draining of its bayous, would make it the best cotton farmland in the world—was the exclusive domain of moccasins, bears, alligators, and panthers.

Thousands of slaves—and, after the Civil War, thousands of tenant farmers, both black and white—labored in cotton fields that reached all the way from the Mississippi levee to the last fringes of wilderness that survived at the eastern borders of the region. It was to Memphis that both the planters and their tenants came for their social and commercial life, to do their shopping, and to indulge in pleasures and vices that could not be addressed in small farming communities.

For the planters, trips to the city meant cotillions and coming-out parties for their daughters, dancing on warm Memphis nights in the roof garden of the Peabody Hotel, drinking gin and bourbon in the lobby where Suzy and I were sitting, amid talk of duck hunting and the price of cotton, shopping for ball gowns and spring frocks at Lowenstein's and Goldsmith's, the big downtown department stores established in the mid-nineteenth century by German Jewish immigrants.

IF BEALE STREET COULD TALK

The black tenants of these same planters flocked to Beale Street, where saloons, gambling dens, and bawdy houses provided employment for musicians from W. C. Handy to Robert Johnson to B.B. King. Young men fresh from the cotton fields of Mississippi got their first taste of the lush life here, gaping at the high-yaller prostitutes and their pimps, alongside gamblers with their zoot suits, long watch chains, and two-toned suede wingtips.

On Beale Street you could buy yourself a live chicken, a bundle of sassafras root, a nickel bag of reefer, or a pint of freshly picked strawberries. A strolling photographer would snap your picture. Gypsies were there to read your palm and tell your fortune; dealers in the occult arts would sell you a black-cat bone, a mojo hand, a John the Conqueroo, or some Dixie Love Oil. The air was fragrant with the irresistible aromas of Memphis barbecue, chicken and chitlins frying, catfish and hushpuppies.

The rise of Beale Street was inextricably linked with Emancipation. When Union troops occupied Memphis in June of 1862 the Hunt house, just east of the party zone of nightclubs and eateries that now pulsates way past midnight on Beale where it intersects Main, was commandeered by General Ulysses S. Grant for his headquarters. Freed slaves gathered around army headquarters, and it was a straight shot west along Beale to the Mississippi River landing with its cluster of warehouses. A steady flow of contraband, soldiers on leave with money to spend, the free and easy life of a river town—it all contributed to the growth of Beale as a good-time street.

But the devil was not the only player on Beale Street. After the war, a freedmen's school taught the three Rs on the grounds of the Hunt house, and black fraternal orders established their lodges in the area. Beale Street Baptist Church first met in a "brush arbor" at the corner of Beale and Main, and the cornerstone for a more substantial structure was laid in 1871. The congregation later moved to Beale and Fourth and subsequently found its permanent home at Beale and Lauderdale.

Memphis and the Delta were always more ethnically diverse than most other parts of the South, with English and Scotch-Irish, Germans, Irish Catholics, Italians, Lebanese Christians, European Jews, Greeks, Chinese, and others migrating to this fast-growing part of what was then the Southwest. One of Memphis's most famous barbecue restaurants, the Rendezvous, located in an alley across from the Peabody Hotel, is run by Charlie Vergos and his family—Memphis Greeks. The Scotch-Irish and English had the cotton business, the Chinese opened laundries and restaurants and established a Chinese Masonic Lodge above a laundry on the street, the Italians operated theatres and saloons, the Jews ran the pawnshops. I bought my first guitar at a pawnshop on Beale. And Beale Street was the site of Lansky Brothers' clothing store, where black musicians and hustlers bought their threads. Elvis Presley, who does not otherwise figure in these pages, outfitted himself at Lansky Brothers too.

But African Americans also proved themselves adept at business, and a thriving black middle class sprang up around South Lauderdale near Beale. Robert Church, who had served as a steward on a Mississippi River steamboat, was what we would now call mixed-race. He set up his own saloon on Beale Street, bought property in the city, and in 1912 became Memphis's first black millionaire. Church was a philanthropically minded man who built a park, playground, and community center near the Beale Street Baptist Church. He went on to open Church's Auditorium, with a seating capacity of two thousand. Booker T. Washington, W. E. B. Du Bois, and Theodore Roosevelt all spoke in Church's Auditorium. Beale Street became known as The Main Street of Negro America.

UP FROM THE DELTA

A good way to get a sense of how the city presented itself to those generations of Mississippians who made the pilgrimage to Memphis is to travel up into the city on the "Blues Highway," Highway 61. I recently did it this way. I have cousins living near Tunica, thirty miles south of Memphis, whom I frequently visit. Their house is a comfortable, welcoming old plantation house about a dozen miles from the DeSoto County line, but it doesn't look a thing like Tara. It's built of cypress logs cut from the surrounding bottomlands and milled on the place. Fields around their house stretch to the horizon across perfectly level land from the river to the Chickasaw Bluffs to the east.

Tunica is where you go to gamble. To me the casinos are really depressing. But I do like the train station the state has transported here and set up beside Highway 61 at the beginning of the conglomeration of casinos. It is from Dundee. Dundee, Mississippi. Casino money has landscaped the highway, and crepe myrtles bloom in the median strip. Cotton is still grown here some years, but the farmers usually plant corn now for ethanol and soy beans for plastic.

From the old plantation system to modern agribusiness. Tenant shacks used to line this highway, but they have become relics of a bygone way of life. Tourism and gaming are how a lot of people in the Delta make their money now. The movie star Morgan Freeman is co-owner of Ground Zero, a blues club in Clarksdale. Some enterprising person has assembled a bunch of these old structures on the Blues Highway and gone into business with the Shackup Inn, a

Delta-themed funky motor court where you can stay in an old tenant farmer's shack and drink beer and listen to the blues in a converted cotton barn. When I was last there, the place was full of English blues fans, perfectly delighted with themselves for having discovered it.

As you travel north into Tennessee the levee ends, and soon the Blues Highway becomes South Third Street. Highway 61 and South Third Street are the underbelly of Memphis. In this stretch of road, the highway is not a highway anymore; it becomes a broad city thoroughfare. The concrete paving is cracked, and ragweed and lamb's quarter grow up out of the fissures. A few homely little churches raise their modest steeples beside the road. A fish market sells fresh perch, catfish, drum, and buffalo.

On the west side of the road stand the brick buildings of the Journey Motor Court, which looks as though it was built in the 1940s. It must have struck people back then as impressively modern. It has been out of business since I can remember, but I think someone lives in there behind the barred windows and doors. Liquor stores are the most popular retail establishments, and they too are guarded by formidable-looking metal bars. Just south of Nonconnah Creek, Ink Stainz, a tattoo and body-piercing establishment, painted purple, stays open late into the night.

EARLY YEARS

As early as the eighteenth century, when the new political entity called the United States of America competed with the Spanish and the French for domination, the desirability of controlling the Chickasaw Bluffs was clear to European explorers. Estaban Roderíguez Miró, at the time an assistant to the Spanish general Galvez, wrote to his superior in 1783, "Your Excellency knows how advantageous it would be to populate the upper part of the river." Gayoso, Governor of Louisiana under the Spanish, bought the land along the river in 1795 from the Chickasaw Indians for $30,000. At first these same Indians continued to live hereabouts. They even built a quarter-mile track to race their ponies. During the presidency of Thomas Jefferson, when the United States bought this part of the country as part of the

Louisiana Purchase, Americans established a trading post on the bluffs to trade with the Chickasaws.

The settlement here thrived off of Mississippi River barge traffic. In 1819 a young lawyer named John Overton, along with Andrew Jackson and James Winchester, two generals of the American army who had defeated the British at the battle of New Orleans, negotiated a treaty of cession with the Chickasaws, who would later be forcibly moved west under the Indian Removal Act when Jackson was elected president. The three men established a town and called it Memphis, after another river city in Egypt, whose name means, we were told in school, "Place of Good Abode." All that remained was to lay out streets and begin selling lots.

A correspondent for the *Western Carolinian* wrote in 1827 that "during the last four months the flow of immigration has surpassed anything of the kind the writer has ever witnessed. It was not uncommon to see eight, ten, or fifteen wagons and carts passing in a single day . . . to the more highly favored climes of the West." An ancestor of mine, Stephen Williford, was one of these immigrants. In 1854 he left Bertie County in coastal North Carolina with his wife and family and three slaves to settle in the new county of Shelby.

Gerald Capers, in his *Memphis, the Biography of a River Town*, writes that West Tennessee's population grew from roughly twenty-five thousand in 1820 to about two hundred thousand in 1840. For this town in a region that was then the Southwest, these were rough and ready days. Murder was common. Even by 1840 the frontier had advanced a scant hundred miles west. It was said that in 1824 there was not enough silver in Memphis "to buy a coonskin":

> . . . a situation which forced merchants to resort to "cut money"; that is, quarters were cut into "bits" (twelve and a half cents). The only coins in circulation were the Mexican dollar, the old Spanish dollar, and the French five-franc piece, while the only paper currency consisted of Tennessee, Georgia, and North Carolina state notes which the Tidewater would accept only at a considerable discount.

"Memphis was then," a traveller in the 1820s wrote, "a small town, ugly, dirty, and sickly. . . . Everything pointed to the certainty that in a short time this squalid village must grow to a great and wealthy city . . . but for many years the population would be uncouth and lawless, and the locality and sanitary conditions of the town promised that disease and death would hold high carnival there." A stage coach line connected the town with Jackson and Nashville to the east.

But by the 1840s the cotton boom was underway, and Memphis, where cotton could be sorted, compressed into bales, and shipped downriver on flatboats to New Orleans and thence to the mills of New England and Liverpool, was part of that boom. In 1853 the town contained "19 groceries; four hat, cap, and boots stores; 37 dry-goods stores; 15 clothing merchants; four auction and commission merchants; two book stores, one musical instrument store, two dentists, five merchant tailors, three millinery establishments, three saddleries, 17 foundries, plumbers, etc.; one flouring mill, five hardware stores, eight drug stores, two real estate agents, nine hotels . . . three factories, two daguerrotypists, three printing offices, six painters, 10 furniture stores . . . three banks, 40 law firms, 32 physicians, three livery stables, three jewelers, Memphis Medical College with eight professors, and four newspapers."

THE WAR

Then war came. Nowadays it is an article of belief from academia to Hollywood that the Civil War was all about slavery. For Abolitionists in the North as well as for the South's wealthiest and most powerful this was surely true. But I am inclined to agree with Gerald Capers's assessment of the situation, at least as far as Tennessee was concerned:

> Had the matter been purely one of protection of slave property, the major issue on which southern and northern civilizations had clashed, the vast majority of southerners could never have been induced to risk their lives in its defense, for four out of five owned no Negroes. The enthusiastic support which the southern cause received outside of the isolated upland regions reveals that men were fighting for more than property—for a way of living which they considered the best way and for their right to live it without interference. Disillusionment and return of reason came with the war; yet

in many cases this conviction was so strong that for four years Kentucky bluebloods and small farmers from Tennessee continued to die on the field of battle rather than betray it.

The disillusionment Capers speaks of came quickly to Memphis. The US Navy blockaded the river early on. "When, after the reverses of the second spring, civilians began to suffer from the shortage of necessaries and the rise in prices which resulted from the blockade, patriotism was no longer rampant. . . . self-preservation became the first concern of all who were not sincerely devoted to the South." On June 6, 1862, in a fierce but brief naval exchange on the river, Memphis fell within a couple of hours and spent the remainder of the war under Federal occupation.

Though the Confederacy suffered significant losses at Shiloh in southwestern Tennessee and at Corinth just over the Mississippi line, and though the Father of Waters itself was slowly but surely coming under Federal domination, few Southern cities suffered as little as did Memphis. Citizens of the occupied city became adept at dealing in contraband. Cotton, gold, and weapons passed profitably through the city's black market.

While the residents of other Southern cities and towns learned to brew their coffee from chicory root, to patch their clothes and twice-turn their frayed collars, Memphians benefitted from the money the Union Army brought to town. For the city's merchants and manufacturers, its dealers in lumber, hardware, and cotton, war on the whole meant that business was booming. By 1863 the population had doubled, swelled by an influx of freed slaves from the surrounding plantations in Arkansas, North Mississippi, and West Tennessee, as well as by carpetbaggers, speculators, and camp followers from the northern states in search of business opportunities.

The aforementioned Hunt house, grandest of the city's antebellum mansions, still stands on Beale Street. With a stout chain-link fence to deter intruders and a For Sale sign out front intermittently, the mansion has somehow survived the ups and downs of urban renewal. In 1862 the Hunts, who made their fortune in the barrel-stave industry, hosted Leonidas Polk, the "Fighting Bishop," a family friend who stayed in Memphis during the first months of the war. From here Bishop Polk, a West Point graduate who took holy orders in the Episcopal Church and was Bishop of Louisiana when war broke out, organized the Provisional Army of Tennessee, planning conscription efforts and laying out a strategy for the war here in its western theatre. After the Confederate defeat at the Battle of Shiloh, the Hunt house was pressed into service as a hospital. Its floors soon became drenched with the blood of the maimed and the dying.

Later, after Memphis fell to the Union Army in June of 1862, General Ulysses S. Grant made his headquarters in the Hunt house. When Mrs. Grant visited, she slept in the house, while the general preferred to bed down in a tent pitched for him in the front yard. Maybe Mrs. Grant didn't like the cigar smoke. As for the house's owners, Grant allowed Mrs. Hunt to take a railroad car full of her furniture and other possessions with her when she left. With these in tow, she followed her husband, Colonel William R. Hunt, in his travels around the Confederacy.

Meanwhile from 1863 to 1865 the wounded from Grant and Sherman's bloody battles in Mississippi were treated here. After the war when the Hunts returned, their carload of chattels was all the furnishings they had left, and they moved it back into their house and began to pick up the pieces of their former life, only to be driven out again by the Yellow Fever epidemics.

During Federal occupation of Memphis, soldiers in the Union Army contributed to the building of a new Roman Catholic church, St. Mary's, and participated in its dedication. Calvary Episcopal Church, built in 1842, is the city's oldest public building. William Tecumseh Sherman, during his time as commanding general in Memphis, attended services at Calvary shortly after the city fell in 1862. When the minister omitted the passage in the prayer for divine protection asking for protection for the President of the United States, Sherman leapt to his feet and loudly supplied the missing prayer.

"HIS NAME IS FORREST"

Naturally the city would prefer to see itself as a center of heroic resistance rather than of accommodation and acquiescence. In this regard the citizens of Memphis differ little from the citizens of Paris, who reinvented what happened during the German occupation of their city from 1940 to 1944. Children of my generation were brought up on stories of daring Confederate raids on the city by guerilla fighters, especially General Nathan Bedford Forrest. "That devil Forrest"—as General William Tecumseh Sherman called him—ranks, along with Stonewall Jackson and Robert E. Lee, among the South's greatest tacticians. He was the only man on either side of the conflict to enlist as a private and rise to the rank of lieutenant general. When asked to name the greatest soldier who fought during the conflict, Lee replied without hesitation, "A man I have never seen, sir. His name is Forrest."

Often when was I was a child in Memphis in the 1940s and 1950s I heard stories of Confederate pluck and derring-do, Federal timidity and ineptitude. I pictured Forrest and his raiders galloping their horses down the streets of the Memphis I knew and into the Gayoso Hotel on Main Street. But Memphis and north Mississippi were quite different places in the 1950s than they had been in the 1840s. Getting into Memphis from the country was not as easy as just driving up the four lanes of Highway 61 in your Honda Accord.

Before he launched his famous raid Forrest was bivouacked in Oxford, Mississippi, eighty highway miles from Memphis. The Confederates, as they would continue to be throughout most of the war, were outnumbered and anxious lest the numerically superior Yankees outflank them and push them farther south. "At the height of this anxiety," in the words of Andrew Lytle's *Bedford Forrest and His Critter Company,* "the order went through the camp for two thousand men to cook rations and prepare for an expedition."

Forrest's approach to fighting, like that of Stonewall Jackson, was to catch the enemy off-guard and attack him when and where he least expected it. Andrew Lytle tells the tale of Forrest's raid with gusto. The story begins when "on August eighteenth, on a night as black as ink and in a pouring rain, the General, fifteen hundred men, and four guns, slipped out of Oxford riding west." He was operating in friendly territory, and to feed his men during the raid, he sent word up ahead asking women between Oxford and Memphis to cook up cornbread and have it ready for the troops as they rode.

One reason for his preeminence as a leader of men was that he didn't simply direct his men in battle, he fought in the front lines. He was wounded many times and had some twenty-nine horses shot from under him. In one such case, during the Battle of Chickamauga, when his horse was shot in the neck he plugged the bullet hole with the finger of one hand while continuing to ride, wielding his sabre with his free hand. Here is how one biographer, John A. Wyeth, describes him:

> Soldier by nature, from earliest boyhood at home on horseback, with firm, erect, and easy seat he rode at the head of the column, an ideal of the *beau sabreur*. From beneath the wide and slightly up-turned brim of the soft felt-hat, which bore no tawdry plumes, the large, deep-set blue eyes were peering with more than usual alert-ness. The look of kindliness which came in moments of repose or gentler mood was gone, and something hard and almost savage had replaced it. The broad, high forehead, the shaggy brows, prominent cheek-bones, and bold, assertive nose told not only the story of his Gaelic origin, but the bull-dog tenacity of the man.

When Forrest's troopers reached Hickahala Creek, swollen to flood stage by the heavy rains, he had his men go to every cabin and ginhouse roundabout and pull up the floors, then carry the planks to the Hickahala Ferry. Others were instructed to cut down telegraph poles and drag them up to the ferry. When they objected that they had no singletrees—those crossbars to which the traces are attached for a horse-drawn wagon or plow—to which the poles could be attached for hauling, Forrest instructed them to tie the traces to their horses' tails.

Having no rope to hand, they stripped muscadine grapevines off the big trees in the forest and used them to tie telegraph poles to the ferry cables, providing a pontoon bridge so the horsemen could ride across the creek. Forrest's scouts, sent ahead into Memphis, ascer-tained the whereabouts of the three Union generals stationed in the town. As his detachment advanced before dawn, a heavy fog settled in.

Captain Bill Forrest, the general's younger brother, hearing a sharp "Who goes there?" replied, "A detachment of the Twelfth Mis-souri Cavalry with Rebel prisoners." He was told to advance. Captain Bill's men proceeded to overpower the pickets the Yankees had posted around the city. Moving forward through fog along the muddy approaches to Memphis, though under orders to keep silent, the men let loose with the high-pitched, spiraling Rebel Yell, their legendarily terrifying battle cry.

Having learned that some of the highest-ranking Union officers were staying at the Gayoso House rather than in their barracks, Bill Forrest galloped to the hotel and right into the lobby itself—in Lytle's witty phrase, "without the formality of dismounting." While one of his fellow officers jumped out of bed, took the time to dress, and ran to the barracks to rally his men, General Cadwallader C. Washburn, who had been left in charge of Memphis while Grant was campaigning in north Mississippi, acted more precipitately. According to the official report made by one of his subordinates, "The general ran away for a safe place in the fort . . . without giving any orders or commands as to what should be done by the troops." The evening I was speaking of at the beginning of this story, as Suzy and I walked from the Peabody Hotel down Charlie Vergos Alley to the barbecue joint, we crossed General Washburn's Escape Alley. It's hard to tell which means more to Memphians, history or barbecue.

Back to 1863. Bursting into the general's room after that officer had absconded, Bill Forrest seized the enemy officer's uniform and sword. After the Confederates had galloped out of town again, they returned these items under a flag of truce. Since Forrest had lived in Memphis before the outbreak of hostilities, Washburn was able to find out who the Confederate general's tailor had been. He had a handsome new uniform made and sent it to Forrest along with a bolt of gray cloth and some gold braid for his staff officers' uniforms. The Union general's fellow officer, General Hurlbut, remarked the next day: "Well, they removed me from command because I couldn't keep Forrest out of West Tennessee; but apparently Washburn can't keep him out of his bedroom."

PLANTATION SLAVERY AND ITS AFTERMATH

The story of Memphis has been a history of racial tensions. The African-American population of the city grew from three thousand in 1860 to fifteen thousand in 1870. After the end of hostilities several thousand black soldiers awaiting discharge clashed in bloody riots with the city's largely Irish-American police force. After several days of rioting, white troops were dispatched from Nashville to restore order, but whole city blocks in the slum neighborhood called Pinch had burned, and in the end forty-four blacks and two whites were slain.

Shortly afterward, the Ku Klux Klan was organized. Nathan Bedford Forrest himself is said to have been the Klan's first grand wizard. The Civil War general whose raid on occupied Memphis was the subject of the previous section of this chapter was the son of a blacksmith from Virginia who had settled his family in the town of Spring Hill in Bedford County in middle Tennessee before moving to the Mississippi wilderness. Forrest grew up to become the kind of self-made man who, contrary to the aristocratic image of itself that the Old South cherished, was probably more typical of this fast-growing and prosperous region in the early nineteenth century.

Much of Mississippi was still a wilderness in those days. The few roads that existed were little more than bridle paths through dense woods. The Forrests lived ten miles from their nearest neighbor, and since Bedford was the oldest son, he became the man of the family. Forrest grew up to become a speculator in property, human and otherwise, and a Mississippi River gambler to boot. For some years he owned a riverboat that ran between Memphis and Vicksburg. As his wealth grew, he engaged in property speculation and at one time owned two Delta plantations near Vicksburg.

By 1861 he was thought to be one of the richest men in the South, with a fortune estimated at $1.5 million, a staggeringly large sum of money at the time. His obituary declares that "He was known to his acquaintances as a man of obscure origin and low associations, a shrewd speculator, negro trader, and duelist, but a man of great energy and brute courage"—qualities that served him well during the war years. Black haired, six foot two, broad shouldered, with piercing blue-gray eyes, he was a commanding presence.

In case you harbor any doubt as to the nature of the slave trade, a flyer from his business, Forrest and Maples, survives, advertising this establishment, which stood at 87 Adams Street between Second and Third (the street we drove up to enter Memphis from Highway 61 in

Mississippi). The flyer makes for chilling reading. Forrest and Maples, according to the flyer, "have constantly on hand the best selected assortment of field hands, house servants & mechanics at their Negro Mart, to be found in the city. They are daily receiving from Virginia, Kentucky and Missouri, fresh supplies of likely young negroes."

"Negroes Sold on Commission," the flyer goes on to declare, with "the highest market price always paid for good stock. Their Jail is capable of containing three hundred, and for comfort, neatness and safety, is the best arranged of any in the Union. Persons wishing to purchase, are invited to examine their stock before purchasing elsewhere. They have on hand at present, fifty likely young Negroes, comprising field hands, mechanics, house and body servants."

"Stock," "supplies"—all kept in their neat, comfortable, and safe jail.

Let's look a little closer and try to picture Forrest's establishment in the city block on Adams between Second and Third, with a jail capable of holding three hundred enslaved Africans whose "comfort, neatness and safety" are advertised in the flyer. It is clear that these miserable people would have been jammed into very tight quarters. As it happens, the father of a friend of mine was involved as an engineer in a construction job on this very site in the late 1930s. When workers dug down into the foundations at number 87, they found manacles cemented into the brick walls.

This is the reality, and the horror, of African slavery in the American South. A military genius Forrest may well have been, but he was also a man who participated willingly and profitably in a monstrous system that treated human beings as property, and he amassed a fortune based on whips and chains. When he fought on the side of the slaveholding South he wasn't just fighting for a way of life; he was also fighting to protect his own personal livelihood.

And yet it is not as simple as that. Though Forrest may have been among the first leaders of the Ku Klux Klan, in 1869 he resigned his position and renounced the organization. Earlier, at the outbreak of hostilities, he offered freedom to his male slaves if they would serve in the army with him. Of the forty-four who accepted his offer, only one deserted, and the remaining forty-three stayed with him throughout the war. A website on Forrest continues:

Part of General Forrest's command included his own Escort Company, his Green Berets, made up of the very best soldiers available. This unit, which varied in size from 40–90 men, was the elite of the cavalry. Eight of these picked men were black soldiers and all served gallantly and bravely throughout the war. All were armed with at least 2 pistols and a rifle. Most also carried two additional pistols in saddle holsters. At war's end, when Forrest's cavalry surrendered in May 1865, there were 65 black troopers on the muster roll. Of the soldiers who served under him, Forrest said of the black troops: Finer Confederates never fought.

After the war, as one of the builders of the Memphis and Selma Railroad, Forrest took the initiative to hire blacks as architects, construction engineers and foremen, train engineers and conductors at a time when, in the North, they were prohibited by law from holding such jobs. In 1875 the former Confederate general was asked to address the Independent Order of Pole-Bearers Association, an early predecessor of the NAACP whose purpose was to promote black voting rights and other issues. They held their convention at the Fairgrounds in Memphis. Forrest was the first white man asked to address a gathering of this organization, and his words to the gathering were recorded on the occasion, including his acknowledgment of a bouquet of flowers given him by the daughter of one of the members:

Ladies and Gentlemen: I accept the flowers as a memento of reconciliation between the white and colored races of the southern states. I accept it more particularly as it comes from a colored lady, for if there is anyone on God's earth who loves the ladies I believe it is myself. (Immense applause and laughter.) I came here with the jeers of some white people, who think that I am doing wrong. I believe I can exert some influence, and do much to assist the people in strengthening fraternal relations, and shall do all in my power to elevate every man, and to depress none. (Applause.) I want to elevate you to take positions in law offices, in stores, on farms, and wherever you are capable of going. I have not said anything about politics today. . . . You have a right to elect whom you please; vote for the man you think best. You and I are freemen. . . . When I can serve you I will do so. We have but one flag, one country; let us stand together. We may differ in color, but not in sentiment. . . . Go to work, be industrious, live honestly and act truly, and when you are oppressed I'll come to your relief. I thank you, ladies and gentlemen, for this opportunity you have afforded me to be with you, and to assure you that I am with you in heart and in hand. (Prolonged applause.)

It is worth noting that at Forrest's funeral in 1877, the ten thousand mourners included, according to newspaper accounts, three thousand African Americans. Maybe they respected him. Maybe they just wanted to make sure he was really dead.

‹‹‹‹‹‹‹

Conflict still simmers in the city around the question of whether to acknowledge or to ignore its Civil War heritage. A park known throughout my childhood as Forrest Park is situated in midtown Memphis. Visitors to the city would scarcely notice it, but it is located right around the corner from Sun Studios, one of Memphis's premier tourist attractions, and it stands in the heart of the medical district, which draws patients from all over the Mid-South. The city's population is now 62 percent African American, and recently the city council changed the names of three parks that formerly commemorated the Civil War.

What we grew up calling Confederate Park is now Memphis Park, what used to be Jefferson Davis Park is now Mississippi River Park, and as for Forrest Park, well, that is now Health Sciences Park, so called for its proximity to the medical center. There have been protests, but Memphis's former mayor, A. C. Wharton, commented, "These are the growing pains of a democratic society"; and no doubt he is right. Mayor Wharton has recently proposed that the city erect a statue of Ulysses S. Grant as a balance to its commemoration of Confederate heroes. By the time my book appears, the equestrian statue of Forrest will probably have been removed.

YELLOW FEVER, COTTON, AND COMMERCE

Just when Memphis was getting on its feet after the ill-advised and catastrophic Civil War, the Yellow Fever epidemics of the 1870s decimated the city's population, and everyone who could afford it fled to healthier places upriver like St. Louis. The disease, a form of typhus, hit the city hard in the late sixties and the seventies. Shallow cisterns located perilously close to privies provided drinking water, which was also drawn from shallow wells and from the Wolf River itself. When it rained the streets became seas of mud. Even when some streets were paved with wooden blocks, the blocks themselves sank into the ooze. Wagons transporting cotton through the downtown streets often sank up to their axles in mire. Rising from the river landing where steamboats unloaded their cargoes, the streets were made deliberately broad so that wagons could zigzag up the slope.

With the profitable trade in cotton resuming once the war was over, Memphis quickly regained her position as the country's largest inland cotton market. Raw and ginned cotton arrived by wagon from surrounding farms and plantations, by the newly repaired railroads, by steamboats on the river. Now that the slaves had been emancipated and the fortunes of those planters who had formerly owned vast fiefdoms consisting of tens of thousands of acres in the Delta destroyed, the economics of the cotton business were altered. Now it was the cotton factor who ran the show.

Operating out of Cotton Row on Front Street in Memphis overlooking cobblestone landings along the river, the factors became bankers, suppliers, and merchants. The buildings of Cotton Row, now home to restaurants and condominiums, are solidly constructed of brick. Rising from dirt basements, their front doors built wide to receive large shipments of cotton, their walls were thick enough to withstand the weight of tons of stored bales.

In their role as bankers, the cotton factors advanced credit to the planters, sold them seed and equipment, and arranged to have the crop sold, making a profit off the brokerage fees they charged. Underneath the factors there operated a small army of workers whose job it was to weigh and class the cotton, run the cotton compresses, gin it, and bind the bales. Around this industry sprang up wholesale grocers and dry goods emporiums, seed merchants, hotels like the old Gayoso—site of Forrest's famous raid—and of course saloons, dance halls, and eateries.

The landmark Peabody Hotel, where our story began, was founded in 1869 with investment capital from the New York financier George Peabody. As far as anyone knows, Peabody himself never visited Memphis, but he was convinced by friends like Colonel Robert Bogardus Snowden—who was himself born in New York but who came to Memphis at the age of three and served under General Albert Sidney Johnston at the battle of Shiloh—that investing in the newly reborn city made sound business sense. Colonel Snowden amassed a fortune in the wholesale liquor trade after the war and was brave enough to stay in Memphis during the Yellow Fever epidemics, when he had the cash to buy up property at a time when most sensible people were packing up and leaving town.

Speculators and investors like Peabody and Snowden, who, as often as not, originally came from other parts of the United States, were typical of Memphis's business climate in the late nineteenth century. Memphis rebounded thanks to its unsurpassable situation on the Mississippi River where the rich farming regions of three states—Tennessee, Mississippi, and Arkansas—come together in the center of vast hardwood forests where timber could be cut, milled, and transported either on the river or on the rail network that connected the city with markets to the north and to the east. Cotton, lumber, and wholesale hardware and grocery businesses were at the heart of the city's recovery.

A PLACE OF GOOD ABODE

Though the city's architectural unity has been violated by decay and several generations of "urban renewal," an impressive array of late nineteenth and early twentieth century buildings still remains. The greatest preponderance of Victorian structures is to be found on Adams Avenue. The river was at the heart of the city's life in those days, and at the foot of Adams stood a public landing stage. Calvary Episcopal and St. Peter's Catholic Church were built on Adams, which was at that time a fashionable part of town. More recently, the neighborhood became a dangerous place to walk at night. Now the surviving mansions that once lined the street have become law offices, one or two of them bed and breakfast establishments. One of the most ornate, the Fontaine House, has been preserved as a museum and is open to the public. My mother used to be a docent there.

A list of those who patronized their construction and lived in these houses is a roster of the city's power structure as it rebuilt in the decades following the Civil War. Captain James Lee owned a fleet of riverboats that ferried passengers from Delta plantations and towns and cities along the Mississippi to and from Memphis, Vicksburg, and New Orleans. Captain Lee's son, James Jr., bought a lot on Adams in 1868 and hired himself an architect from Philadelphia to build the fine Italianate Victorian mansion at number 239.

Later, as the family grew, the Lees moved into a still larger place at the corner of Adams and Orleans, and it was here that I first experienced Italianate Victorian—equal parts fantasy and ostentation, borrowing ideas from the Italian Renaissance, French chateau architecture, and God knows what else. This place is sometimes referred to as the Goyer-Lee House, because it was built by a merchant from Indiana named Goyer who dealt in sugar and molasses and was the president of a bank.

When the Lees moved here from their previous location, they set up the bell from the steamer *James Lee* on the property to remind themselves of the source of the family fortunes. A nice gesture. They lived at this location from 1890 to 1925, the year the daughter of the family, Miss Rosa Lee, started an art school here which in 1942, two years after I was born, became the Memphis Academy of Art.

During summers while I was in high school and in my first years at Sewanee, I studied drawing and painting there. The rooms were dusty, windows were broken, and to climb the staircases and wander through what had once been one of Memphis's most luxurious residences was almost as much fun as learning how to paint. One of my teachers was the visionary Memphis painter Burton Callicott, who liked to talk theosophy while on warm, firefly-lit evenings we drank cokes during our breaks from doing our still lifes, landscapes, and life studies. Mr. Callicott was at first a commercial artist working in his father-in-law's studio. People used to say he made the two plaster owls that sat atop the Owl Café at the corner of Cooper and Peabody a few blocks from where I grew up.

Just down the street on Adams from the old Art Academy stands the Mallory-Neely house. On the outside it resembles the houses the

Lee family built. The beauty of the interior is that so little has been changed since the 1890s. The front door is fitted out with Tiffany-style stained glass, and the showplace of the house is its double parlor, every inch decorated with gilded surfaces, heavy draperies, patterned carpets, crystal sconces and chandeliers, and Victorian bric-à-brac. A grand arch leads to the opulent dining room, its heavy mahogany table set for sixteen with Haviland china and sterling silver flatware.

Miss Daisy Mallory lived in the house until her death in 1969 at the age of 98. The house is now open to the public. Construction probably began in the 1850s, but later owners in Victorian times included James Columbus Neely. The Neelys were a well-known West Tennessee family who made their money partly from raising cotton, partly from the wholesale grocery business, and partly as cotton factors on Front Street.

A series of Memphis's avenues are named after the presidents, so if you walk one block over from Adams you find yourself on Jefferson, the site of other fine late-nineteenth-century residences. One of the most striking is the Lowenstein House at the corner of Jefferson and Manassas. The Lowenstein family's history is a typical American rags-to-riches story. Elias Lowenstein, so the story goes, arrived in Memphis in 1854 with thirty-five cents in his pocket. His ship docked in New Orleans and he came upriver to join two of his brothers who had preceded him here. They opened a dry goods establishment in 1861 and prospered during the war years. By the time of his death Lowenstein had become the owner of a cotton mill and an insurance company and was the director of two banks.

In 1890 this pillar of the community built a fine brick mansion with a massive Richardson Romanesque entry arch, terracotta ornamentation, and round-arched windows, surmounted by a square Italianate tower topped with a pyramid-shaped roof. The Lowenstein House exudes North-European bourgeois solidity, an impression partially mediated by the fanciful Tiffany-looking stained glass. Particularly charming among these windows are the broad demi-lunette double windows on the facade and the bull's-eye window, also on the facade, set right underneath the square tower.

This prosperous merchant's house squarely faces the street that runs along the front of it, and it is every inch a declaration of respectability, even of smugness. Inside the house stand fireplaces with carved over-mantles and decorative tiles. Magnolia trees in the yard and a vaguely New Orleans-looking latticed porch that turns the southeast corner of the house are its only notes of Southern charm and breeze-worthiness.

Among public buildings, my favorite secular structure remaining from this period is the Tennessee Club at the corner of Court Square and Second Street, built one block from Calvary Episcopal Church by an architect from Ohio in 1890. One of my uncles who was in the lumber business belonged to the club, and he took me to lunch there occasionally when I was a boy. Constructed of reddish ashlar sand-stone, the building is a gloriously over-the-top exercise in Victorian eclecticism.

True, the Tennessee Club lacks aesthetic unity. The Romanesque arches and the big round opening rising from a third-floor balcony would lead one to call the architecture Richardson Romanesque. But there are also flamboyant Moorish touches like the Venetian-looking windows and especially the huge bulbous dome that tops the structure over what at one time was a ballroom.

Originally housing a library and an art gallery, this in its heyday was a men's club. The balconies facing onto Court Square, which was considered Memphis's civic center, were designed "for watching parades or whatever was passing by." Of the two big tables in the basement grill, the lawyers sat at one and the lumbermen at the other. Presidents Grant, Taft, and Teddy Roosevelt were entertained at the club, and in 1931 the Memphis *Commercial Appeal* pronounced that "To have free access to it, to be of the company that gathers there daily for lunch, bridge, or to loaf and read, is to have 'arrived' in Memphis."

MISTER CRUMP

With the rebirth of the city's fortunes in the final quarter of the nine-teenth century, the antebellum population of Memphis was replaced by newcomers, some of them investors from the North, most of them plain people from the surrounding countryside. "In 1900, conse-quently," according to Gerald Capers's book, "Memphis presented a strange paradox—a city modern in physical aspect but rural in background, rural in prejudice, and rural in habit." This provincialism made Memphis vulnerable to the political machine masterminded by E. H. Crump from the late teens through the 1950s.

Mister Crump—I never heard any Memphian refer to him as "Boss Crump"—came here from his hometown of Holly Springs, Mississippi in the early 1890s, and his first job in the city was a modest one. He signed on as a clerk in one of the cotton companies on Front Street. From these modest beginnings, he moved up quickly, marrying Betty McLean, daughter of a socially prominent Memphis family, in the process. This marriage gave him access to the interconnected social circles that have always run things here.

Crump was first elected to office as a reform candidate for mayor, and one of his appeals was that he cleaned up the city and made it safer. As long as the city was run well, voters did not seem to care that it was run undemocratically. The old blues song, "Mister Crump don't 'low no easy riders round here," dates from this period. W. C. Handy later took the tune, changed the words, and turned it into his "Memphis Blues."

It is no accident that Martin Luther King was assassinated in the city of Nathan Bedford Forrest and E. H. Crump. Not that Mr. Crump was a racist—by the standards of the day he was more progressive than most. But his half-century domination of Memphis resulted in a political vacuum where there was an absence of an experienced, democratically elected governing class. No one outside Mr. Crump's immediate circle learned how to govern because every detail was dictated from the top. Thus when the city's sanitation workers went on strike in 1968, the city government in the post-Crump era was clueless as to how to deal with a movement among what it regarded as uppity Negroes. The city's white business and civic leadership was drawn from the same class that had owned cotton plantations in the Delta and West Tennessee.

And since most of Memphis's black residents descended from workers on the old plantations, they brought the same dynamic and the same mutual incomprehension from the plantation to the city. A saying attributed to Mr. Crump was: "Negroes do not vote in Memphis. They are voted." And the black vote would not have been a reliable source of support for the Crump machine without the coop-eration of his black allies. All of this history was real to me as a boy. In my childhood I saw school buses pull up to the door of Lenox School in my all-white neighborhood with busloads of African Americans who went into the polling place and cast their votes as directed. They certainly were not registered to vote in my part of town. It is said that these serial voters were rewarded for their day's work with a five dol-lar bill and a half pint of whiskey.

>>>>>>>>

Mr. Crump was a popular figure around town. He attended all the Central High School football games at the stadium in midtown that was renamed for him after he died. He had seats, naturally, on the fifty-yard line. We boys knew that if we went up and greeted him, he would reach into the pocket of his big overcoat and hand each of us a brand-new shiny silver dollar. Part of his high reputation among or-dinary citizens was due to his responsiveness to their day-to-day con-cerns. More than once I overheard my grandmother, whose husband had been active in local politics, call him up on the telephone and give him a piece of her mind about one thing or another. He listened politely and thanked her for her advice. When Crump died in 1954, a school holiday was declared, and a friend of mine and I attended his funeral. I remember how shrunken he looked, laid out there in his open casket at his house on Peabody, his trademark bushy eyebrows more prominent than ever.

A lowering bronze statue of Mister Crump stands in Overton Park near the Brooks Art Museum. The inscription reads, "To the great public benefactor Edward Hull Crump, Memphis dedicates this tribute. Erected by the people of the city of Memphis in memory of Edward Hull Crump, 1874–1954. His was a life of dedicated public ser-vice, wise council, human understanding, designed to make Memphis the city of good abode." I wonder how many informed citizens would agree with this assessment of E. H. Crump's motives. Still, though his reign was decidedly undemocratic, he did make Memphis a quiet, safe, and enjoyable city in which to live, truly a "place of good abode."

Any life is touched, colored and shaped by what surrounds it. It was that way for me, growing up in Memphis and West Tennessee. As with most people in this part of the world, there was a farm in our family—sixty miles from Memphis, near Brownsville in Haywood County. My playmates out there in the country were let out of school in the autumn during cotton-picking season, and I remember the farm workers coming in from the fields lugging their long "lebben-foot" sacks of cotton, loading my cousin's wagons with the white fluffy stuff, still gritty with cotton seed and the dirt of the fields, and driving it down the road to the cotton gin. Bringing the cotton to the gin was a social event of great moment in the black community. They gathered to gossip while the wagons were unloaded and the ginning began.

My father was a practical-minded Yankee from Massachusetts who had been lured south by a job offer as a young industrial engineer. Working here, Daddy introduced innovations into the business of processing cotton, inventing a revolutionary method of compressing and bailing it designed to streamline the procedure. I remember the blueprints and scale models of his inventions that filled his office at the Sterick Building, one of the first tall buildings in downtown Memphis. Occasionally I accompanied him on business trips to machine shops in places like Forrest City, Arkansas (named after Nathan Bedford Forrest), and Byhalia, Mississippi, getting a glimpse of the practical side of how cotton underlay the way most of Memphis and the Mid-South made their living in those days.

When I was a teenager I went to dances and parties during Cotton Carnival, Memphis's paler but still exciting version of Mardi Gras. For my father, cotton meant a slide rule and blueprints; for the tenant farmers in west Tennessee it meant long days chopping and picking cotton in the blistering heat. For me it meant a dinner jacket, a shiny white Buick, and good-looking girls at the dance.

When I left Memphis to go into the larger world of college and graduate school, the first thing I wanted to do was to get as far away as possible from what seemed to me at the time a quite ordinary and even stifling and benighted place. In retrospect Memphis seems anything but ordinary. It's a storied place with a narrative that belongs more in the pages of a novel than a history book.

Now I see how lucky I am to have grown up in this singular place, with a history altogether unlikely and at the same time quintessentially American. When I lived in Ireland, I remember how impressed people were when they learned I was from Memphis. That surprised me. Our history is a strange one—conflicted and untidy, familiar and strange, brutal and beautiful, boring and tinged with glamor all at the same time.

>>>>>>>>

When I return to the city today, things are the same and not the same. Though the Owl Café has been gone for years, I do find places where I can still get those four-vegetable lunches with cornbread and iced tea that are one of God's gifts to Southerners. And yet at other old-favorite spots, like a little lunch place on Monroe near the corner of Front Street, things have changed. I am greeted by a nice man named Omar, and one of the servers is wearing the hijab. How nice, I think—change! Memphis has become multicultural! At the same time I am cheered by the sight of a couple of men with white hair and red faces wearing white shirts and silk-rep neckties. Decades ago this lunchroom would have been filled with the likes of them, come from their downtown offices, talkin' bidness. The cornbread was great, but the turnip greens didn't taste right. The new owners didn't cook with pork—it was against their religion—and everybody knows you don't want to be cooking greens without fatback or ham hocks.

Suzy and I visited in July, and it was hot. The sun-beaten cracked sidewalks and urban weeds on Front Street said something about ennui. Downtown alleyways where twentieth-century asphalt had worn down to nineteenth-century brick were an emblem of the city's decline. No one could deny the feeling of decrepitude in this old Mississippi River town, but changes have come, and a sense of rebirth is in the wind. Memphis is forever optimistic.

What I once thought of as provincialism and determined me to leave Memphis resurfaces as charm. I love this old city. The Carpenter

Gothic bungalows I hardly noticed when I passed them on the way to school, the cracks in the pavement, are now soaked with the warm glow of memory. I love sitting around the supper table with my relatives. Registering the traits we all share, passing a dish to a second cousin once removed, I experience what Carroll Cloar wrote of as a "joy in the sense of belonging, of possessing and being possessed by the land where you were born."

Nathan Bedford Forrest:
Born to Fight

In the previous chapter we looked at Nathan Bedford Forrest mostly through a Memphis lens. Forrest made his mark beyond the Bluff City, though, and he remains one of the Civil War's most controversial figures. According to his biographer Jack Hurst, he was both "a soft-spoken gentleman of marked placidity and an overbearing bully of homicidal wrath." Here let's look at him primarily as a soldier.

Of his military genius there can be little doubt. And yet his abilities were never fully appreciated within the Confederate government. In 1877 Jefferson Davis sat by Forrest's bedside in Memphis the day before he died of diabetes, wasted down to one hundred pounds, "broke up," the old warrior confessed, "broke in fortune, broke in health, broke in spirit." The next day the President of the Confederacy served as a pallbearer. Riding to Elmwood Cemetery in the funeral cortège, Davis spoke of Forrest's martial greatness and commented that "the generals commanding in the Southwest never appreciated him until it was too late. Their judgment was that he was a bold and enterprising raider and rider. I was misled by them, and never knew how to measure him until I read the reports of his campaign across the Tennessee River in 1864." Of Brice's Crossroads, Forrest's most enterprising and daring victory, "That campaign was not understood in Richmond," the former president admitted. "The impression made upon those in authority was that Forrest had made another successful raid. . . . I saw it all after it was too late."

What is our final evaluation of Nathan Bedford Forrest as man and soldier to be? What was it like to serve as a trooper under Forrest's command, or to be among the out-smarted Union officers and common soldiers who had the misfortune to go up against him? How did his slaves see him—those gangs of men, women, and children force-marched along dusty or muddy Southern roads from Alabama to Mississippi, from Mississippi into West Tennessee during the years before the war when Forrest was in the business of buying and selling human beings? These are questions I have attempted to answer to my own satisfaction, though probably we shall never get a clear answer to that last question, never plumb the depths of that rage, fear, frustration, and pain.

›››››››››

When Forrest was free to fight without having to follow orders from above, he was most himself, and he usually won, often against heavy odds, earning his nickname, The Wizard of the Saddle. But he hated serving under other officers, even when, as with "Fighting Joe" Wheeler—whom we will see briefly again in the skirmish at Sewanee in a later chapter—his ranking officer liked and admired him. After he fought under Wheeler in 1863 at Dover on the Tennessee River and Wheeler was dictating his official report on the battle, Forrest was lying in pain on the floor in the cabin they were using as a temporary headquarters, propped up on a cane-bottom chair. He had been thrown from his horse that day, his ribs bruised. Forrest said to Wheeler that he meant "no disrespect to you; you know my feelings of personal friendship for you; you can have my sword if you demand it; but there is one thing I do want you to put in that report to General Bragg—tell him that I will be in my coffin before I will fight again under your command."

Wealthy planters like Harry St. John Dixon from Mississippi chafed under Forrest's ascendancy. After the death of General Earl Van Dorn in 1864, Forrest was put in charge of all cavalry in Hood's ill-fated invasion of Tennessee. Dixon, who was serving as a private soldier, wrote: "The dog's dead: finally we are under N. Bedford Forrest." Sarcastically alluding to his nickname, Dixon speaks of "The Wizzard" and notes his "distaste [at] being commanded by a man having no pretension to gentility—a negro trader, gambler,—an ambitious man, careless of the lives of his men so long as preferment be *en prospectu*. Forrest may be able & no doubt is, the best Cav officer in the West, but I object to a tyrannical, hotheaded vulgarian's commanding me."

EARLY YEARS

Born in 1821 in Middle Tennessee, as I have mentioned, young Bedford moved with his parents to the wilderness of Tippah County in North Mississippi, between Memphis and Corinth. The Forrests rose early and breakfasted by candlelight so as to be in the fields at dawn. Bedford's evenings were spent in front of the fire, sewing "buckskin leggings, coonskin caps, or shoes . . . for his younger brothers," according to Jack Hurst, whose biography of Forrest is the most balanced I have found.

In his mid-twenties this resourceful young man began making the transition from farming to more lucrative activities, moving to Hernando in DeSoto County, just south of the Tennessee line. Operating between Hernando and Memphis, he went into business with his uncle as a building contractor, owned a brickyard and a livery stable, and operated a stage line between Hernando and Memphis, soon gravitating to the booming river town of Memphis. By the outbreak of the war, he had become a dealer in farm supplies, buyer and seller of slaves, real-estate speculator, Mississippi River steamboat owner, and planter.

Forrest neither drank nor used tobacco; his vices were swearing and gambling, the latter often for enormous stakes. Though he had the self-made man's envy of the more refined and better educated Delta planters and Memphis merchants in whose company he moved as his wealth increased and his station in life rose, he distrusted and feared the written word. "I never see a pen but what I think of a snake," he would often say. Later in life there were educated men on his staff to render his dispatches, orders, and speeches into proper English, but his actual command of the language may be surmised from his written refusal of a soldier's request for leave: "I told you twict Goddammit Know."

Raised on what was then the southwestern frontier, Forrest was a natural-born fighter, a violent man living in a society where you had to fight to protect yourself, your family, your property, and above all, your honor. Anyone or anything that injured Forrest stood to regret it. When a panther attacked his mother and sister as they were returning to their farm with a basket of baby chicks, killing Mrs. Forrest's horse and tearing the clothes from her back, her son declared, "Mother, I am going to kill the beast if it stays on the earth," and he set out with his dogs at midnight, treed the animal, and waited until dawn to get a clear shot. By nine o'clock in the morning he returned home with the panther's scalp and ears.

Fortunately for the student of history, plentiful journalistic documentation exists about Nathan Bedford Forrest. In 1845 the *American Eagle,* a newspaper covering Memphis and the Mid-South, recounted a "most bloody affray" in nearby Hernando, Mississippi, wherein a "young Mr. Forrest"—he would have been twenty-four at the time— became involved in a dispute with one T. J. Matlock, Esq., his brother, and his plantation overseer. When, according to the *Eagle,* one of the Matlocks drew on Forrest, the latter "immediately drew a revolving pistol and set it to work as fast as possible, shooting both of the Matlocks through." In the "affray," Forrest's uncle Jonathan was killed by a stray bullet.

In 1864 a Lieutenant Gould made an attempt on Forrest's life, unhappy at having displeased Forrest and being transferred to another unit. Gould shot Forrest in the left side, after which the general grabbed Gould's pistol hand, took his penknife from his pocket, opened it with his teeth, and stabbed Gould between the ribs. Two doctors brought the wounded lieutenant into a tailor's shop, laid him out on a table, and tried to staunch the bleeding. The man's desperate condition did not deter Forrest, however, even when the Confederate provost marshal, Colonel J. Lee Bullock, tried to stop him, saying "I think you need not pursue Gould, for I believe that he is fatally wounded." "Get out of my way," Forrest shouted, "I am mortally wounded and will kill the man who shot me." Forrest recovered; Gould did not.

SLAVE TRADER

In 1808 an act of Congress made it illegal to import enslaved persons into the United States. The humanitarian impulse, however, clashed with an almost simultaneous contradictory development in industry. Eli Whitney's cotton gin made it possible to easily separate fiber from seed, and suddenly cotton became hugely profitable. Production in the United States expanded from 750,000 bales in 1830 to 2.85 million bales in 1850. "Cotton and Negroes are the constant theme—the ever harped upon, never worn out subject of conversation among all classes," wrote a Mississippian in the 1830s. "Slaves were seldom kept... for the sake of raising crops, but crops were often cultivated for the sake of raising slaves," another observer wrote.

In the old-fashioned, romantic view the Old South was a paternalistic agrarian society where slaves worked the fields, providing the wealth to sustain a cultivated and leisured society where chivalry, religion, fine manners, and good conversation could flourish. There were brutish and cruel masters, true, but there were kind masters too. And surely this picture is not completely the stuff of fantasy. At Leighton, Bishop Leonidas Polk's sugar-cane plantation in Louisiana, a former governess recalled, "The household, white and black, assembled every morning before breakfast in the parlor. The psalms for the day were read, a psalm or hymn was sung by all; the bishop read and expounded a chapter of the Bible, and then prayed."

Recent thinking puts slavery more in the context of capitalism than of agrarianism. The economist Robert Evans Jr. wrote in 1962 that "the slave market performed for the antebellum South some of the functions now performed by the New York Stock Exchange, i.e., it served in the eyes of the public as a sensitive reflector of current and future business prospects." Evans claims—somewhat improbably, it seems to me—that if one had purchased a number of twenty-year-old male slaves at market prices and held them for twenty or thirty years, the return on one's investment would have been greater than that on stock in railroads, North or South, greater even than "three- to six-month bankable paper money market in Boston."

Agriculture was on the decline on the Eastern Seaboard and Kentucky, while the Mississippi Delta, its soil enriched by thousands of years of soil runoff from the Father of Waters, was being cleared for cotton plantations. The wilderness, with its stands of fine old first-growth forests, was being cut down, the timber sold from Memphis, which in addition to its commerce in slaves, hogs, and mules, was becoming the nation's largest inland market for hardwood lumber.

Since Forrest started out as a dealer in farm supplies, it made sense—if anything about slavery can be said to make sense—to expand that business to include slaves. He scoured the countryside in search of slaves who could be bought at bargain prices and re-sold in Memphis at a profit. Auction Square on North Main Street was near the Mississippi River landing, where planters could transport their human property to their land in the Delta. Forrest and his partner, a man named Hill, built a "Mart," which is described in the previous chapter.

As we have seen, Forrest's views on race would change radically in the last few years of his life, but there's nothing to indicate that his conscience bothered him at this point in his career. The Southern economy was based on slavery, Forrest was intent on making his fortune, and he was a very good businessman. As an indication of the kind of money to be made, in 1854 he bought three slaves for $1,450 and sold them again two weeks later for $1,600, a profit of 10 percent. Everything I have read about the man convinces me that he was above all a realist. There is every indication that he treated his slaves well, just as later on he would take good care of the soldiers who fought under him. This doesn't mean that the milk of human kindness flowed through his veins—it was just good business.

THE WIZARD OF THE SADDLE

Though originally he opposed secession, Forrest joined up as soon as Tennessee and Mississippi cast their lot with the Confederacy. Despite having no military training, in a conflict where officers on both sides were West Point men and veterans of the Mexican and the Indian wars, he was a quick study who became exceptionally adept at his *métier*. He disdained the by-the-book tactics of his colleagues from the regular army. When asked by General Stephen D. Lee if he had any ideas about the defeat the Confederates had just sustained at the battle of Harrisburg in north Mississippi, he replied irascibly, "Yes, sir, I've always got ideas, and I'll tell you one thing, General Lee. If I knew as much about West Point tactics as you, the Yankees would whip hell out of me every day."

He is known to have personally killed thirty enemy soldiers. Left-handed by nature, he taught himself to use both hands with equal strength so he could fight ambidextrously with a sword in one hand and a revolver in the other. A powerfully built, broad-shouldered man standing six foot two inches—extraordinarily tall for those times—he cut an imposing figure. Leading his men into combat, he would rise in the stirrups, waving over his head his saber, honed to a razor-sharp edge on both sides. It is not surprising that so many enemy troops panicked and fled.

William Tecumseh Sherman declared that Forrest needed to be "hunted down and killed if it costs 10,000 lives and bankrupts the treasury." His soldiers revered him, but they also feared him, more than they feared the enemy. His orders to his staff were: "Shoot any man who won't fight." He was no sentimentalist: if one or two of his men had to die in the effort to shore up the courage and morale of the rest, Forrest was willing to pay that price. He shot at least one deserter himself, and another time he attacked a retreating soldier with a tree limb, thrashed the man to within an inch of his life, and ordered him back into the fray. At Murfreesboro in 1864, when one of his regiments stampeded toward the rear, he shot the standard-bearer, seized the flag, and rallied the troops.

≫≫≫≫≫

In addition to his reckless daring and split-second battlefield decisions, he meticulously and single-mindedly planned out his tactics. War is sometimes described as a chess match, but people of

Forrest's background did not play chess. On the other hand, no one ever beat him at checkers, a favorite pastime in the rare moments when he found time to relax. Describing his victory over the Federal commander in the battle of Brice's Crossroad, Forrest used a metaphor from checkers: "I saw Grierson make a 'bad move,' and then I rode right over him." Once, when someone attempted to engage him in conversation while he paced back and forth making plans for the next day's action, he knocked the man down with a single blow, stepped over him, and continued to cogitate, uttering not a single word the entire time.

Once given a commission, the ever-resourceful Forrest became his own recruiting agent, running ads in the Memphis papers like this one:

200 RECRUITS WANTED!

I will receive 200 able-bodied men if they will present themselves at my headquarters by the first of June with good horse and gun. I wish none but those who desire to be actively engaged. . . . Come on, boys, if you want a heap of fun and to kill some Yankees.

N.B. Forrest
Colonel, Commanding
Forrest's Regiment

Nor did he neglect the practical aspects of arming and mounting his troops. A week after being commissioned to raise a regiment, Forrest traveled up to Kentucky, where he bought with his own money five hundred Colt navy pistols, one hundred saddles, and other gear, transporting it clandestinely back to Memphis. Throughout the war he was adept at finding horses for his troopers, and hogs and cattle to feed them.

During his first engagement, northeast of Bowling Green, Kentucky, he (in Shelby Foote's words) "improvised a double envelopment, combined it with a frontal assault—classic maneuvers which he could not identify by name and of which he had most likely never heard—and scattered the survivors of a larger enemy force." His characteristic tactic was to take the offensive and catch the enemy off guard. Even when the enemy charged him, he would charge back rather than waiting to be attacked.

At Parker's Crossroads, when informed that the enemy had been reinforced and was attacking him from the rear, he ordered (probably apocryphally), "Charge them both ways!" The reckless courage of these charges caused many an opponent whose forces outnumbered Forrest's to turn tail and flee. "Whenever you meet the enemy," he instructed his men, "no matter how few there are of you or how many of them, show fight. If you run away they will pursue and probably catch you. If you show fight, they will think there are more of you, and will not push you half so hard."

After positioning sharpshooters around the enemy's flank and rear, he would attack frontally, then be ready to enfilade the panicked Federals as they fled. Technically Forrest's troops were cavalrymen, but if we picture mounted saber charges, this does not give an accurate picture of how the general fought. No one can shoot accurately while mounted on horseback. Forrest used his horses to transport troops quickly; once in position, he would dismount them and use them as infantry. Rather than keeping his artillery at a safe distance behind the battle line, he moved it up right up to the front and fired close-range, which terrified and killed more of the enemy than if his artillery had fired from the rear.

"War means fightin'," he famously said, "and fightin' means killin'." He loved to "put the skeer" on an opponent—an early example of "shock and awe"—and then relentlessly and tirelessly pursue the enemy forces until they were destroyed or forced to surrender. In his famous rout of the expedition against the Confederate rear guard in Georgia and Alabama under Colonel Abel Streight in 1863, he ordered his troops to "shoot at everything blue and keep up the skeer."

DECISIVE BATTLES

Unless the Confederacy succeeded in exhausting and outlasting the North, the South had no realistic chance of winning the Civil War. The Confederate states had only 12 percent as much industrial capacity as the North. According to James M. McPherson, "Union states had eleven times as many ships and boats as the Confederacy and produced fifteen times as much iron, seventeen times as many textile goods, twenty-four times as many locomotives, and thirty-two times as many firearms."

But the Confederates also made tactical blunders that hastened the inevitable. Forrest took part in many crucial battles in the western theatre, and it is clear in retrospect that had his views prevailed, some of these battles might have been won. At Fort Donelson in 1862 the CSA command was divided among three generals: Floyd, Pillow, and Buckner. The first two were political appointees with little military sense. This conclave of incompetents decided to surrender the fort to Union forces, skillfully commanded by a new star in the Union Army, Ulysses S. Grant. Losing the fort meant losing control of the Cumberland and Tennessee Rivers and made the loss of Tennessee virtually inevitable.

But the Confederate triumvirate could not see the big picture. Colonel Forrest had found an escape route via a riverside road to the south of the fort and thought that the entire army could be evacuated. In the conclave where surrender was determined, he spoke up: "I did not come here for the purpose of surrendering my command," he declared. Forrest got his whole regiment out. "Not a gun [was] fired at us," he reported. "Not an enemy [was] seen or heard."

>>>>>>>>>

At Shiloh, Confederate forces carried the first day's fighting, pushing the Federals, under Grant, back to bluffs overlooking the Tennessee River. Confederate General Albert Sidney Johnston was killed in action, and Pierre Gustave Toutant Beauregard, that grandiloquent, beplumed Louisianian, took over. Before retiring for the night he sent a telegram to Richmond, declaring that he had achieved "a complete victory, driving the enemy from every position." While other commanders had retired to their tents, Colonel Forrest crept along the bluff to reconnoiter. He saw Buell's army arriving during the night and thousands of fresh troops being unloaded from riverboats. Let Shelby Foote tell the story:

> For Forrest this meant just one thing: the Confederates must either stage a night attack or else get off that table-land before the Federals

charged them in the morning. Unable to locate Beauregard, he went from camp to camp, telling of what he had seen and urging an attack, but few of the brigadiers even knew where their men were sleeping, and those who did were unwilling to take the responsibility of issuing such an order. . . . Forrest stomped off, swearing. "If the enemy comes on us in the morning, we'll be whipped like hell," he said.

He was right. The next day the Confederates were driven from the field. Outnumbered as they almost always were, they sorely missed the more than 12,000 troops and 48 artillery pieces captured earlier at Fort Donelson. Disobeying orders during the retreat, Forrest flung his three hundred and fifty Tennesseans, Kentuckians, Texans, and Mississippians against his pursuers at a place called the Fallen Timbers, where he was outnumbered five-to-one. In the heat of battle he outrode his men and was surrounded by Union troops shouting "Kill him! *Kill* the goddam rebel! Knock him off his horse!" One Union rifleman pushed the muzzle of his weapon into Forrest's side and pulled the trigger, knocking Forrest out of his saddle, lodging a bullet at the base of his spine and rendering his right leg useless. But Forrest had the strength to grab a Union soldier by the collar, swing him onto the crupper of his horse, and gallop back to safety, using the hapless Yankee as a shield.

Forrest's attack stopped the Federal pursuit, further fueling his reputation. As for the wound, the musket ball was removed from his spine without anesthesia, which was unavailable—though the teetotaler was probably given a dose of whiskey. With his seemingly supernatural strength he recovered quickly, and though still in pain, he returned to his command within three weeks.

>>>>>>>>

The third of three battles whose outcomes might have been altered had Forrest been in command was Chickamauga, fought in September 1863. The unfortunate Braxton Bragg had allowed himself to be maneuvered out of Tennessee by the wily William S. Rosecrans after fighting the Federals to a bloody standoff at the battle of Murfreesboro on Christmas Eve, 1862. Despite written pleas from the officers on his staff, including General Leonidas Polk, President Jefferson Davis had refused afterwards to relieve his old friend of his command.

Now, south of Chattanooga, Bragg chose to do battle. Forrest had been promoted to the rank of brigadier general by this point in the war, and he commanded a cavalry brigade on Bragg's right flank. The Confederates, in savage and bloody fighting, carried the day. Casualties amounted to 18,454 on the Southern side and 16,170 among the Federals. Bragg, in a funk because his orders had not been carried out to his satisfaction, sulked in his tent like Achilles before the walls of Troy and refused to order the hot pursuit that might have destroyed Rosecrans's army, and at the very least, have kept him out of Chattanooga.

But Forrest pursued on his own, so quickly that he overtook a party of Federal observation troops in a tree, ordered them down, and used their field glasses to observe the Union retreat. The message he dashed off to General Polk, requesting it be forwarded to Bragg—"I think we ought to press forward as rapidly as possible"—brought no response, and the Yankees were once again allowed to escape. Later Forrest went to Bragg's tent, but again received no satisfaction. "What does he fight battles for?" the Wizard wondered out loud. To Bragg he said, "You have threatened to arrest me for not obeying your orders promptly. I dare you to do it, and I say to you that if you ever again try to interfere with me or cross my path it will be at the peril of your life."

TRICKSTER

Stonewall Jackson once said: "Always mystify, mislead, and surprise the enemy if possible. When you strike and overcome him, never give up the pursuit as long as your men have strength to follow; for an army routed, if hotly pursued, becomes panic-stricken, and can then be destroyed by half its number." He might have been describing the tactics of Nathan Bedford Forrest, one of military history's great tricksters. One of his favorite ploys was to send a courier under a flag of truce to his opponents, who more often than not outnumbered him, demanding surrender. Here is the note he sent in 1862 to Colonel Parkhurst, commander of a Michigan regiment:

Murfreesborough, July 13, 1862

COLONEL: I must demand an unconditional surrender of your force as prisoners of war or I will have every man put to the sword. You are aware of the overpowering force I have at my command, and this demand is made to prevent the effusion of blood.

I am, colonel, very respectfully, your obedient servant,

N.B. FORREST,
Brigadier General of Cavalry, C.S. Army

Never mind that Forrest was a colonel at the time, not a brigadier general. He must have thought that Colonel Parkhurst would be more intimidated if he thought he was facing a general.

‹‹‹‹‹‹‹

Invading West Tennessee during the winter of 1863, Forrest brought kettledrums along and kept them beating at all times, giving the enemy the impression that large detachments of infantry were gathering. As a result, Colonel Ingersoll of the Eleventh Illinois Cavalry overestimated his strength at "at least 5,000 strong," when Forrest's troopers actually numbered only two thousand. During the same campaign, Forrest arrested a number of Union sympathizers, kept them under guard, and ordered the drums beaten night and day while his troops marched past in sight of the prisoners, informing them that this was Cheatham's infantry division, which was in fact nowhere near. Then he would mount his troops and have them file by to exaggerate, in the captives' mind, the numbers of cavalry on hand. Later he let the prisoners escape. They hurried to Union headquarters to report on the numbers they thought Forrest had on hand. As a result, General Grant sent 25,000 troops from Memphis who were thus diverted from more useful duties.

‹‹‹‹‹‹‹

One of the more amusing campaigns of the war was the excursion Colonel Abel Streight launched across Alabama and Georgia in 1863.

Though Streight's men outnumbered Forrest's three to one, the Rebel commander "put the skeer" on him and pursued the Yankees so relentlessly, day and night, that Streight's men were run ragged, falling asleep with their rifles in their hands. Requesting a parley, Forrest, who was travelling with only two artillery pieces, stood with his back to a ridge while he and Streight talked, and had his men wheel the same two pieces over and over again along the ridge within Streight's field of vision.

"Name of God!" Streight exclaimed. "How many guns have you got? There's fifteen I've counted already." Forrest glanced casually over his shoulder and drawled, "I reckon that's all that has kept up." During the parley Forrest would occasionally interrupt himself and issue orders to a subordinate concerning non-existent units. Finally Streight gave in and surrendered his 1,466 soldiers to Forrest's fewer than 600. Once he had turned over his men and their weapons to the Rebels, it became clear that he had been tricked, and he furiously demanded that Forrest return all surrendered weapons and further insisted that the two sides resume the fight. Forrest chuckled, patted his captive on the shoulder and remarked, "Ah, Colonel, all is fair in love and war, you know."

Greek Revival and
Double Dogtrot

As a child walking to Lenox School in Memphis—half a block from home—I was intrigued by the house two doors down from us. It had a porch that curved gracefully around and a little fairy-tale turret topped with a conical hat of a roof. "What kind of house is that?" I asked my mother, who knew everything about this sort of thing. They call that "Queen Anne," Mother said.

Which Queen Anne this was, I had no idea. Was it the same Queen Anne as in the wildflower called Queen Anne's lace? I learned at some point that our own house had been built in 1888 in the Victorian Gothic style that was once the fashion in towns all over the United States and Canada. The house itself was small, and nobody's idea of grand. But its lines were pleasing, its rooms were spacious, and the fourteen-foot ceilings kept the place breezy and cool all through the Deep South summers.

By the time my grandparents had decided to expand and remodel, people in Memphis had begun building in the Arts & Crafts style. So the remodeling my grandparents did gave the house some Arts &

Crafts touches as well: fireplaces with tile surrounds, bookcases built on either side of them with mullioned glass doors. The front porch, meanwhile, sported round wooden columns—a bow to Old South notions of antebellum Greek Revival grandeur.

When we look at buildings, it seems to me natural to start wondering who built them and why, and where the money came from. Art is bankrolled by commerce, and architecture even more so, since the architect, if there is one, the carpenters, the roofers, and so on must be paid. The extraordinary nineteenth-century residences and churches in Holly Springs, Mississippi—fifty miles southeast of Memphis—were built by people who made their money from the cotton economy of the American South, an economy that took off around 1820 and then crashed and burned in the Civil War.

The Memphis and Charleston Railroad, the first rail line to link the Atlantic Ocean with the Mississippi River, opened for business in 1857. When war broke out, the Grand Army of the Republic made a point of putting the torch to Southern towns that came within their line of advance, but General Ulysses S. Grant spared Holly Springs because he made his headquarters there and the people he met were too nice for him to destroy their town—or so the story goes.

>>>>>>>>

After having read William Faulkner as teenagers, my girlfriend and I drove the eighty miles from Memphis to Oxford in my powder-blue-and-white '54 Chevy coupe to make a pilgrimage to the great man's house. We were too diffident to impose on his privacy, and so we contented ourselves with peering at his house, Rowan Oak, down its *allée* of cedars, paved with old bricks in a herringbone pattern. Whether he was at home working, I don't know, but just being there, and being that close to him, meant something to us. It was the first of many literary pilgrimages.

They say Faulkner had some carpentry skills and did a lot of the fixing up with his own hands. Rowan Oak is a Greek Revival mansion dating from the 1830s. The columns on its porch are square rather than rounded, reflecting the rudimentary fashion with which American builders imitated classical styles in the early nineteenth century. Faulkner's reasons for buying the house probably had a lot to do with finding a house he could afford, but he couldn't have chosen a place more harmonious with the novels he was writing. Rowan Oak suggests those aspirations to grandeur that flourish side by side with down-home plainness in the best Southern writing.

The Mississippi home of Caro Armstrong, a family friend, sort of an adopted aunt, who taught history in a public high school in Memphis, was a plantation house built in the same early nineteenth-century style as Rowan Oak. It stood deep in the woods near Columbus in the Tombigbee River watershed in Lowndes County. Cotton money, slave labor, paid for the house. It dated from the 1840s and its columns were square like those William Faulkner may have driven a few nails into. When Miss Armstrong's brother Linley died, the *Memphis Commercial Appeal* headed his obituary, "Linley Armstrong, Mississippi Planter." My father, a plain-spoken Yankee from Massachusetts, said with a smile, "I doubt if Linley ever planted a seed in his life." But that didn't keep him from being a "planter."

After she retired from teaching and had her pension she moved back down there and worked tirelessly to keep the house in good repair, and in the family. A portrait of Robert E. Lee draped with Confederate banners hung above the landing. I thought of her devotion to that old house recently when re-reading Frank O'Connor's *Irish Miles.* "Women," he writes,

> sleeping in one room of some great house in its woods, going to bed hungry rather than part with granddad's cracked portrait, women lost to the world like mystics in the contemplation of God, know how hard that service can be . . .

The novelist and essayist Andrew Lytle's "double dogtrot" log house in Monteagle, Tennessee was a living link to an earlier period of history. On warm evenings a group of Mr. Lytle's students and friends would sit out on the broad front porch drinking bourbon, passing the guitar around and singing old ballads and Carter Family songs. Andrew had bought the house from one of his cousins at the Assembly Grounds in Monteagle.

The Monteagle Assembly had been founded as a kind of Methodist Chautauqua for people from Nashville and other parts of the middle South. They built a collection of vintage summer homes in a place Peter Taylor described in a letter to a college friend as "a little, old fashioned mountain resort where the same fine old families have been going for seventy-five years." Later he would fictionalize the resort as Owl Mountain Springs and make it the setting for several of his stories. Mr. Lytle's house was one of the oldest in the Assembly Grounds. His family roots had been firmly planted in Middle Tennessee since the eighteenth century, and Andrew cherished the rough-and-ready aspects of Tennessee history. He liked to remind us how close in time and spirit we were to frontier days.

A "dogtrot" house is one of the simplest of frontier houses. At first the pioneers would cut down trees and build a one-room log cabin, chinking the logs against the cold. When they wanted to add another room, they would leave a space between it and the existing room as a breezeway or "dogtrot." As the family grew, they might add two more rooms behind the first two, with another breezeway or hall running crossways to the first. Thus, a Greek cross design with four rooms divided by two halls. A porch could be thrown up across the front of the house, and in the case of Mr. Lytle's log house, broad porches surrounded the house on all four sides.

Like Andrew Lytle, the house was rustic and elegant at the same time, and its owner's love for it was typical of a sensibility many Southerners share. Given the choice between saying "Greek cross" or "Double dogtrot," a real Southerner will also choose the latter.

Peter Taylor and Tennessee's Three Kingdoms

While my father piloted the family Oldsmobile from Memphis to Nashville, my mother pointed out the limestone outcroppings and arrow-like cedars that began to appear alongside the highway a few hours into the trip. "Look, boys. Now we're in Middle Tennessee," she said to my brother and me. Cedars flourish in acid soil nourished by limestone. The alluvial plains where we lived in West Tennessee were not rocky country, and cedars were uncommon. We were still in the same state, but something had changed.

Though I grew up in Tennessee, I did not fully understand my native state until I read the stories and novels of Peter Taylor. In his novel, *In the Tennessee Country*, he talks about "the long green hinterland that is Tennessee." Within that long green hinterland lie Tennessee's "three Grand Divisions," West, Middle, and East—so different from one another they could almost be three separate states.

Born in 1917 in the small West Tennessee town of Trenton, Peter Taylor spent his childhood there and in Nashville, the urban center of

Middle Tennessee, which was the first part of the state to be settled. He also had roots in East Tennessee, where part of his family originally came from. His parents were both named Taylor, but the families were unrelated. Peter's maternal grandfather, Robert Love Taylor (1850–1912), a Democrat, served the state both as senator and as governor, defeating his own brother Alf, a Republican, for that office in 1886, in a campaign that became known in the annals of our state as the War of the Roses. In Tennessee Senator Taylor was known as Our Bob.

My own grandfather, A. J. Williford, a municipal judge, was active in Democratic politics, and named one of his horses Our Bob. Before I was born, before the Memphis city limits extended to include our part of the county, Our Bob used to graze in the field beside our house. When my brother David and I sold the family home in 1987, I found among the judge's papers in a trunk in the attic a letter from the senator, informing my grandfather that he was making a campaign stop in Memphis and asking him to "round up some of the boys" for the occasion.

Senator Taylor was one of the state's genuine heroes in the period between the Civil War and WWI, a time when we badly needed leaders who could guide the divided state through the troubled days of Reconstruction. East Tennessee had been pro-Union, while the state as a whole had seceded as part of the Confederacy. Robert Love Taylor was renowned as an orator, known for his set pieces such as "The Fiddle and the Bow" and "Yankee Doodle and Dixie." Here is a sample of his style as an orator:

> Mason and Dixon's line is still there, but it is only the dividing line between cold bread and hot biscuits, and there it will remain as long as the Yankee says, "You hadn't ought to do it," and the Southerner says, "I've done done it!"

This was the age of the orator in America, and Our Bob had the gift. After serving two terms as governor he traveled the lyceum circuit as a sideline to his legal practice. A living link to the state's frontier past, Senator Taylor was also a renowned fiddler, and to this day his instrument is on display at the Museum of Appalachia near Knoxville.

›››››››

Peter Taylor grew up with an awareness of historical background, a grounding in politics and oratory, a sense of inheriting as a birthright the important events of his state's history. An awareness of the state's history and geography are never far from the surface of the fiction written by Robert Love Taylor's grandson. This is how Phillip Carver's mother in *A Summons to Memphis* describes the family's move from Nashville to Memphis:

> With her ironic cast of mind and her sense and knowledge of local history she kept comparing our removal to the various events of early Tennessee history. We were like the Donelson party on the voyage down the Tennessee River, making their way through the flocks of swans at Moccasin Bend. We were like the Watauga men setting out for the Great Powwow on the Long Island of the Holston. Or what she liked best of all, we were like the Cherokees being driven from their ancestral lands on the notorious Trail of Tears.

The body of lore I have briefly sketched here formed the heroic past for Peter Taylor. His Tennessee had historical depth; its regions had their roots in the period before statehood, starting in the east with "the tiny, northeast corner of the state, which was sometimes referred to by erstwhile historians . . . as The Lost State—or the Lost State of Franklin." To the west were "the Miro District, an area of Middle Tennessee, and so called allegedly under the hegemony of the Spanish." Then there was "the westernmost part of the state, which is often . . . referred to as the Purchase."

From the Nashvillian point of view Memphis had its own "peculiar institutions . . . the institutions, that is to say, which one associates with the cotton and river culture of the Deep South," as the narrator of his Pulitzer Prize–winning novel *A Summons to Memphis* explains. In the same book a Nashville society lady puts it this way: "Nashville . . . is a city of schools and churches, whereas Memphis is—well, Memphis is something else again. Memphis is a place of steamboats and cotton gins, of card playing and hotel society." Before reading this book I had no idea that Middle Tennesseans looked down on us. We were always inclined to look down on *them*.

"The Old Forest," one of Taylor's most celebrated stories, is a study of power in a medium-sized American city in the late 1930s, in which the central character, Nat Ramsey, son of a prominent Memphis family, learns several lessons about his place in the scheme of things, becoming considerably less arrogant in the process. After a minor traffic accident, a young woman in the story disappears into

> a densely wooded area which is actually the last surviving bit of the primeval forest that once grew right up to the bluffs above the Mississippi River. Here are giant oak and yellow poplar trees older than the memory of the earliest white settler. Some of them surely may have been mature trees when Hernando de Soto passed this way, and were very old trees indeed when General Jackson, General Winchester, and Judge John Overton purchased this land and laid out the city of Memphis.

By such means Peter Taylor turns a relatively trivial automobile accident into a quasi-mythical surround informed by the deep history of the region. The Old Forest? I had never heard those woods in Overton Park called by that name before, though I had grown up six blocks away and had often as a boy ridden my bicycle on paths through those huge old trees, alive with the music of mockingbirds, cardinals, and brown thrashers.

During a visit he paid to Allen Tate in Tennessee as a young man, Robert Lowell saw how alive the South and its legendary Confederate past were to Tate and the other Southern writers. Lowell wrote that by contrast with Tate and his friends, "I began to discover what I had never known. I, too, was part of a legend. I was Northern, disembodied, Platonist, a puritan, an abolitionist." Peter Taylor, as a native of my own city, helped me through his writing and conversation to place myself, just as Allen Tate had given Robert Lowell, Peter's roommate at Kenyon College, the gift of seeing himself as a New England Yankee. With Peter's help I came to realize I was not only a Southerner and a Tennessean: I came from Memphis, in the westernmost of the state's three kingdoms.

Sewanee and
the Civil War

On the morning of the Fourth of July I cycled along Break-field Road in Sewanee, a ſtone's throw from my house here. The scene was tranquil. In the sunshine a young mother pushed her child along in a ſtroller, and several joggers were out. Behind white wooden fences, the Equeſtrian Center's little herd of horses that ſtudents at the University of the South board here cropped the summer grass. Swallows swooped and glided overhead, and on the telephone wires I ſpotted one or two bluebirds, evidence of a gentle and success-ful campaign to provide habitats for ſpecies that were once endan-gered on the Cumberland Plateau in Tennessee. Everything ſpoke of proſperity and ease and kindness. The scene could have been an il-luſtration for a contemporary book of hours. The legend underneath the picture would have read "Peace."

An observer on the morning of July 4, 1863, more than one hun-dred and fifty years ago, would have witnessed an entirely different scene along the Breakfield Road. He would have seen the dirt of that road churned to mud, malodorous with the smells of gunpowder, sweat, and carnage, a horse shot dead every fifty yards or so, abandoned rucksacks, canteens, uniforms with CSA stitched onto the breast and shoulder.

In "River Town," my chapter about Memphis, we caught a glimpse of Leonidas Polk, Episcopal bishop and Confederate general, as a recruiter for the Southern cause in the war's early days. A few days before the skirmish at Sewanee, General Polk's and General William J. Hardee's corps of Braxton Bragg's Army of Tennessee had taken up defensive positions at the foot of Sewanee Mountain to cover the Confederate Army's retreat from Tullahoma toward the Tennessee River and Chattanooga as these corps moved south and east across the plateau.

A force of Union cavalry engaged two regiments of General Joseph ("Fightin' Joe") Wheeler's cavalry on the western approaches to the mountain in a running battle that ranged from Tunnel Point, where the road from Cowan reached the plateau, to University Crossing, where the Cowan Road met the Sewanee Mining Company's railroad. All this during an unrelenting downpour.

You may remember General Wheeler as the officer whom, earlier in 1863, Bedford Forrest vowed never to serve under again. Of New England stock, Wheeler was born in Georgia but grew up in Connecticut and went to West Point, where he graduated nineteenth in a class of twenty-two. A short man barely tall enough to meet the academy's specifications for height, he served with distinction in the Indian wars and joined the Confederate Army at the beginning of the war as a lieutenant in a Georgia regiment.

THE BATTLE OF MURFREESBORO

The story begins an hour's drive north of Sewanee at Murfreesboro. I occasionally drive up there to walk the quiet fields where few traces remain of the Battle of Stones River (Confederates called it the Battle of Murfreesboro), one of the bloodiest of the war, fought in the waning days of 1862 between the Confederate Army of Tennessee under General Braxton Bragg and the Union Army of the Cumberland under the wily and resourceful command of General William S. Rosecrans.

Rosecrans was forty-three years old—tall, both a heavy drinker and a devout Catholic who wore a crucifix on his watch chain and carried a rosary in his pocket. His men liked him. He was mercurial in temperament, prone to fits of anger that blew over quickly. The soldiers called him "Old Rosy," because of his unusual name and his remarkably red nose. Rosecrans was meticulous in his preparations for battle, refusing to move or engage the enemy unless and until he had everything in readiness. His finicky nature drove President Lincoln to distraction, and the president constantly sent letters and telegrams urging the general to action. Though as we shall see, this commander's meticulous planning saved the day for the Union Army.

On the Confederate side the Christmas season had been festive with card parties, dances, and horse races arranged by the town's patriotic citizens. Murfreesboro, where the Southern army was headquartered, was eager to show its heroes a good time. The highlight of that Christmas was a visit from His Excellency Jefferson Davis, President of the Confederacy. The day after Christmas saw the wedding of Brigadier General John Hunt Morgan, the Kentucky cavalryman famous for his daring raids into enemy territory, to a local belle who had set her cap for him as early as the summer before, when Union troops occupied Murfreesboro.

After she had given some invading Yankees a piece of her mind one day on the square in Murfreesboro and suggested they go back where they came from, one of them demanded to know her name. "It's Mattie Ready now," she replied. "But by the grace of God one day I hope to call myself the wife of John Morgan." Hearing about this when he returned to the Confederate base in Murfreesboro from a raid into Kentucky, General Morgan lost no time in getting himself introduced to the aptly named Miss Ready. (In truth, the name was pronounced Reedy.)

Cupid's arrows hit their mark, and soon the two became engaged. General Morgan's relatives from Kentucky came down to Tennessee for the nuptials, and his fellow officers joined in the wedding party too, as well turned-out as they could make themselves after their many months on campaign. Sewanee's own Bishop-General Polk was present in Murfreesboro during the holidays, and he married

General Morgan and his bride, pulling his Episcopal surplice on over his gray Confederate uniform to perform the ceremony.

Chief among the officers at the wedding was General Braxton Bragg. At the age of forty-five, Bragg was two years older than his opposing general. Both he and Rosecrans had graduated fifth in their respective classes at West Point. A visiting Englishman, Colonel Arthur James Lyon Fremantle, described him in the diary he kept during a visit to the United States at this time.

"This officer," wrote the Sandhurst graduate, who had commanded a brigade of Coldstream Guards during the Sudan campaign, "is the least prepossessing of the Confederate generals. He is very thin; he stoops; and has a sickly, cadaverous, haggard appearance; rather plain features, bushy black eyebrows which unite in a tuft on the top of his nose, and a stubby, iron-gray beard; but his eyes are bright and piercing. He has the reputation of being a rigid disciplinarian, and of shooting freely for insubordination. I understand he is rather unpopular on this account, and also by reason of occasional acerbity of manner."

Those officers in the Confederate Army with the means of getting away over the 1862 Christmas holidays had done so, and some officers returned to camp with hangovers. "I felt feeble," one lieutenant from Georgia wrote in his diary, "but, being anxious to be with my men, reported for duty." From New Year's Eve in 1862 to the second of January 1863, on the outskirts of Murfreesboro, the opposing armies fought what the Yankees called the Battle of Stones River. (Confederates called it the Battle of Murfreesboro—or Murfreesborough in the old spelling.) Casualties in this battle ran higher for both armies than in any other battle of the war.

The night before the conflict, the music of both armies' military bands was clearly audible on either side of the line. After a spirited rendition of "Yankee Doodle" from the Yankees, the Rebels replied with "Dixie." After "Hail Columbia," the Southern musicians came back with "The Bonnie Blue Flag." But when one band started to play "Home Sweet Home," the opposing side joined in, and more than one soldier in both armies must have felt a lump in his throat when men from both above and below the Mason Dixon Line joined in singing the words to Stephen Foster's song.

Tennessee winters can be severe, and on the night before the battle soldiers on both sides tried to get some sleep on the frozen ground. At dawn on New Year's Eve, the sixteen thousand Union troops on the right wing of Rosecrans's army were just starting to wake up, kindling their camp fires and making coffee, when rabbits and quail burst out of the woods, followed by deer crashing through the undergrowth and birds of the forest flying startled from among the trees. Almost immediately afterwards came the sound of advancing soldiers, and long lines of Confederate troops attacked them unprepared and, firing volley after volley, swept them backward through the fields.

The Confederates under Generals McCown and Cleburne numbered only about ten thousand, but they had the element of surprise. In the homespun words of Sam Watkins, a private from Tennessee whose memoir, *Company Aytch: Or, A Side Show of the Big Show,* is a Civil War classic, the men in gray "swooped down on those Yankees like a whirl-a-gust of woodpeckers in a hailstorm." One dead Union soldier was later found holding the handle of a coffee pot in his hand, his grip stiffened by rigor mortis.

The attack on the Union Army's far right was followed up by an advance of troops under General Polk. As a churchman Polk did not hold with the use of strong language, so when his subordinate, General Benjamin Cheatham, a native Tennessean and seasoned veteran of the Mexican War, yelled to his men, "Give 'em hell, boys!" Polk yelled, "Give them what General Cheatham says, boys, give them what General Cheatham says!"

General Cheatham, though a brave and effective commander ordinarily, was drunk the day of the battle. When an officer later remarked to Sewanee's Charles Todd Quintard, who was serving as Chaplain to the First Tennessee Infantry Regiment, that Cheatham was "on his high horse" that day, Quintard replied, "Yes, I'm sorry to say, he was on his low horse too." Asked what he meant by that, the chaplain replied that when Cheatham had ridden out in front of his troops to rally them before the advance, he "rolled off his horse and fell to the ground as limp and helpless as a bag of meal—to the great humiliation and mortification of his troops."

By 10:00 a.m. the rout was well underway, and the Rebels had captured three thousand Union troops and twenty-eight cannons, abandoned in haste as the Union troops retreated. Only stubborn resistance in what the soldiers dubbed "the slaughter pen" was able to prevent a complete rout. The Union Army regrouped along the Nashville Pike and the Nashville and Chattanooga rail line that ran parallel to each other down from the Tennessee capital, which had been under Union control since February. At this point in the proceedings the Rebels attacked the Union left flank as well, driving the Federals back to what was called the Round Forest. But on this side of the battle line, faced with imminent defeat, troops from Illinois, Indiana, Kentucky, and Ohio stiffened their resistance and finally stopped the Confederate advance on a piece of ground that soldiers called "hell's half-acre."

On the elevation of the Round Forest Rosecrans, exhibiting the thoroughness for which he was known, had massed fifty cannons hub to hub. When the Confederates came charging toward the Federal position, these heavy guns opened fire point-blank. A brigade of Mississippians, attacking through a cotton field, plucked cotton from the stalks of bedraggled plants left from the harvest to protect their ears from the deafening roar of artillery. Their attack was "without doubt the most daring, courageous, and best executed attack which the Confederates made on our line between pike and river," according to a Union veteran of the battle. But it was broken by the savage cannon fire into which they valiantly and vainly charged.

Confederate casualties for that one day amounted to nine thousand. And yet, as night fell and the fighting stopped, it appeared as though victory was in Southern hands. Whereas at the start of hostilities the two armies had faced each other in parallel lines, now both wings of the Union formation had been wrenched back, at a heavy cost in human lives, so that it resembled a jackknife almost closed on itself. The wounded and dying were carried back to improvised field hospitals on both sides of the battle lines.

Harried and overworked doctors did what they could to stanch the bleeding, and they freely amputated limbs, "then threw," as a soldier from Ohio observed, "the quivering flesh into a pile." Quintard, a medical doctor before being ordained as a priest, rolled up his sleeves and went to work with the other surgeons. Shelby Foote describes the aftermath of the first day's fighting: "Except for the surgeons and the men they worked on, blue and gray, whose screams broke through the singing of the bone saws, both sides were bedded down by now amid the wreckage and the corpses, preparing to sleep out as best they could the last night of the year."

During the night, Bragg's scouts reported wagons rumbling north toward Nashville along the turnpike. The Confederate general inferred that the enemy, having been defeated in the field, was retreating to his fortified entrenchments around the Tennessee capital. Bragg was counting his chickens before they hatched. He began planning to have his cavalry fall upon the retreating army the next day while it was strung out along the road. Before retiring for the night he dispatched a triumphant telegram to President Davis in Richmond, reading "The enemy has yielded his strong position and is falling back. We occupy the whole field and shall follow him. . . . God has granted us a happy New Year."

God had, as it turned out, done no such thing. The wagons the Confederates heard were not those of an army in retreat, but medical wagons transporting some of the twelve thousand Union casualties back to hospitals in Nashville. While the wounded were being evacuated, Rosecrans gathered his generals for a council of war at his headquarters, a cabin on the Nashville pike. General George Thomas, who would later win fame as "the Rock of Chickamauga" for standing firm when the rest of the Union Army was routed on that battlefield in Georgia, slept through most of the council, but he woke up when the word "retreat" was mentioned. He opened his eyes and muttered, "This army doesn't retreat," then fell back to sleep.

Bragg awoke on New Year's morning fully confident of victory and ready to begin the mopping up. But with both armies in position and stalemated, little happened on New Year's Day. Neither commanding general seemed to have a notion of what to do next. Bragg was concerned with getting his army lined up properly so as to resist a Union attack if one should come, and he ordered General Polk to prod the enemy's left wing to determine how things stood on that side of the field.

One thing that history is not very good at rendering from a distance in time is how things smelled. And yet, among the catalogue of war's horrors, its gut-wrenching smells rank high on the list. Soldiers who have gone through combat have unforgettable memories of the stench. The odor of decomposing bodies, excrement, and the smoke from exploded munitions in the aftermath of the Normandy invasion in World War II was so strong that veterans of the campaign could never forget it even years later. As Polk's men moved through the Round Forest, the scene of the previous day's slaughter, the stench of the dead bodies of Union troops sickened the advancing Confederates. Before they withdrew, the bishop-general ordered his men to bury the bodies.

On January 2 the only thing that Bragg could think to do was attack the Round Forest. General Breckinridge of Kentucky, who was ordered to move forward that afternoon with the forty-five hundred men under his command, could see that the mission was doomed to fail, and he said as much to his second in command. But the men in gray followed orders and charged valiantly up the hill. Halfway up, they fired their first volley and broke into a run toward the top, screaming out the Rebel Yell as they crested the hill. The terrified Union troops broke and ran. This, however, was just the moment that Captain John Mendenhall, in charge of Union artillery, was waiting for.

He commanded his fifty-eight double-shotted cannon to open fire. "The very forest seemed to fall before our fire," one artilleryman wrote afterward, "and not a Confederate reached the river." Many of the Southern men were crushed under fallen limbs brought down by heavy cannon fire. As they withdrew, seventeen hundred of the forty-five hundred men had fallen. That night Bragg's staff counseled retreat. The enemy had proved to be lodged in an unassailable position, and meanwhile rain was falling harder and harder, rendering impassable Stones River, which divided the two wings of Bragg's army. Bragg called retreat. The hapless general, who was gaining a reputation as an expert in snatching defeat from the jaws of victory, declared that "the army retired to its present position behind Duck River without giving or receiving a shot," as if that were some consolation.

His soldiers, officers and men alike, having lost fully one-third of their number, were now severely demoralized and soaked to the skin. "What does he fight battles for?" some of them muttered under their breath. And a civilian wrote in his diary, "It was a small surcease to the sob of the widow and the moan of the orphan that 'the retreat to Tullahoma was conducted in good order.'" This brave but now spiritless army, worn out, many of them shoeless and lacking overcoats in the bitter cold, retired back to the towns north of Sewanee—Wartrace, Shelbyville, Tullahoma, and Winchester—to lick their wounds and regroup. Rosecrans stayed at Murfreesboro. The two armies rested there until the following June, "lying," as a contemporary observer wrote, "like two bull dogs crouched and facing each other."

LEONIDAS POLK

The retreat must have been especially poignant for Leonidas Polk, Lieutenant General, CSA, and Bishop of the diocese of Louisiana before his friend Jefferson Davis offered him a commission in the Confederate Army. Along with Bishops Stephen Elliott and James Hervey Otey, Bishop Polk was one of the founders of what had been envisioned as the grand Southern University, one that would rival Oxford, Heidelberg, and Harvard, here in an idyllic setting in the Cumberland Mountains.

Polk, a member of one of Tennessee's most distinguished families and a distant cousin of President James K. Polk, graduated in 1827 from West Point, where he was eighth in his class. But soon after graduation he resigned from the military and enrolled in the Virginia Theological Seminary. In 1831 he was ordained in the ministry and assigned a church in Maury County, Tennessee. Polk combined his spiritual duties with the life of a wealthy planter. Census records show that in 1840, with 111 slaves, he was the largest slaveholder in Maury County.

When he was appointed Missionary Bishop of Louisiana, Polk relocated from Middle Tennessee to Thibodaux, Louisiana, where he purchased Leighton Plantation on Bayou La Fourche, for $100,000.

Here Polk produced an average of 692 hogsheads or 761,200 pounds of sugar per season, and in 1844 Leighton ranked as the largest sugar plantation in La Fourche Parish. Census records indicate that Polk owned 215 slaves in 1850, but agriculturalist Solon Robinson estimated 370 and Frederick Law Olmsted estimated 400 during their respective tours of 1849 and 1854.

Southerners of the slaveholding class had a view of the South's "peculiar institution" that presented, deliberately or unconsciously, a view of what life was like for "the darkies" that was, to say the very least, euphemistic. Work in the cane fields would have been just as punishing or even more so than in the cotton fields of Mississippi. But Polk hired a chaplain to minister to his slaves, and unlike most other plantation owners, he did not work them on Sundays.

It should be remembered that the accounts we have of life at Leighton are largely confined to the lives of the house servants, whose duties were easier than for those who worked the fields. Still it is clear that the Polks were among those plantation owners who tried to treat their servants humanely. A Miss Beauchamp, the Polks' Irish governess, wrote her impressions of Leighton, bringing a British perspective to the scene:

> I knew before I came to this country that slavery existed here, and I expected to see the black servants treated with much less consideration than the white domestics in my own country; to my surprise, I found that quite the contrary was the case. There was a host of servants at Bishop Polk's; they were on more familiar terms with the family, were more kindly nursed in illness and more carefully watched over at all times, than I ever knew servants to be in the old country. The familiarity at first somewhat shocked my European notions. I did not, I confess, like all the shaking of black hands that I found was the fashion. The household, white and black, assembled every morning before breakfast in the parlor. The psalms for the day were read, a psalm or hymn was sung by all; the bishop read and expounded a chapter of the Bible, and then prayed.

To this might be added the testimony of one of the bishop's daughters:

> The greatest efforts were made by the bishop to preserve among his servants the sanctity of family life. Their weddings were always

celebrated in his own home; the broad hall was decorated for the occasion with evergreens and flowers, and illuminated with many lights. The bride and groom (all decked in wedding garments presented by Mrs. Polk) with their attendants, were ushered quietly into their master's presence. The honor coveted by the bishop's children, and given as the reward of good behavior, was to hold aloft the silver candlesticks while their father read the marriage service. A wedding supper always followed (in a large room used on such occasions, where were spread every variety of meats, cakes, and sweets, provided by the master and mistress), after which all invited guests joined the bride and groom in making merry, to the sound of "fiddle, banjo, and bones," until the small hours of the night.

For those slaves whose desires forestalled the ceremony of marriage and who could not wait to consummate their unions, however, their master took a different approach:

If the couple had misbehaved, they were compelled to atone for it by marriage. In that case there was no display, but the guilty pair were summoned from the field, and in their working-clothes, in the study, without flowers or candles, were made husband and wife.

Clearly, for all his genuine kindness, generosity, and charity, Bishop Polk remained blind to the evils of slavery, and was not shy about imposing his own morality on those over whose lives he had absolute power. In his politics Leonidas Polk was uncompromisingly an upper-class Southerner of his time—proud, paternalistic, and scornful of Abolitionists, who he felt did not understand slavery as it was practiced in the feudal South, where in his view the slave owner was as bound to his charges as they were to him. He wrote in a letter to his colleague, Bishop Elliott: "Talk of slavery! Those madcaps at the North don't understand the thing at all. We hold the negroes, and they hold us! They are at the head of the ladder! They furnish the yoke and we the neck. My own is getting sore, and it is the same with those of my neighbors in Church and State."

From this distance in time, it is hard to understand how the bishop could have deceived himself so thoroughly. And yet from our historical vantage point it is probably impossible to appreciate how the institution of slavery must have appeared to those who were born into a society where it was taken for granted. After all, slavery had existed at least as far back as Biblical times. There are many references to the institution in both the Old and the New Testaments. As J. H. Bills, a Tennessee slaveholder, observed in 1843, "I found the institution here when I came upon the stage of life. I have bought many & sold few; never bought one but that I thought I had bettered his or her condition & most of those I bought I have done so at their own request." The historian Eugene D. Genovese writes in his book, *The World the Slaveholders Made,*

> There is no reason to believe that for every guilt-stricken, inwardly torn slaveholder there were not many who went about their business reasonably secure in the notion that they did not create the world, that the world existed as it existed, and that their moral worth depended on how well they discharged the duties and responsibilities defined by the world in which they, not someone else, lived.

These observations probably describe Leonidas Polk's view of things.

FOUNDING OF THE UNIVERSITY OF THE SOUTH

One function of the University of the South as its founders perceived it was to educate planters' sons in a manner commensurate with the role they would play as slave owners and leaders of a society where the "peculiar institution" was the law of the land. For Bishop Polk it was important that "the ruling race of the South should realize the greatness of the trust which has been providentially committed to them in the care of an ignorant and helpless people." (He conveniently ignores the fact that laws in practically all the Confederate states made it a crime to teach slaves to read and that the institution of slavery was what made these people helpless.) Sewanee graduates would be Christian gentlemen who ran plantations worked by slave labor. This is implicit in the Board of Trustees of the Southern Dioceses' report in 1858, making the case for a winter rather than a summer vacation:

> For the South, the proper vacation of a University is the winter; that season when our planters and merchants and professional men are

surrounded by their families upon their homesteads; when the cheer-
ful Christmas fire is burning on the hearth, and mothers and sisters
and servants can receive the returning student to his home . . . when
he can engage in the sports which make him a true Southern man,
hunting, shooting, riding; when he can mingle freely with the slaves
who are in the future to be placed under his management and control.

The founding of the "Southern Oxford" in 1860 was a grand occasion
that stirred the hearts of those who gathered on the Mountain. "Nine
bishops in their robes," an observer wrote in his diary, "and 50 or 60
clergymen in surplices and gowns and some 5,000 people formed a
procession and headed by a band playing Hail Columbia marched to
the spot where the main building of the university was to be. Here
Old Hundred was sung by the vast multitude."

Even in those early days, Sewanee had a knack for rising to the
challenge of a great occasion: "The hogsheads of hams, the barrels,
and boxes, and bags of groceries, the cartloads of crockery and glass,
the bales of sheeting and blankets, and acres of straw beds, indicated
that Southern hospitality for once had entered upon the difficult un-
dertaking of outdoing itself." But many among the throng were uneasy
about the political situation, and the happy occasion carried an un-
dercurrent of foreboding: "Even then, there was a feeling as of a great
danger near at hand, a yawning chasm which all feared to look upon."

THE WAR FINDS ITS WAY
TO SEWANEE MOUNTAIN

By the time the opposing armies fought to their stalemate at Stones
River, the South's, and Sewanee's, idyllic days had ended. The two
armies were moving south along the Nashville and Chattanooga Rail-
road, which was of primary strategic importance to both sides. The
Cumberland Plateau runs roughly perpendicular to the north-south
line of the tracks. As the railroad descends into southern Tennessee,
it turns southeastward toward Chattanooga, and the armies turned in
that direction too.

Nowadays when I drive back to my house at Sewanee from Nash-
ville or Winchester over broad plains where golden tassels wave over

fields of ripening corn, I feel Sewanee Mountain looming above me, forested, wreathed in blue haze, inscrutable. For me this is, for at least part of the year, home. But in the early 1860s the Mountain was a no man's land, a dangerous place to be, no matter where your loyalties lay. Even before Bragg's slow retreat, or "retrograde movement," as he euphemistically called it, this part of the South was aflame with irregular fighting. Cavalry units from both armies, as well as Southern partisans and guerillas, used the forests of the Mountain as places to retreat to and hide when push came to shove.

Before the cataclysm of war, farmers in the valley would drive their livestock up the mountain to graze in summer pastures. But once war had gripped the country, these dense woods of oak, tulip poplar, pine, and hemlock became the dens of men who owed little loyalty to either side—opportunistic and often brutal outlaws and bushwhackers who preyed on defenseless civilians.

The state voted for secession in 1861, but while Middle Tennessee voted seven to one in favor of joining the Confederacy, in poorer, mountainous East Tennessee the vote was two to one against. Franklin County raised three regiments of infantry, a battalion of cavalry, and one artillery company to fight for the Rebel cause. But a sharp divide separated those who lived in the rich flatlands from those who lived in the mountains. According to a Union officer who led a foraging operation toward Midway and could find only potatoes, "Most of the people living on the mountain are poor, and mostly Irish. They came here for the purpose of digging coal." It is hardly to be expected that these poor people would find common cause with the prosperous farmers, slaveholders, and plantation owners in the flatlands. Union sympathizers hid out in remote coves and hollers to avoid Confederate conscription agents.

The actual nature of the Mountain's sparse, ragtag population contradicts Sewanee mythology, which presented the place as an unspoiled and unpopulated wilderness. In an address he gave in 1898, decades after the event, George R. Fairbanks described the domain as follows: "The primeval forest in its solitude and its grandeur surrounded us. These noble oaks, mute witnesses of the long, unbroken solitude, overshadowed us then, as now, and paths trodden only by the kine, the wild deer, or the occasional hunter, left scarce a trace on the surface."

The nucleus of a Sewanee community had begun to form around the few rough academic buildings of the nascent university as well as at the road and rail junction known as University Place. A large assembly hall, as well as a dining hall, had been constructed for the students whose presence was anticipated. By 1860 one William Tomlinson was operating a hotel at University Place where visitors including Bishops Otey and Green stayed when they came to visit. In the summer of 1860 Bishops Polk and Elliott built houses for their families there, and Major George Fairbanks built a house for himself on a bluff overlooking the valley.

‹‹‹‹‹‹‹‹

What brought the differing political persuasions of the Mountain's diverse population to a crisis point was the burning of Bishop Elliott's and Bishop Polk's houses in April of 1861. Coincidentally it was the same day a Confederate battery opened fire on Fort Sumter in Charleston harbor: April 12. But there is no indication that the news reached Sewanee right away. Fairbanks, Polk, and Elliott were off the Mountain, but Bishop Polk's wife, Fanny, and three daughters were in residence. Mrs. Polk was awakened by a "horrible roaring and light."

Her house was in flames. Having alerted the servants, who slept at the top of the house, and her daughters, she set about saving what she could—a few family portraits, the bishop's papers, the family silver, and a few other items. One of her house servants, a man named Attimore, entreated her, "Mistress, you must leave the house, this roof may fall in a moment," and she got out, fifteen minutes before the roof collapsed.

Clearly the fires were deliberately set by individuals who targeted the residencies of the two bishops, both of whom were known to be ardent pro-slavery secessionists. On the sixteenth of April, Mrs. Polk wrote her sister: "On the night of Friday the 12th our house was destroyed by fire with its whole contents. . . . The fire was evidently the work of an incendiary." She goes on to blame abolitionists, and if her suspicions were correct, this proves that such sentiments did exist in this part of the South at the time.

〉〉〉〉〉〉〉〉

Rosecrans's tactically brilliant flanking movements against Bragg's forces continued to threaten his line of supplies from Chattanooga and further south. As warm weather returned, Bragg got his army in motion again and continued his retreat along the rail line, burning bridges and railroad trestles behind him wherever he could. Lacking the imagination of a Stonewall Jackson or a Lee or a Bedford Forrest, Bragg could think of only one thing to do: retreat.

Just as it was the severe winter of 1812 that defeated Napoleon in his attempt to conquer Russia, weather was almost as much a factor in the campaign of 1863 as were the two armies. Either the day would dawn misty and drizzly, or the sky split open with one of those fire-and-brimstone thunderstorms that rake across Tennessee in midsummer—enjoyable if one has a sound roof overhead, but not for the men who slept out in the open under what flimsy shelter they could improvise. One soldier wrote that "it was hard to tell, sometimes, whether the rumbling noises which accompanied the heavier rains were the artillery of earth or heaven, for sometimes both were at work simultaneously."

Rations were issued to the troops along the way, but as they were constantly on the move, they could not stop to prepare a meal. So they would find a big leaf, bend it into a concave shape, put flour in, carefully mix it with water, and then try to cook it over whatever fires they were able to build in the constant rain. Their only meat was bacon, and this they wrapped around sticks or the ramrods from their rifles and roasted it over their faltering fires. According to one soldier,

> We pushed on—men, horses, artillery, ammunition and supply-wagons plunging and floundering through the mud. Onward, through the deep mire and bridgeless streams, swollen by the incessant rains, over the hills, through the dense woods, out on the open, swampy plain.

Eventually the Confederates would have to stand and fight, if only to slow the enemy down. Bragg telegraphed General Polk with this question: "Shall we fight on the Elk or take post on the mountain near to Cowan?" What if anything Bragg knew about Polk's connections with Sewanee we have no idea. Polk replied that the army should withdraw to the foot of the Mountain at Cowan and offer resistance there, protecting the railroad and giving the wagon trains time to withdraw over the Mountain in the direction of Chattanooga. The army was followed, according to a private from Arkansas, by a rout of refugees who choked the roads.

> There were streams of people, mostly women and children with faithful servants, fleeing back from the invaded country, back into the recesses of the ever contracting Confederacy. Rather than even come in contact with the despised Yankees, they often abandoned everything and went "naked among strangers," but with perfect confidence because they knew they were their own.

Nowadays only one road climbs Sewanee Mountain from the west: Highway 41A, which splits off from Highway 64, the road that runs all the way from Memphis in the southwest corner of the state through Winchester and Cowan here on the verge of the Cumberland Plateau between Middle and East Tennessee. Fifty or more years ago Highway 64/41A was my route from Memphis to college, and I never ascend the twisting road up to Sewanee without feeling I am coming home.

But back in the 1860s traffic on and off the Mountain traveled by foot, or by horse, wagon, or mule up multiple routes. Many trails, tracks, and footpaths wound through the coves and over the ridges and valleys, giving outlaws, moonshiners, guerillas, and bushwhackers many hiding places and escape routes. Yet the two main approaches were by the Cowan Road and the Breakfield Road mentioned at the beginning of this story. The troops under Hardee, which had camped at Decherd, came up the Mountain along the Breakfield Road. Polk's troops trudged up the Cowan Road, but in those days it did not follow the same route, and it was not the easy ascent that it is today:

> Another night march [one soldier wrote], and that up the tortuous, rocky and precipitous road which scaled the mountain. It was here, on this night march, that fatigue, loss of sleep and wet clothing began

to tell on the powers of the strongest. When morning came we had progressed three miles.

After their all-night forced march the vanguard of Polk's men made it to the top of the plateau by dawn on the 3rd of July. Part of his corps kept moving toward the Tennessee River near Battle Creek, where it crossed on pontoon bridges.

General Polk himself reached the top of the Mountain around 2:00 a.m. on the 3rd of July. Here, while his troops, artillery pieces and supply wagons filed past across the mountaintop, he stopped to rest at the spring which has come to be called Polk Spring, continuing on toward Jumpoff to the northeast before dawn. The image we get of the bishop-general here is haunting. The charred embers of the house he had built lay soaked with rain only a few dozen yards from the spring. His son William, who served under him in the Army of Tennessee, wrote after his death: "[No] man can read the mystery of that glimpse of the vision that came to him . . . when as general he passed with his army corps in retreat over this same mountain."

When Bishop Polk first came to Sewanee he, like the other founders, saw the domain as a place of idyllic, unspoiled natural beauty. Now the roads and tracks up and across the Mountain lay trampled into depressing morasses of mud, scattered with the abandoned equipment, knapsacks, tents, bedrolls, and uniforms of the retreating Confederates. Many of these deserters were Tennesseans who felt no loyalty to Bragg's army once it left their native state. They stayed home to work their farms and defend their families. Many others were simply defeated, exhausted, hungry, shoeless, sick of the whole thing. In the woods around Sewanee ragtag deserters lurked, hiding out.

THE SKIRMISH AT SEWANEE

The year 1863 was when the tides of war turned irrevocably in favor of the Union. From July 1863 to Robert E. Lee's surrender at Appomattox Courthouse in April 1865, the Confederacy's defeat was not a question of if but of when. Though in public he put a brave face on it, after the defeat of his armies at Gettysburg Lee was forced to admit, at least to himself, that his invasion of the North had failed. His dispirited troops, leaving some twenty-eight thousand of their dead and wounded comrades behind, set off on the long trek home to Virginia.

As if some master plan were being orchestrated, on this same Independence Day Vicksburg surrendered to Grant's army, and Union troops and gunboats once more controlled the Mississippi from Minnesota to the Gulf of Mexico. Geographically Sewanee lay somewhere between Vicksburg and Gettysburg, those two axes of defeat. While the outcome of the skirmish here gave little or no strategic advantage to the victorious Union Army, there is some symbolic rightness in the clash having occurred at this decisive time on the site of the University of the South—"the grand Southern university," wrote a private from Indiana whose unit bivouacked on the ountain later in the month, "that was to have been."

On July 3 Rosecrans set in motion up the Mountain a reconnaissance mission of cavalry and infantry. On the Confederate side, two regiments of Wheeler's Cavalry were in place, stationed at University Place to screen the withdrawal of Southern troops across the Mountain and from Sewanee across the Tennessee River in the direction of Chattanooga.

A skirmish between cavalry units evokes images of mounted troops charging and counter-charging, sabers drawn. But here the terrain was rocky and the ground uneven, so the cavalrymen on both sides fought dismounted in the steadily falling rain, their guns as likely to fizzle out and misfire as they were to hit their targets. The day before, Wheeler's men had wielded axes to cut down trees across the trails and roads ascending the mountain. Now his two regiments waited at the top of the Cowan Road to oppose any Federal unit that might attempt to cross the Mountain and impede Polk's withdrawal. These regiments included Terry's Texas Rangers, an elite unit of volunteers that had figured in several important earlier engagements of the war.

Rain continued to fall heavily as Independence Day dawned. Just as the Texas Rangers were poised to withdraw from University Crossing, three companies of Union cavalry from Kentucky attacked the Texans' positions in the dense woods. The Rangers opened fire from behind fallen logs and through thickets. The initial encounter lasted only ten or fifteen minutes. This began a running battle during the course of which the Texans withdrew in an orderly and disciplined fashion, attacking and counter-attacking as they fell back.

The Rangers reported the loss of twenty-five horses killed and wounded, while the Kentucky companies reported the loss of twenty-six. One of the Rangers was killed, seven wounded, and two were missing. Union losses were roughly equivalent. And that was it. The Union reconnaissance mission stopped attacking at about nine in the morning and withdrew down the Mountain to their headquarters in Cowan. The Confederates, having accomplished their mission of protecting Polk's withdrawal, withdrew during the day to Jumpoff and from there off the plateau, across the Tennessee River in the rearguard of Bragg's army. The skirmish at Sewanee may not have been one of the war's major engagements, but still, as Sergeant Rabb of the Texas Rangers commented, it was "a rite sharp little fight."

>>>>>>>>

General Polk himself would be killed at Pine Mountain, Georgia less than a year later, shot clean through the chest with a cannon ball. Privileged even in the manner of his death as a soldier, he was lucky enough to die instantly. "I saw him while the infirmary corps were bringing him off the field," Sam Watkins wrote:

> He was as white as a piece of marble, and a most remarkable thing about him was, that not a drop of blood was ever seen to come out of the place through which the cannon ball had passed. My pen and ability are inadequate to the task of doing his memory justice. Every private soldier loved him. Second to Stonewall Jackson, his loss was the greatest the South ever sustained. When I saw him there dead, I felt that I had lost a friend whom I had ever loved and respected, and that the South had lost one of her best and greatest Generals.

AFTERMATH

Back in Cowan, in observance of Independence Day, a "National Salute" was fired, and a similar celebration was mounted in the

Union camp on Elk River. General Wheeler reported "considerable firing of cannon, which we could not tell whether intended for shelling the woods or Fourth of July guns." By the 5th, Wheeler had withdrawn from the Mountain, and Colonel Watkins of the Union Army reported laconically back to his commanding officer: "No rebels here."

War, in addition to its dramatic turns of events, its horrors, tragedies, and outrages, sometimes occasions absurdities. In his official report Watkins notes that his men have captured "15 prisoners and a set of brass musical instruments." Where did these come from, these musicians and these instruments? Nothing seems less likely than that the bedraggled, retreating Confederate Army, many of them shoeless and undernourished, would have needed a brass band as part of their entourage. Maybe the music had cheered them up as they retreated.

For a few days the mountaintop was a perilous place to be. The Confederates had fled, and the Federals had not yet firmly established control. While the Mountain "remained," in one historian's words, "largely empty of organized military units, it teemed with stragglers, deserters, draft-dodgers, guerillas, escaped slaves, refugees, and other, more sinister fauna."

Many of these men were on the brink of starvation. They dug up edible roots, and shot with their service revolvers or smooth-bore muskets whatever game they could scare up, stealing provisions wherever they could. Men must have shot and knifed each other in these now peaceful woods, too, and no one would know what became of their remains. Skeletons of these stragglers and irregulars lie, I am sure, in shallow and unknown graves all over Sewanee Mountain.

On July 13 it was reported that "Bragg's men [were] still coming in by companies and taking the oath." The rains of June and July continued on into August. Once the US Army had established control—even though Union troops were still not safe from occasional raids by guerilla units and the ambushes and sniping of bushwhackers—the Mountain largely reverted to its previous condition as an island of calm in a sea of turmoil, "the eye of the storm" that raged all around it. Edwin Williams of the Indiana Fourth wrote:

This is one of the best camping-grounds I know of. Near our quarters is a very large spring of the clearest and finest water I ever drank. . . . This place is so delightful and cool that I had hoped we might be permitted to spend the whole summer here, but I fear it is not our lot to enjoy such a luxury. . . .

After the war's end, Major George Fairbanks was among the first to return to the Mountain. When, "in 1865," the Major wrote, "I came to this spot and pitched my tent for a few days, all was gone but one small cabin." Both the dream and the nightmare had passed. Now the time had come to rebuild. Among the churchmen who came to the Mountain was Charles Todd Quintard, whom we saw back at Stones River doing double duty as chaplain and surgeon to the First Tennessee Infantry Brigade, later to serve as Bishop of Tennessee and the University of the South's first Vice Chancellor. Dr. Quintard was known for his kindness to the foot soldiers, known as "webfeet." Private Sam Watkins, writing in his memoir, *Company Aytch,* notes in passing, "The next day Dr. C. T. Quintard let me ride his horse nearly all day, while he walked with the webfeet."

As for Bishop Polk's widow, Fanny, she who had escaped barefooted and almost possessionless from her burning house at Sewanee, it has been hard to gain any information about what happened to her after the War. Sada Elliott, the novelist and daughter of Bishop Polk's friend and colleague Stephen Elliott of Georgia, wrote a letter to her brother Habersham in 1871, giving a caustic survey of the university community at Sewanee as it struggled to get back on its feet.

Many "distressed gentlefolk"—to use a British expression—took in student boarders, and among them was one "Widow Polk," who, according to twenty-two-year-old Sada's description,

is a commonsense, proper, dignified, kindhearted widow-woman, who never meddles in other people's business. She lives in a melancholy, mulatto-colored, wooden house with pink blinds, named Waverly. The front yard is trampled into a desert, only redeemed by the shade trees, a dilapidated rail fence and no gate. She has three little children and keeps house for 26 boys.

It is tempting to identify this Mrs. Polk as Fanny Polk, the bishop's widow. But I don't think she is our Mrs. Polk. Instead of returning to Sewanee after the War, it appears that the former mistress of Leighton plantation on Bayou La Fourche, Louisiana settled back in Middle Tennessee and taught at a girls' school, Columbia Institute. She died in 1875.

<<<<<<<<

The Mississippi planter and poet William Alexander Percy enrolled in the University at the turn of the century. In his memoir, a Southern classic called *Lanterns on the Levee*, he describes Sewanee as Arcadia:

> It was a small college, in wooded mountains, its students drawn from the impoverished Episcopal gentry of the South, its boarding-houses and dormitories presided over by widows of bishops and Confederate generals. Great Southern names were thick—Kirby-Smith, Elliott, Quintard, Polk, Gorgas, Shoup, Gailor. The only things it wasn't rich in were worldly goods, sociology, and science. A place to be hopelessly sentimental about and to unfit one for anything except the good life.

Percy's characterization is admittedly sentimental. Those widows, those impoverished gentry, those great Southern names were for him the stuff of romantic idealization—as they were for me in 1958 when I first came here as a student. Almost sixty years on, Sewanee remains "a place to be hopelessly sentimental about and to unfit one for anything except the good life."

<<<<<<<<

As for the Civil War period, the passage of years and the dreamy haze of recollection that comes with it soften the reality of what actually happened in the South one hundred and fifty years ago. As a result of Emancipation, several million freed slaves were trying to find new ways to subsist, farming small plots of land, sharecropping for their former masters, or taking to the roads in search of new homes. Among the whites, for those who participated and suffered—and this meant more or less everyone—the war was less a time of gallantry and glory than an agonizing ordeal of loss, betrayal, pain, sacrifice, and bereavement. For both populations it meant a new life, and a hard one. Some of the survivors returned to this wooded mountaintop. Serenity and peace were to be found here, along with an echo of the old, privileged life people had lived before the ill-advised war they should never have been so foolish and arrogant as to fight.

Yet for many in the late 1860s, old at twenty, or forty, life seemed a phantasmagoria. Walking through the graveyard with its tall oaks and crosses hewn from local sandstone, reading the names and dates on old markers and registering the finality of the inscriptions, I sometimes sense these old Southerners' bewilderment and disappointment. The adjustment must have been hard, even for those who had not lost an arm, or a leg, or a hand in battle. As for soldiers returning damaged to their sweethearts and wives, there was an expression—a bitter one: "Cupid stumps on crutches."

They gathered mint from limestone springs at the mouths of caves and drank juleps in the warm afternoons and toddies in the cool evenings. The ruined ladies, the widows, dozed and dreamed among lavender and orrisroot and plain pine boards. Everything so different from how it had been before the war. And if some of these ladies sought the solace of a grain of opium from a small silver box, would we be inclined to reproach them? Some of these old Confederates died early, and the families died, leaving us only initials on a well-made old steamer trunk or a curious name cut into stone above a grave, and two nineteenth-century hands clasping in marble.

Scarcely a good word is spoken or written about the Confederacy nowadays, but for me and some of us the Civil War remains a conflict in which our people fought bravely and with élan in defense of what they thought of as a nation of their own—tragically flawed and based on the evil system of slavery as it was. I have always liked it that there is a flower Southerners call Confederate violets. But probably as each generation succeeds the previous one, there are fewer and fewer people who can recognize that flower.

HAWAII

Introduced Species on
the Hamakua Coast

Our string band sets up at the farmers' market in Wailea. While people "talk story," buy food for the week, and catch up on the latest gossip, we entertain. Small growers from along the Hamakua Coast bring lemons and limes, apple bananas from their own trees, sweet corn, beets, and carrots from their gardens. Papayas, Thai basil, turnips, and avocados are arrayed on the sellers' tables, along with many kinds of greens—all the bounty of this fertile land. Some people bake and bring *mochi* and mango bread for sale. A Vietnamese lady sells green papaya salad and spring rolls. A local fisherman has brought in a big *ahi* today—the Hawaiian name for yellowfin tuna—and cuts slices off it, which people are eating raw as a kind of sashimi, dipping it into spicy shoyu sauce.

A man with a rotisserie grill cooks chickens on a spit. An older man from the mainland and his Thai lady sell limes and papayas, and they also make delicious limeade with mint that cuts the thirst from singing for a couple of hours. These folks offer their produce, we entertain the shoppers. The native Hawaiians, the *haole* (Caucasians), the Japanese, Portuguese, Puerto Ricans, Okinawans, and Filipinos, the Thais and Vietnamese, and the old hippies who have ended up out here in the islands are part of the changing world of Hawaii in the twenty-first century, where light-skinned folks like me are in the minority—a position from which there is much to be learned.

Wailea was a Japanese camptown, one of many that sprang up along the Sugar Coast north of Hilo when the sugar cane plantations brought in foreign workers in the middle of the nineteenth century. The native Hawaiian population had been decimated by lack of immunity to diseases brought in by European and American seamen. And in any case most Hawaiians preferred their traditional way of life—fishing, working their own little patches of taro, occasionally trapping a *pua'a* (wild pig), wrapping the pig in banana leaves and layers of wet burlap, digging a pit in the ground, and roasting it. Working for wages on the plantations did not appeal to these free spirits.

In many ways native Hawaiians have adjusted to being citizens of the fiftieth state, but some part of them is still attuned to an older sense of things, a familial attunement with the earth. Last evening I went for a walk with my neighbor Charlie, and as we were standing on the camp road, smoking some of his homegrown *pakalolo* and gazing down toward the horizon over the ocean, he said, out of the blue, "We're waiting for *Mahina*." For a moment I thought he was talking about a person, and then I remembered that *Mahina* is the Hawaiian word for the moon. Charlie and I were waiting for the moon to rise.

CAPTAIN COOK, THE *MIKANELE*, & LIFE IN THE CAMPTOWNS

Captain James Cook, who rediscovered these islands for England in 1778, named them the Sandwich Islands, after the fourth Earl of Sandwich. The first sugarcane plantation in Hawaii was established some sixty years later by William Hooper, a Bostonian who was given permission to do so by King Kamehameha III. Hooper's timing was good, because when the Civil War broke out on the mainland, sugar produced on the large Louisiana plantations was no longer available in the United States.

In 1863 the American Board of Commissioners for Foreign Missions (ABCFM) closed the Sandwich Islands Missions. The *mikanele,* as they were called in Hawaiian, had accomplished what they set out to do. Christianity was widely and enthusiastically accepted on the islands. Their mission work done, it is not surprising that many missionaries and their descendants went into the sugarcane business. They also intermarried with the Hawaiian *ali'i,* or nobility, engendering a well-connected ruling class that would dominate life on the islands up to the present day. Samuel Thomas Alexander and Henry Perrine Baldwin, both sons of missionaries, founded Alexander & Baldwin, one of the largest of the sugar firms, in 1870.

At first, Chinese workers were brought in to labor in the cane fields, but those who were recruited came from towns and cities on the Chinese mainland, and after a season or two cutting cane they left the fields for Chinatown in Honolulu. They didn't like life out in the country. When I first arrived here I was puzzled by the presence of people I would meet who were called "Portagee." Turns out they are the descendants of Portuguese immigrants from the Azores and Madeira, off the west coast of Africa. These workers were recruited in the 1870s, and they brought their wives and families with them when they came. Their features are Caucasian, but they speak the pidgin-inflected English of the locals.

〈〈〈〈〈〈〈

To be employed on the plantation was to enter a paternalistic world where, in exchange for very hard labor, the worker's every need was provided for. The company gave him and his family a house to live in, with utilities, water, and free medical care included. Most of the workers were Japanese. The cane companies recruited them in the 1880s once it was clear that the Chinese weren't panning out. The plantations paid for their transportation to the islands, provided free food and housing, and paid fixed wages of $12.50 a month for men and $8 a month for women. Once the Philippines were ceded to the US after the Spanish-American War, Filipinos became American nationals, and they were recruited in a similar fashion to the Japanese before them. By 1931 the Filipino population in Hawaii had risen to almost seventy thousand.

Unlike the Portuguese, who brought their wives with them, and the Japanese, who sent home for "picture brides" who came here sight unseen to marry Japanese plantation workers, most of the Filipinos were single men, and they soon began to intermarry with the native Hawaiians.

Every camp along the Sugar Coast shared a way of life: the common life of labor, church—whether Christian or Buddhist—clubs, sports, gossip, births, and deaths. The plantation workers quickly became Americanized—in a uniquely Hawaiian way—and there were Boy Scout troops in the camps, paper drives to help the war effort in the 1940s, church socials, Lions Clubs, and baseball teams. Gardening was pursued enthusiastically, as Tadao Okimoto, who grew up in a camptown, recalls, with each ethnicity growing its own special foods:

> The plantation provided garden space for families. The Japanese grew daikon (turnip), beans, taro, chicken, and some had pigs and bamboo patches. Filipinos grew marungay, bitter melon and fighting chickens, pigs and goats.

The countryside along the Sugar Coast is dotted with beautifully simple churches, the legacy of the New England missionaries, their modest steeples rising above the houses of the towns. At the same time, many Japanese homes contained shrines to the ancestors, incense burners and little statues of the Buddha. The Japanese also built Buddhist temples, and some of them will take your breath away. The roofs of the towers on the pink, two-towered Odaishisan temple in Honomu, another nearby plantation town, curve up at the edges in pagoda fashion. The temple subtly alters the feel of the place, bringing gravitas to a row of storefronts that in the rawness of their wooden construction could almost have come freshly sawed, hammered and nailed from the set for a Western movie.

And so does the domed Hongwanji mission temple next door to the Odaishisan temple. These Japanese follow the Jodo Shinshu school of Buddhism. Their temple mixes Palladian details with the overall Oriental impression. Broad steps rise to a classical portico—four Doric columns surmounted by a triangular pediment. Two round-headed windows flank the entrance, and the building is topped with a leaded dome. Amid the clapboard utilitarianism of the camps' frontier simplicity, these temples allude to the ancient traditions of the East. Clearly they speak to a deep nostalgia among the Japanese for what they left behind when they came here to work.

Pidgin was the common tongue through which these disparate groups communicated. Like immigrants in any other part of the US, they shared a common dream of being American—whatever that meant. The public schools encouraged the adoption of American first names by all ethnicities. Tadeo Okimoto writes:

> In those days, Japanese students came to school with Japanese names, Filipinos had Filipino names, Puerto Ricans had Spanish names, and even the Portuguese children had Portuguese names. For many of us our teachers gave us English names, or we named ourselves. Takayoshi named himself James, Akiko-Alice, Florentino-Clarence and so on. Then when we in turn became parents, we gave our children *haole* names on their birth certificates.

There is a big parade on the Fourth of July in Hilo where the few tottering old veterans from WWII put on their uniforms and march, and the Vietnam Vets, some of them rumbling past on Harleys, fly their hippie flags. Old Chevrolets and Fords are lovingly restored and preserved on the island, just as they are in backyards in Southern California. There was and is as much enthusiasm for baseball here as in Brooklyn or Havana. It's like watching cricket on Corfu or the Indian subcontinent.

Behind us at the park in Wailea as we play and sing today is a ball field, well groomed, with a closely mowed baseball diamond and soccer pitch. Some kids are kicking a football across its broad expanse. On the other side of the road in front of us rises a huge barnlike building that must have been used to warehouse machinery, tools, and equipment. Structures like this one are what remains from a multibillion-dollar industry, an agribusiness empire that once defined the economic and cultural life of Hawaii, giving jobs to immigrants from all over the Pacific and making fortunes for the cane companies.

I love these big hulks, many of which stand as reminders of the island's old economy, which began disappearing in the 1960s as sugar production became more profitable in far-flung places such as Venezuela and Pakistan—an early example of globalization. In some cases the old-fashioned refining machinery was shipped lock, stock, and barrel overseas. The machinery and infrastructure were still in working condition, even though the markets had pulled up stakes and moved elsewhere.

The old buildings, at once utilitarian and imposing, have their charm, sometimes even a rough grandeur of their own. Spiders spin their webs in spaces where work used to go on from before dawn to sundown. Or if the buildings don't stand empty, they house community centers and art galleries or are used to warehouse other materials for today's economy. In Papaikou where we get our mail, one of the big warehouses looms next door to the post office, and the former office of the Onomea Sugar Company, one of the largest, is now occupied by the local credit union.

WAILEA TODAY

The center of Wailea lies just down the road from the ball field. A dozen households still inhabit this old plantation settlement. The heart of the resurging town is Akiko's Buddhist B&B. Akiko Masuda has converted Motonaga's garage into a *zendo* or meditation hall where the market is held when the rains come. I love Motonaga for a garage—Dickensian in a Japanese-Hawaiian way. A single word, "Lubrication," is still emblazoned on the facade of the building. Everyone in Wailea knows Akiko. Though she is a relative newcomer from Honolulu, this enthusiastic, good-looking, no-nonsense lady has become a pillar of the community and is by way of being unofficial mayor of the town. Her establishment consists of a congeries of structures surrounding the kitchen, dining room, and meditation hall, all oozing funky charm. Akiko is helping to preserve the old wooden houses and storefronts that line the little main street of the town.

One thing I like about Hawaii's vernacular architecture is its provisional nature. It makes little sense to build here with anything but wood, and the warm climate keeps things basic. Simply constructed, with pitched roofs to let rain stream off over broad eaves, and porches for sitting out in hot weather, the town's houses breathe an air of simplicity and ease. *Ti* plants grow in profusion alongside banana trees, palms, and flowering plants. Wailea in the early evenings after the market has closed and we have packed up our instruments and are driving home, takes me right back to the neighborhood where I grew up in Memphis. This old plantation town is a theatre of rot and renewal, some old structures moldering in the steamy rain, renovation projects underway as old houses are rescued and brought up to code, repairs made, fresh lumber sawed and nailed in to replace the old. Renewal has gained the upper hand over rot.

Near Akiko's, several storefronts give a sense of what the town's modest commercial center must have been like in plantation days. A sign points to the H. Fuji Bakery, now no longer in business. At one time townspeople could buy a cold Coke and a malasada or a mango *mochi* and sit on the shady porch to chat in Japanese or pidgin with the neighbors. License plates tacked up in front of an abandoned house tell of travel to and from far-flung places on the mainland. A New Hampshire license, so many thousand miles from home, gives its quixotic advice: "Live free or die." An old rhomboid-shaped license plate from Tennessee, seven hundred and fifty miles from Bristol in the northeast to Memphis in the southwest, harks back to a more fanciful age. A hand-painted sign on the wall of a recently occupied house proclaims its robust mantra: "Live, Love, Farm."

The word that inevitably comes to mind when one thinks about Hilo and the sugar towns along the coast is "funky." The bench I sit on in front of Mr. Ed's Bakery in Honomu is a church pew, curved to face front and center like they often are in Congregationalist churches. Someone has painted the pew Chinese red. The paint job must have been applied a good few years ago, because now the bench is peeling and flaky, with the red paint scraped off in spots.

Summer evenings in warm climates have something in common the world over—the relief people feel when the day's work is done, the enjoyment of sitting on the porch with conversation and a cold drink while the children play out in front. Hawaiians love the *pau hana*—

"work's done"—hours. The houses are close enough together in these plantation towns to allow a sense of neighborliness. Hawaiians spend as much time as possible outdoors, and the carport or garage or *lanai* is perhaps more important than any room in the house. Nothing is quite as much fun as a party in someone's open-air garage on a warm evening, with sushi, rice, a bowl of *poke*, fresh salads from the garden, slow-cooked Kalua pig, plenty of cold beer, music from all and sundry, ladies getting up and dancing an impromptu hula. It reminds me of Johnny Mercer's lyrics to the old Hoagy Carmichael song:

> In the cool, cool, cool of the evening
> Tell 'em I'll be there.
> In the cool, cool, cool of the evening
> Better save a chair.
> When the party's getting a glow on
> And singin' fills the air . . .
> If I'm still on my feet
> And there's something to eat,
> You can tell them I'll be there.

PLANTATION DAYS

Before roads were built along the coast, goods got shipped by boat from town to town and cove to cove. Then the cane companies ran a rail line up the coast from Hilo, spanning the deep ravines with daring bridges. Now the railroad too is gone. In this fecund climate, with its torrential rains and year-round growing season, many plantation-era buildings have disappeared into the jungle without a trace. Along the coast road stands a formidable concrete building on the *makai* side of the highway, half overgrown with creeper. The date 1910 is emblazoned on its portico, but what its purpose was I could not tell you. Off the pebble beach at Papaikou loom the ruins of what was once a sugar mill, now rusting away, collapsing inch by inch into the sea.

I wouldn't have thought so, but there is considerable nostalgia on the island for those old days. This puzzles me, because the plantation system here would seem to have uncomfortable parallels to plantations in the old South, run with slave labor. At first the *lunas*, or overseers, many of Portuguese descent, kept an eye on the field hands from horseback, and they carried whips they were not shy about using. Garrett Hongo, a Japanese-American poet who was born in Volcano on the Big Island and grew up on the mainland, has explored the history of his family, who were brought to Hawaii from Japan to work the cane fields.

If Hongo's accounts are accurate—and they have the ring of truth to them—life for the field workers on the plantations must have been a kind of slavery. Some of the chapters in his 2011 book of poems, *Coral Road*, tell the story of workers who broke their contracts with the cane company: "In 1919, twenty Japanese laborers once fled their contracts, the first in the islands who dared strike." Among these workers were members of Hongo's own family:

> My ancestors fleeing Waialua Plantation,
> Trekking across the northern coast of O'ahu, that
> whole family / of first Shigemitsu
> Walking in *geta* and sandals along railroad ties
> and old roads at night,
> Sleeping in the bushes by day, *ha'alelehana*—runaways
> From the labor contract with Baldwin or
> American Factors

Working conditions gradually improved, and some of the plantations unionized in the forties and fifties. The work was hard, but for people escaping the desperate poverty of their homelands, the money was good. Hawaiians who grew up on the plantations harbor fond memories of that old way of life. Here is the way Tadeo Okimoto recalls the life they led:

> Free bus transportation was available if the walking distance was at least 3 miles. Though it would seem far, we certainly had lots of pleasant memories walking, making stopovers for sweet guavas, chewing sugar cane or swimming in the ditches. Our memorable school event was the May Day Program where the whole school performed songs and dances, many wearing leis and costumes with our parents in attendance.

"Plantation Memories" is a familiar theme. In Papaikou a Portuguese gentleman who grew up during the plantation era has moved his collection of memorabilia into one of the old warehouses and hired a local artist to paint a mural across the front of the building. Her mural evokes the immense labor of those bygone days: men and women in straw hats with their arms and legs stoutly covered to protect them against the sharp cuts of the cane plants—think how hot they must have been!—the men in overalls with their machetes, the women chopping with hoes, the overseer on horseback, the workers' grass shacks nearby.

INTRODUCED SPECIES

We live on land that at one time sat in the middle of a sugar cane plantation. The cane companies have left their imprint. An antiquated crankshaft, gears from some vanished old machine, rust in the new-growth woods. Plantation roads are solid and durable, laid down over the fertile soil and surfaced with crushed lava rock. The companies needed these roads to be open and passable no matter how hard the rain fell, no matter how drenched the ground became. We drive up one such road to get to our house, and though it is rough and steep, we get through in all weathers. Some of the land has been leased to entrepreneurs who grow ginger and sweet potatoes here.

Today a truck drives up into a neighboring ginger field, and the workers—Korean these days, not Filipino or Japanese—wearing coolie-style straw hats, spread out along the rows, congregating at noon for their midday meal. Lunch is lunch the world over, but digging into a bowl of *poke* and rice and *kimchi* with your chopsticks must feel quite different from wolfing down a baloney sandwich, a bag of potato chips, and a Coke. These men and women settle down with their tidy bento lunches and flasks of tea in the shade of the *hau* trees that border the fields, remnants of the forests that covered these hillsides before cane was planted.

The flowers of the *hau* punctuate the dense green of the remaining forest with small explosions of yellow. The African tulip trees blaze with blossoms a shade of red like a rooster's comb when it catches the sunlight. The African tulips are an introduced species, like the Japanese, the Portuguese, the Filipinos, the Korean workers, and me and my friends who play in the market band.

Many of the common birds are introduced species too, like the Japanese White-Eye, *Zosterops japonicas*, which was brought to the islands in 1929, and the Nutmeg Manikin or Spice Finch, *Lonchura punctulata*, a perky, wren-like bird that travels in small flocks and feeds on the seeds of field grasses. Commonly called the Rice Bird, it was introduced to Hawaii more than one hundred and fifty years ago. The Saffron Finch, *Sicalis flaveola*, brilliant yellow with a popsicle-orange crown, has lived on the Big Island only since the 1960s. The birds feed busily, the field hands do their work; at my laptop, I do mine. The workers call back and forth to each other in Korean across the rows of ginger. Our *genius loci*, the guardian of the place, is a native bird, the Hawaiian Hawk or 'Io, now an endangered species. *Buteo solitarius* is the bird's Latin name. A family of them nest in what is left of the forest.

‹‹‹‹‹‹‹‹

The old-timers say a dance hall for the plantation workers once stood alongside Kalaoa Camp Road, a graveled track that runs through fields near here that have now reverted to grassland and scrubby forests or are planted with new crops: ginger, sweet potatoes, or row upon row of ornamental plants that are harvested and shipped off-island in big containers to adorn office and hotel lobbies on the mainland. My friend Ray's father was among those hired to demolish the old dance hall once the plantation had gone out of business. In the process of salvaging boards and posts, Mr. Navarro found old coins that had fallen through the cracks of the dance floor—Japanese yen, Philippine pesos and centavos, American pennies and quarters, Buffalo nickels, Roosevelt dimes, one or two heavy silver dollars.

Histories of Paradise

Friends on the US mainland tell me I live in paradise—often enviously, sometimes mock-scoldingly, as though by not shoveling snow or wearing long underwear I have opted out of life's unpleasant but character-building rigors. I do like to spend the day wearing shorts and no shoes. I do love the ocean, and the beach, and the breezy hills where I live. But paradise? Paradise is a timeless place, with no history. Hawaii does have a history. It has several competing histories. These narratives tell the story not just of the island chain's native people, but also of the colonizers, traders, and merchants who developed and exploited the riches of the land. One of the most interesting histories is that of the *mikanele,* the missionaries who brought Christianity to this island chain in the middle of the Pacific Ocean.

FIRST EUROPEAN CONTACTS

From the beginning of time Hawaii was uninhabited, and then sometime between 300 and 800 AD, historians estimate, Polynesians set sail from further south and settled here. It was not until the eighteenth century that European explorers "discovered" the islands. First came Captain James Cook, an Englishman who was received with lavish hospitality upon his arrival in 1778. He called Hawaii the Sandwich Islands in honor of the Earl of Sandwich back in England. The Hawaiians presented him with presents and accorded him the status of a great chief.

But on his last visit Captain Cook overstayed his welcome. He never understood the islanders' code of mutual gift-giving. They assumed that the many presents they gave afforded them the privilege of taking whatever they wanted from Cook's ship. By the Europeans' lights, this was theft, and the Hawaiians were severely punished. After having gone ashore for supplies on his second and last visit, Cook was murdered in a confused melee.

Once Westerners had discovered the Sandwich Islands, attempts to extract and make a profit from the islands' natural bounty quickly followed. Hawaii's fragrant 'iliahi, or sandalwood, was cut down and shipped west, selling for a profit in China, where it was used to make perfume, incense, and fans. Sandalwood dealers traded the chiefs European luxury items like clocks, mirrors, brocades, crystal, European clothing, and furniture in exchange for the valuable wood.

In the heyday of the Pacific whaling trade, Hilo, near where I live on the Big Island, with its secure natural harbor, became a port of call for ships from as far away as New England in search not only of whales but a place to come ashore and bring on board fresh water, coconut oil, rope for ships' riggings, and salted meat. Sailors, who were often away from home for three or four years at a time, came ashore looking for women, and the *wahines* eagerly swam or rowed out in their canoes to board the ships. Before the missionaries came, the Hawaiian approach to sexuality was open and spontaneous. Brothels and bars lined the harbor. Syphilis devastated the islanders.

But this story is not a simple one of European exploitation of the native culture, with a cast of characters made up of predators and naïfs. The history of Hawaii is one of give and take. The Europeans brought cash, and the island economy began to shift from barter to capital. In 1795 Captain George Vancouver made a gift to King

Kamehameha I of five cows and a bull that he had brought onboard ship from California. Kamehameha put the animals out to graze, emaciated and sickly though they were from the long voyage, and placed a ten-year *kapu,* or taboo, on them to prevent them from being killed.

These six were the basis of the island's cattle industry. Spanish *vaqueros* were brought in from California to teach the Hawaiians how to rope and ride. Sailors who tired of life at sea signed on as ranch hands, and so did adventurous native Hawaiians, as well as Portuguese from the Azores who had experience with cattle. Thus were born the Hawaiian cowboys, or paniolos—from Spanish *Español*—colorful, rough-and-ready characters. They are still here. When a poster appears for one of their rodeos, we get in our truck and go.

From the island's cattle ranchers the ships bought hides, butter, beef to make into jerky, tallow for candles. Laundries, stores, and barber shops opened to service the sailors' needs, and natives served as messengers and guides for the newcomers. The Hawaiians learned new trades, setting themselves up as blacksmiths and carpenters. The skills they already had as builders of traditional outrigger canoes and sailing boats translated into new crafts of ship building and sail making. Though the white men did bring rum and venereal disease, they also brought money, enterprise, and new horizons.

Life under the old system was paradisiacal only if you belonged to the *ali'i*—the nobility and royalty. For commoners, things were rough. The elaborate *kapu* system made it a capital crime for a commoner even so much as to touch one of the *ali'i*, and they had to prostrate themselves in the presence of their rulers. It's not surprising that hundreds of Hawaiians joined the crews of whalers and shipped out in search of more freedom and wider horizons. These realities are, of course, lost on those who feel nostalgia for the old system of kingship. No doubt it is preferable to be tyrannized by your own than to be exploited by strangers, even if those strangers have brought with them a system of laws and greater opportunity for ordinary people.

Travelers' accounts exist of European contact with the islanders. Here is an excerpt from the journal of one Peter Corney, first published in the *Literary Gazette* of London in 1826, that describes the great Hawaiian King Kamehameha (sometimes spelled Tameameah), who conquered all the islands and united them into one kingdom:

> On the 16th January, 1815, made the island of Owhyee [Hawaii], ran close in shore; some natives visited us and informed us that Tameameah was at the village of Tyroa [Kailua, on the opposite side of the island from Hilo]. We made all sail for that place. . . . The natives came off in great numbers, bringing with them hogs, vegetables, rope and the cloth of the country; we allowed a few to enter the vessel and took a chief woman on board who acted as pilot. About midnight we reached Tyroa, where we anchored and . . . saluted the king. . . . Tameameah was dressed in a colored shirt, velveteen breeches, red waistcoat, large military shoes and worsted stockings, a black silk handkerchief round his neck, no coat. He is a tall, stout, athletic man, nose rather flat, thick lips, the upper one turned up . . .

MISSIONARIES & ROYALTY

A powerful force in Hawaii from the nineteenth century on were the American missionaries who came from New England to spread the news of the gospel. Hawaiians today are very religious people. Churches are everywhere you look. And the success of the missions seems the oddest thing, because no two groups would appear to have less in common than the warm, fun-loving, generous Hawaiians, accepting of life and its many pleasures, and rock-ribbed puritans from the stony coasts of Massachusetts and Rhode Island.

After reading a good bit in various sources about the missionaries, I have reluctantly arrived at a not unqualified respect for them. For one thing, they brought literacy, for which the people were grateful, as the notion of expressing speech or thought on paper and being able to keep records was something they had previously not conceived of. The missionaries wanted the Hawaiians to be literate so they could read the Bible. One of their number, the Rev. Hiram Bingham, developed an alphabet for the language, and he was shrewd enough to understand that if the royal family learned to read, it was only a matter of time before literacy was passed along to the population at large.

Here is his account, complete with all the prejudice and arrogance of the day, of the Queen and how she learned to read:

> She was nearly fifty years of age. She was tall and portly . . . had black hair, a swarthy complexion, a dark commanding eye, a deliberate enunciation, a dignified and measured step, an air of superiority, and a heathen queen-like hauteur; yet sometimes a full-length portrait of her dignity might have presented her stretched out prostrate on the same floor on which a large black pet hog was allowed unmolested to walk or lie and grunt for the annoyance or amusement of the inmates.
>
> She would amuse herself for hours at cards or in trimming and stringing the bright yellow nuts of the pandamus for odoriferous necklaces or rude coronets, listen to vile songs and foolish stories, and sometimes make interesting inquiries. Her stiffness toward the missionaries, to whom her little finger, instead of a right hand, had been sometimes extended, had unbent. . . . Mrs. Bingham and myself called at her habitation in the center of Honolulu.
>
> She and several women of rank were stretched upon the mats playing at cards. . . . Being invited to enter the house, we took our seats without the accommodation of chairs, and waited till the game of cards was disposed of, when the wish was expressed to have us seated by her. We gave her ladyship one of the little books, and drew her attention to the alphabet printed in large and small Roman characters. . . . She followed me in enunciating the vowels one by one, two or three times over in their order, when her skill and accuracy were commended. Her countenance brightened.
>
> Looking off from her book upon her familiars with a tone a little boasting or exulting. . . . the queen exclaimed, "*Ua loaa iau!* I have got it." . . . She had passed the threshold, and now unexpectedly found herself entered as a pupil. Dismissing her cards, she accepted and studied the little book, and with her husband asked for forty more for her attendants.

Missionary influence over the royal family continued for the duration of the monarchy. Nostalgia for these rulers is widespread throughout the islands. Second only to Kamehameha in popularity is King David Kalakaua, known familiarly as the Merrie Monarch for his fondness for parties and drinking. Henry Adams, on a visit in 1885, found him agreeable, noting that he "talks quite admirable English in a charming voice; has admirable manners. . . . To be sure, his Majesty is not wise, and he has—or is said to have—vices, such as whiskey and—others." Austin Strong, son of an artist who came to Hawaii for a few years to paint, describes, as a child, meeting a man who turned out to be the Merrie Monarch, riding in

> a shining C-spring victoria which smelled of elegance, varnish, polished leather, and well-groomed horses.
>
> In it rode a fine figure of a man, calm and immaculate in white ducks and pipe-clayed shoes. He sat in noble repose, his strong face, his hands, and his clothes dyed crimson by the tropical sunset. My heart began to jump about, for I recognized the face which was stamped on all the silver coins of his island realm. He wore his famous hat made of woven peacock quills as fine as straw, with its broad band of tiny sea shells.

A MISSIONARY FAMILY

"I was born in my father's bamboo cottage, in Hilo, at half-past eleven o'clock A.M., November 26, 1835," writes Henry M. Lyman, MD, in his *Hawaiian Memories,* dated 1906. Dr. Lyman was the son of an early missionary. He wrote *Hawaiian Memories* before the era of political correctness, and his accounts of the missionaries' encounters with the native Hawaiians abound with phrases like "copper-skinned barbarians," "aboriginees," and "heathens":

> When the early missionaries of my father's time embarked for heathen shores, it was the universal understanding that they went for life. No return was at all probable, unless failure of health should render their labor useless. And, in fact, there were few men or women who, having once made a voyage of six months round Cape Horn, would ever care to repeat that experience. But this was not the root of the matter. It was expected that the devoted missionary, arrived at the scene of his future labors, should house himself in a dwelling of aboriginal construction, and should, so far as possible, nourish himself and his family with the native provisions of the country in which

he abode. Thus cast out upon the remote Hawaiian Islands, the pioneer missionaries found themselves compelled to seek shelter in straw huts, without floors or glazed windows or proper ventilation. The native food, though abundant, was coarse and ill adapted to the adequate nourishment of refined and educated men and women.

The Lymans' dwelling place is preserved with its original furniture as part of the Lyman Museum in Hilo. It gives off an aura of plainness and austerity. The missionaries brought with them the culture of New England in the early Victorian age, with its rigid standards of morality, propriety, and dress. Here is an account by the missionary Jonathan S. Green of how native girls were trained in the Wailuku Female Seminary on Maui:

> The little girls, of whom there are now 42, spend two hours daily in sewing and braiding; they are taught to arrange their sleeping apartments, prepare the table for eating, and wash their dishes. They are becoming industrious and are making considerable progress in their studies and in the knowledge of the usages of civilized life.

Throughout the nineteenth century many Hawaiians referred to the continental United States simply as "Boston." That was where most of the Americans they met had come from. The broad, roofed lanais or porches on missionaries' houses are among the few architectural acknowledgments that we are not in frosty New England but rather on a subtropical island. Here is the Rev. Mr. Lyman's son Henry's account of the house where he lived as a child:

> Thus placed in the midst of such magnificent scenery, our new home was by no means luxuriantly furnished. Every article was of the cheapest and plainest description . . . There was a large arm-chair for my father, a rocking-chair for my mother, a high-chair for the baby, and a lot of red-painted kitchen chairs. No carpets of any kind covered the floors, no paper the plastered walls, no blinds were at the window— only some plain white cotton sash-curtains. The sole decoration consisted of a looking-glass with a gilded frame that hung in the dining-room, and a few coarsely colored lithographic cards, representing incidents in the life of Jesus, suspended on the walls in the bedrooms.

SEADOGS

These pious folk were not the only white people who came to the islands. Sailors and whalers arrived in great numbers. From the very beginning there was a conflict between the missionaries and the seadogs. "Licentiousness and drunkenness are their besetting sins," wrote Sarah Lyman, "and most of them are profane in the extreme." Here is what Henry T. Cheever, a clergyman, had to say about the whalers:

> It is painful to go out among them here at sundown when liberty expires and, drunk or sober, they must be off to the ships or into the fort. Liquor and lust have done their best to inflame many of them, and your ears would be shocked by ribald oaths and the language of lewdness, caught up and repeated by native boys; and you see some reeling to and fro at their wit's end, and hustled along by some less drunken comrade; and others without shame caressed and hung upon by native girls, who flock here in the ship season from other parts to get the ready wages of sin.

Henry Lyman was of much the same opinion:

> Such were some of these rovers of the sea; but our parents welcomed them kindly, for they generally came from New England, and many of them were excellent people. But some were ruffianly fellows, scarcely above the level of pirates and buccaneers, who made a deal of trouble among the unsophisticated Hawaiians. . . . Peace be with those ancient mariners! They have gone the way of all the earth, and are asleep with their fathers—wherever that may be.

Perhaps an even more galling thorn in the sides of the missionaries were those beachcombers and other *haoles* who had jumped ship and gone native, because they were not seasonal irritants like the whalers and traders, but a regular presence. One such is described by Dr. Lyman:

> Another Englishman also dwelt near us,—one of the lowest and stupidest of his kind. He lived like a pig, in a miserable hovel with a slatternly native woman for a wife; and, professing to have been a

carpenter's mate on the ship from which his residence had been—accidentally, of course—transferred to the shore, he occasionally earned a few honest dollars with the help of sundry borrowed tools that were not always returned until replevined by the lender. After such wearisome labor he would remain in the seclusion of his stye . . .

REVIVAL TIME

Visible from the Lyman House is Haili Congregational Church, another bit of New England transplanted to Hawaii. It is among my favorite buildings in Hilo. I love seeing the church poke its austere steeple up above the modest skyline of the town. On this site occurred one of the most momentous developments in the story of religion in Hawaii. David Lyman's colleague, the Reverend Benjamin Coan, arrived from New England in the 1830s and proved to be a more effective preacher than Mr. Lyman. Mr. Coan appears to have had all the zeal, single-mindedness, and energy we associate with missionaries at their best.

While Mr. Lyman had managed to recruit only a score of Hawaiians for his church, Coan's ambition was to meet and talk personally with every single Hawaiian in his hundred-mile-long parish, which ranged across steep hills and deep gullies down which plunged fast rivers and streams running down from the volcanic mountains. So off he went through the length and breadth of the Big Island's windward side, talking to them all. But he found them unreceptive. "This people are . . . dead," he wrote, "but God can raise them. Is it not *time for him to work?*"

Though Hawaiians enjoyed the novelty of going to church, they were not ready to commit themselves yet, be baptized, and become church members. According to Gavin Daws in *Shoal of Time,* his history of Hawaii,

> a good many Hawaiians had come to accept and even approve of Christianity. They kept the Sabbath well, far better than the average foreigner did. They enjoyed dressing up for church (though admittedly they liked undressing afterwards too). Their ability to memorize

long passages of Scripture was amazing. They had an appetite for oratory that amounted almost to an addiction, and they enjoyed a good sermon immensely—the longer the better, or so it seemed.

And though the female chief Kapiʻolani, a devout convert, had urged her fellow countrymen to join the new religion, they were at first not inclined to do so. Kapiʻolani was a force for Christianity in the early days of its introduction here. In 1824 she and an entourage of fifty traversed the island from Kona on the leeward side to Hilo on the windward side. Along the way was the volcano at Kilauea, whose crater holds a massive lake of molten lava. Pele, the goddess of fire, is said to preside over the volcano.

According to the account written by the missionary Joseph Goodrich, the local people "tried to dissuade Kapiʻolani from going up to the volcano. They told her that Pele would kill her and eat her up if she went there. She replied that she would go up, and if Pele killed and ate her up, they might continue to worship Pele, but if not, i.e. if she returned unhurt, then they must turn to the worship of the true God." Kapiʻolani proceeded to the crater's edge, prayed, and led her followers in the singing of a hymn. Unscathed by the wrath of Pele, she continued on her way to Hilo.

On Sundays, thousands of worshippers began to turn out to hear Mr. Coan preach, but perhaps Hawaiians were too content, too well adjusted, too lacking in that sense of sin and guilt necessary for the heart-wrenching personal crises that foster the born-again experience. As Daws puts it, the missionaries "knew from their own personal experiences, too, that genuine conversion was usually accompanied by sharp anguish." If so, then nature cooperated wonderfully with the New England puritans. One Sunday in 1837 a massive tsunami struck while he was preaching, and Mr. Coan interpreted this as an admonition from God to the islanders. It is worth quoting him at some length, because his vigorous prose shows what a great preacher he must have been:

On the 7th of November, 1837, at the hour of evening prayers, we were startled by a heavy thud, and a sudden jar of the earth. The sound was like the fall of some vast body on the beach, and in a few seconds a noise of mingled voices rising for a mile along the shore thrilled us like the wail of doom. . . . The sea, moved by an unseen hand, had all of a sudden risen in a gigantic wave, and this wave, rushing in with the speed of a racehorse, had fallen upon the shore, sweeping everything not more than fifteen or twenty feet above high-water mark into indiscriminate ruin. Houses, furniture, calabashes, fuel, timber, canoes, food, clothing, everything floated wild upon the flood. . . . The harbor was full of strugglers calling for help, while frantic parents and children, wives and husbands ran to and fro along the beach, calling for their lost ones. As wave after wave came in and retired, the strugglers were brought near the shore, where the more vigorous landed with desperate efforts, and the weaker and ex-hausted were carried back upon the retreating wave, some to sink and rise no more till the noise of judgment wakes them. . . . Had this catastrophe occurred at midnight when all were asleep, hundreds of lives would undoubtedly have been lost. Through the great mercy of God, only thirteen were drowned.

This event, falling as it did like a bolt of thunder from a clear sky, greatly impressed the people. It was as the voice of God speaking to them out of heaven, "Be ye also ready."

High drama. The forces of nature at their most powerful, the compelling call of a new religion in a country that was fast aban-doning the old ways, and the persuasiveness of the convinced human voice in the service of old-fashioned oratory, all working together. The people heeded the preacher's call, and the following year nearly two thousand Hawaiians were baptized into the faith as part of a reli-gious awakening that is remembered as The Great Revival—a mirror of what was happening on the mainland. Eventually the Haili Church had a congregation of some seven thousand souls.

<<<<<<<

Religion continues to be a strong force in these islands. Christian-ity seems as powerful here as it is in the Southern states on the US mainland. Pride in native Hawaiian traditions, even the feeling that Hawaii should be an independent kingdom again as it was in the days of Kamehameha the Great and King David Kalakaua, do not appear to conflict with Hawaiians' embrace of Christianity. Performances of hula dance and chanting are often prefaced by prayer invoking the Christian God, and my impression is that respect for the ancestors, a sense of the sacredness of the land and an awareness of spiritual presences in and of the land, blend harmoniously with Christian faith.

The social mission embraced by local churches would impress anyone, believer or non-believer. There is poverty in Hawaii, and homelessness, drug addiction, problems within families. The churches take seriously their obligation to address these needs. They feed hundreds of people every week. The explorers, the missionaries, the seadogs, the kings and queens may be gone, but traces of them and what they brought have blended harmoniously in a continually evolving way of life on this island chain. Hawaii is not paradise and never will be, but to a transplanted mainlander like myself, it may be the next best thing.

Hilo, My Hometown

Fan-like crowns of palm trees wave over the corrugated tin roofs of Hilo. Rows of wooden storefronts project an improvised rawness, as though the carpenters had just put away their hammers and saws. You can almost smell the pine resin. After a rain, steam rises from the sun-warmed streets. I like it that you can buy leis at Walmart and the Sack 'n' Save here. I enjoy the raffish street life in this city on the Big Island of Hawaii—free spirits, burnouts, beachcombers with bad teeth and bloodshot eyes, old hippies with venerable beards and Hari Krishna clones in dhotis with shaved heads and little pigtails, *tilakas* painted on their foreheads, pounding their hand-drums and wailing out their bhajans.

I like the dreadlocks and aloha shirts, Polynesian tattoos on legs and forearms, people going about their daily errands in flip-flops and cargo shorts, carrying furled umbrellas. Sometimes paniolos from the upland ranches up near Waimea walk by bow-legged in cowboy boots and ten-gallon hats.

Hilo feels like a sleepy South Seas port off the pages of a Somerset Maugham story. Fronting Hilo Bay, the town climbs the slope leading up to the volcano, Mauna Kea, and looks out over the sea. Life moves to the rhythm of the trade winds that stir the fronds of palm trees lining the bay and help to blow away the "vog" from the still-active volcano. The town's more substantial buildings exist in a kind of time warp—the vaguely Egyptian-looking art deco Bank of Hawaii, the classic revival Federal Building, and the Hawaiian Telephone Company building, which mixes island style with California Mission.

Lyman House was originally a one-story thatched-roof structure of ōhi'a and koa wood. As the family and the mission grew, the Rev. Mr. Lyman expanded his house in 1855, adding a second story and an attic. The house would not look out of place in small-town Vermont. Now roofed with corrugated tin instead of thatch, it still stands in Hilo as part of the Lyman Museum. Most of the furniture was hand-crafted in the woodshop where the missionaries taught carpentry to young men of the island.

Nearby stands Haili Church, constructed in the late 1850s. Taken together with Lyman House, it stands as a statement about the impact the missionaries made on the Big Island. Architecture is always so much more than building. Haili Church's sparse, spare spire, competing with the baroque, domed steeple of St. Joseph's Roman Catholic church further up the hill, rises above the low buildings of downtown Hilo, and when my friends and I go fishing off Coconut Island we see it from the bay. Both Haili Church and St. Joseph's are imports, introduced species, bringing New England Protestantism and Roman Catholicism to the islands.

Architects and builders have responded to the challenge of establishing something man-made and beautiful in this humid temperate climate of cooling ocean breezes and sudden showers. The architects, known and unknown, who have worked in Hilo have taken seriously their mission to adorn, please, and delight. And because the buildings of note here are sprinkled throughout the town among plainer vernacular structures, they do not compete with each other as skyscrapers do in New York and other big cities. Here buildings stand alone against the low skyline and can be viewed from many different angles and perspectives.

THE MERRIE MONARCH & HIS LEGACY

One of my favorites in Hilo is the Federal Building, a handsome, white, three-story structure that faces onto Kalakaua Park. The park that the Federal Building overlooks is named after King David Kalakaua. The king, who will be familiar from my previous chapter, reigned from 1874 until his death at the age of 54 in 1891 at the Palace Hotel in San Francisco. Having experienced the most stringent of missionary asceticism during his schooling at the Chiefs' Children's School in Honolulu, Kalakaua became a supporter of native Hawaiian culture, with its pleasure-loving ways and its roots in ancient Polynesia.

The King championed the hula and ukulele music and helped popularize the ancient Polynesian sport of surfing—hard as it may be to picture the portly monarch hanging ten. His fondness for drinking, gambling, and carousing, and his love of the *wahines* also contributed to his merriment. But Kalakaua was fighting a losing battle against the Americanization of the islands. His last words were, "Tell my people I tried."

A bronze statue of King David Kalakaua by Henry Blancini has been erected in the park. Bronze is the perfect medium for showing a youthful glow on the King's features, a brightness and innocence in his eyes. A taro plant grows on one side of the monarch, and on his knee he holds an *'ipu heke*, the hourglass-shaped Hawaiian double-gourd drum used to beat out the rhythm for hula.

A merrie monarch is not necessarily an honest monarch. As Sarah Vowell puts it in her book, *Unfamiliar Fishes,* "Kalakaua's weaknesses and strengths were of a piece." He accepted hefty bribes from the sugar magnate Claus Spreckels, who because of his influence over Kalakaua, became known as "the uncrowned king of Hawaii." According to a biography of Spreckels, the King's cashbook shows that he received promissory notes from Spreckels for $40,000 at the same time that Spreckels was granted a lease on water rights on Maui that would make it possible for the German immigrant to dominate sugar production. The transfer of the $40,000 coincided with a card game between Spreckels and the King. Robert Louis Stevenson records being present when in a single afternoon the king downed three bottles of champagne and two bottles of brandy.

During the election of 1886 the King plied the voters with copious amounts of cheap gin. He was able to get it through the Custom House duty free because of royal franking privileges. The electorate dutifully if not soberly returned a slate of legislators loyal to the king and his cronies. This legislature passed a bill allowing the king to issue a license for the importation of opium. Kalakaua sold the license to a Chinese merchant for $71,000, then assigned the license to another bidder instead and pocketed the first man's money.

Chinese workers had brought the drug to Hawaii. In his book *Pau Hana* ("After Work"), Ronald Takaki describes how workers used the drug to alleviate the tedium of work in the fields: "A Chinese plantation worker recalled how the cook for his gang would bring their hot lunches to the field in a bucket: 'In the top of the bucket was a little paper or envelope with the dope in it. All the men . . . took their dope that way with their dinner.'"

Many members of the Anglo-Saxon elite on the island were the children of missionaries. Is it surprising that they would bridle at this level of corruption, particularly when it interfered with their business interests? The "bayonet constitution" of 1887 by which they seized power took away most of the Merrie Monarch's prerogatives, creating a constitutional monarchy, the real upshot of which was to solidify power in the hands of the missionaries and *haole* industrialists.

For all his flaws, the King left a great legacy to his people and has won an unshakeable place in their hearts. The rediscovery of Hawaiian culture has been gathering steam since the 1960s and 1970s, producing beautiful dance, music, and traditional crafts, as well as giving younger generations pride in their heritage.

In 1893, two years after King Kalakaua's death, his successor, Queen Lili'uokalani, was deposed and the monarchy abolished. In 1895, for her alleged part in a failed counter-revolution, a military tribunal sentenced Lili'uokalani to five years of hard labor in prison and fined her $5,000. But the sentence was commuted to imprisonment in an upstairs bedroom of 'Iolani Palace. While confined there, she composed songs, including The Queen's Prayer (*Ke Aloha o Ka Haku*) and started writing her memoirs.

When the King and other *ali'i*, or nobility, visited Hilo they stayed in Nilolopua, a royal compound on the *mauka* or upland side of the park—the side of the park toward the mountain. King David Kalakaua presented the city with a sundial that still stands in the park. In the old days sailors and townspeople set their watches by it. On the site of Nilolopua now stands the former Hilo Hotel, a hideous essay in 1950s modernist style, now dilapidated and uncared for, its air conditioners rusted out, screens torn. The asphalt of its parking lot is broken and crumbling. Weeds grow out of cracks in the pavement.

ARCHITECTURE & RULING-CLASS POWER

The Federal Building, built in 1917, is well kept and its grounds are well groomed. It has suffered no decline during the century succeeding its foundation. The two wings added in 1936 during the Roosevelt administration project forward from the main block of the building, forming a U-shaped surround whose white Doric columns front open balconies, or loggias, on three sides. The imposing proportions of the ground-level elevation and the one above it in every way deserve the noble framing of the big columns. These wings frame a little courtyard and fountain in the center that is roofed with glazed tile the color of ripe avocado—if the flesh of the avocado had a glossy sheen. A marble plaque attached to the front of one wing declares:

1936 Post Office
Henry Morgenthau
Secretary of Treasury
James A. Farley
Postmaster General

I like the stone eagles that stand above the windows. I like the bronze frogs that spout water into the fountain. I like the pebble mosaics, and the pennies that people have thrown into the fountain. I toss one in too, and make a wish.

Palm trees line up along both sides of the Federal Building, and magnolias grow in front. Every detail of the workmanship of this public building, its classical urns and brass and cast-iron fittings, bespeaks a level-headed solidity. No expense has been spared, and yet nothing is ostentatious. It is a pleasure to post one's mail here. The postal clerks' windows open to breezes that blow up from the sea in the morning. Hawaii likes to live outdoors, even when going to the post office. At the foot of the palm trees on the *makai* (toward the sea) side of the building, little bronze commemorative shields have been set into the ground. Here are three of them:

James Nahale, Died at Front
Thomas Smith, Died at Front
James B. Todd Dead at Sea. Feb. 21, 1816

Across the way stands the East Hawaii Cultural Center, a pleasant hip-roofed Arts and Crafts structure whose leaded, mullioned windows look out over the park and the statue of King David Kalakaua. A huge banyan tree trailing its hanging fronds down to the ground takes up most of the *mauka* end of the park. Along the *makai* side runs a rectangular pond where water lilies grow—a monument to Hawaiian servicemen who died in WWII. As one sits on a park bench and looks across the park's barbered lawn, the eye falls on an octagonal window fitted into one wall of the Carlsmith Building, with baby palm trees softening its geometrical art deco symmetry. Structures like the Federal Building, the East Hawaii Cultural Center and the Carlsmith Building, all of them in the Kino'ole Street part of town, went up when civic pride among the ruling class was the order of the day in Hawaii, when there was no lack of sugar money for construction, when the orderly, sober Anglo-Saxon oligarchy that had deposed the Hawaiian royal family called the shots and got rich.

Farther down, facing the *makai* side of the Federal Building, are two more fine structures. One of them is the pink, blue-roofed C. C. Kennedy Annex, once part of the Waikea Sugar Mill. C. C. Kennedy was manager of the mill and a philanthropist. The annex's staunch postage-stamp-sized portico fronts a solid, one-story building, pink, with round-headed windows. Its tin roof, painted the color of periwinkles, is buttressed by a course of arching corbels that hold up the cornice. Down at the end of the street, past the white turrets of the old armory, now a gym, the bay glows emerald green or turquoise, depending on the changing moods of sea and sky.

One block closer to the Bay from the Federal Building stands the Kaikodo Building, or Hilo Masonic Hall, built in the second decade of the twentieth century. Like the Federal Building, this solid citizen employs the Renaissance Revival style. Round-headed windows face all around from its second and third stories—distinguished looking and tall, with octagonal mullioned lights at the top of each window. A granite stairway with a carved oak balustrade leads from the lobby to the second and third floors. At one time a roof garden with a view of the bay topped the Masonic Hall.

During Hawaii's years as a US territory, when fortunes were being made on the Hamakua Coast's sugarcane plantations, the Masons who built this edifice ruled the roost. John Troup Moir (1859–1933), manager of the Onomea sugar plantation in Papaikou, near where I live, was master of the lodge. At the dedication ceremony in 1910, Moir announced that he had fired one architect and hired another because the first one was skimping on the quality of the materials. "Nothing but the best would satisfy the boys," he assured his listeners, calling the Masonic Building "a substantial, fireproof, earthquake-proof, up-to-date building, first class in every respect, a credit to the town of Hilo and the Territory of Hawaii."

ASIAN BREEZES

In contrast to what the missionaries and sugar bosses built, one of the most pleasing architectural notes in Hilo is Asian. Hongwanji Mission temples built by the Japanese community look like hybrids between churches and pagodas. They are topped with domes where, on churches, you would expect to see steeples. And inside, geometrical stained-glass windows in glowing primary colors look like what you would see in a Methodist or Presbyterian church. Many residences sport the upturned eaves of pagodas. My favorite is the lime-green and Chinese-red pagoda faced entirely with glossy ceramic tiles of extraordinary beauty at the Chinese cemetery on Ululani Street. Graves, neatly tended, fill the hillside behind the pagoda.

If these up-curving eaves really do serve the purpose, as some commentators seem to think, of discharging rain water further from the house, it would make sense to have them here in Hilo, which has an average annual rainfall upwards of 150 inches. Christianity and Buddhism meet on this rainy island without apparent friction. A building on the south side of town that looks for all the world like a pagoda has a notice-board in front declaring it to be the United Community Church.

Across town at the Suisan fish market, fishermen bring their catch up to the shore: *ahi* (tuna), *mahi mahi* (dolphinfish), *tako* (octopus), and other seafood selling at a quarter of the price one pays on the mainland. *Le tout* Hilo shows up down near the waterfront for the twice-weekly farmers' market to talk story, catch up on the day's gossip, and sample the fragrant offerings of fresh exotic fruit and vegetables, juices, local coffee beans, homemade tamales and sushi, and flowers like anthuriums and ginger blossoms. On Saturdays I like to skip breakfast at home and have an ambulatory breakfast at the market.

Wherever you go—to the Saturday market, to the mall, wherever—it is hard not to be struck by Hilo's racially mixed population. As "Hilo, My Hometown," a song from the 1930s, an era less self-conscious about such things, puts it, "See the smiling faces / Of the many races, / And you'll be smiling too." I don't know of any other song about a city that makes that particular boast! Statistically, 17 percent of Hilo's population is Caucasian, 14 percent Native Hawaiian, 10 percent Hispanic, and 34 percent of Hilo's residents are of Asian descent. In addition, nearly 32 percent of its population classify themselves as being of two or more races, while 12 percent claim three or more races. Good luck in making all this add up! Native Hawaiians have intermarried with Filipinos, Chinese, Caucasians from the mainland, and the "Portuguese." More recently Samoans, Koreans, Thais, Vietnamese, and other Asians have made their way to the islands.

Between the market street and the bay the city created a large park on Banyan Drive after the ruinous tsunami of 1960, which devastated what had been a warren of houses, mostly Japanese. The waterfront park is dotted with ornamental ponds, little pagodas, pavilions, and Japanese-looking bridges and islands. It is a Blue Willow plate come to life. The park honors the many Japanese who perished in the tsunami and fills at all hours of the day with strollers, joggers, families with their *keikis*—little children—and people doing tai chi.

DOWN-HOME HILO

So much of Hawaii has been turned into a tourist paradise that I am glad to live near a town that still works for a living. Hilo, in some regards, is refreshingly ordinary. Its waterfront is a reminder of what seaside cities like New York and San Francisco that have lost their working harbors are missing. I like going down to the docks to see the inter-island cargo barge load up with freight containers, forklifts scooting busily around the wharf. Those enormous triple-decker cruise ships that debouch tourists for a day are a magical sight from the hills where we live above the town, when we see them steaming out of the harbor in the early evenings, their decks illuminated like something from a maritime fairytale.

School kids flock together after class here like everywhere else, and they are polite and well spoken. Most locals are brought up in large families, and they learn their manners early. Hilo has its homeless population, too, but somehow they don't seem as desperate or put upon as they do in New York or London or Dublin or San Francisco—perhaps because the climate is clement. It must be easier to live outside here, to shelter under a banyan tree when it rains, to drink your wine or smoke your pakalolo out in the open.

The impression that Hilo exists in the backwash of vanished Sugar Coast prosperity is inescapable. I am not invoking anything like vanished grandeur—Hilo is much too down-home for that. But clearly there was money here once. In addition to the institutional buildings in the Kino'ole part of town I have described, the museum-piece, art deco Woolworths building on Bayfront now houses a down-at-the-heels multiplex on one side and a little Indian restaurant on the other. And what used to be the Hilo Ironworks down by the harbor, art deco witness to bygone industry, now houses a frame shop, a dance studio, a gun shop, and a massage therapist.

Another of my favorite places in Hilo is the Palace Theatre, an authentic temple of cinema from Hollywood's high and palmy days. Its marquee and the vertical neon sign for the theatre are green. At night the letters spelling out P-A-L-A-C-E come alive in red—not a brash, declarative scarlet, but a mellowed neon vermilion in keeping with the town's faded but still stylish aura. At one time the theatre filled with workers from the plantations on their days off, eating popcorn, chatting in pidgin, and marveling at the exploits of Tom Mix and Laurel and Hardy, enraptured by Theda Bara and Carole Lombard, impressed by Clark Gable's masculine sexiness and sense of command. The men's room, piss whiffy as it is, has a little anteroom with chairs and, of all things, bookcases. I think this must have been a smoking lounge. The Palace is a grand building, less a barn than a drafty basilica.

HULA

Hilo is the center for the practice of hula, widely popular here. Hula means traditional Hawaiian dance, music, and drumming. This culture, and the Hawaiian language itself, was passed down orally through families (*'ohana*) such as the Kanaka'oles, during the many years it was suppressed by the missionaries. A hula troupe is called a *halau*—though to call it a troupe is misleading. A *halau* is more than an organization of dancers; it is a family, an *'ohana* of its own under the guidance of a *kumu*, with a spiritual philosophy and an orientation toward the living traditions of this ancient art.

While mainstream American popular culture has created its own clichéd ways of seeing Hawaii and its arts, trivializing the ukulele as an instrument and making hula almost a joke, the *kumu hula* practice and teach in its purest form this combination of dance, chant, song, drumming, and music. There are two kinds of hula: one ancient and tribal, called *kahiko*, and one more recent and familiar, called *'auana*, with music rather than drumbeats—more focused on feminine grace. The root of the word *'auana* means to wander or drift.

Kahiko is the branch of hula with the deepest roots in tradition. Taupouri Tangaro, *kumu hula* of the Unukupukupu Halau and a professor at the University of Hawaii in Hilo, is an articulate spokesman for the hula tradition, and for him and his *halau*, hula is a holistic discipline. When members of the *halau* go into the forest to gather greenery for their costumes, they ask permission from the plants they pick. Along the way, the dancers and musicians learn something about plant ecology and sustainability. If a plant starts becoming rare, *halau* members are among the first to know.

Hula in its purest and most traditional form is intertwined with the spiritual traditions of the native Hawaiians. Respect for one's ancestors plays an important role. And it goes beyond respect: the individual is seen as *embodying* his or her ancestors. They live in and through us. One *kumu hula* told me that he keeps his house filled with mirrors so that he can see in his own face the presence of the ancestors as they visit. "Oh, it's you," he says to one of them when they appear on his own features. "What brings you here today?"

‹‹‹‹‹‹‹

To see hula, particularly at a down-home venue or a party, is to witness an altogether joyful experience. It is a pleasure and a privilege to be part of an audience whose members are knowledgeable and appreciative of the many nuances of the art. Often the crowd includes relatives, parents, and grandparents of the dancers. The Hawaiian custom is to applaud as soon as dancers start to dance, as soon as singers start to sing. A really good hula dancer in the 'auana style enters into the dance with all the sinuosity her body is capable of. She never stops smiling—and her smile is genuine, because she dances for joy, and she shares that joy with those who witness the dance.

Recently, at a party launching a new CD by Mark Yamanaka, a Hawaiian singer famous for his falsetto, two old aunties, relatives of one of the musicians, were invited up to dance the hula while Mark sang and played. As beautiful as it is to watch a dancer with a beautiful body, in a way I take more pleasure in watching an older woman who really knows the hula. Her body may have thickened, her perfections may be tarnished, but if she is a great hula dancer, these flaws are quickly forgotten. In addition, she may be less self-conscious than a younger dancer might be about sexuality and the curves of her body.

Easter brings The Merrie Monarch festival, an annual week-long showcase for traditional dance, music, and crafts. The Merrie Monarch is the high point of the social year in Hilo, eagerly antici-pated and talked about. Tickets to the hula competition go on sale the day after Christmas and are snapped up before the day is out. It's as hard to get Merrie Monarch tickets as it is to get tickets to the World Series. The performances are televised as well. Large hula troops, sometimes with more than 100 girls and women in one *halau* on stage at a time, dance in perfect unison, wearing long dresses with orchids in their hair and leis of *maile* leaves, gathered from the high forests, which reach almost to the floor of the stage.

Almost as much an attraction as the performers in terms of put-ting on a show are the audiences of aging *kumu hula* from the old families as they try to outdo each other with their vintage gowns and profusion of orchids in their hair and strands of *ti* leaves braided into their leis. It is not unusual to see three generations of women dressed to the hilt in 1940s-style grandeur, all as smart as a whip, the daugh-ter proud to be the center of attention, the mother with dark lipstick looking like a film star, the grandmother in rhinestone glasses and a vintage silk muʻumuʻu to die for.

The festival is capped by a parade through downtown Hilo, a funky kind of Tournament of Roses spectacle with lots of bands in aloha shirts and palominos draped with flowers. Participants and sponsors go all out to produce the most beautiful and showy floats, decked with flowers grown locally. Queens from the Polynesian is-lands and Pacific Rim countries wave to the crowds lining the streets from vintage American convertibles. If the missionaries had never come, if the United States had not extended its reach into the Pacific and seized power from the Hawaiian royal family, if Hawaii had not become the site of a hugely profitable sugar-producing industry—if, if, if!—one of these queens might be ruling her own independent is-land kingdom here.

Index

Brahms' String Sextet No. 1 in B-flat major, 76
Breakfield Road, Sewanee, 267
Breathnach, Caoilite, 84
Breckenridge, General John C., Confederate States Army, 258
Brice's Crossroads, Mississippi, 230, 235
Brideshead Revisited, by Evelyn Waugh, 186
Bridge of Sighs, Venice, xiv
Bridges, Alvilde. *See* Lees-Milne, Alvilde
Bristol, Tennessee, 283
Bristol, Virginia, 5
Britain, 9, 12, 42, 105, 124, 150, 151, 154, 165, 183, 189, 190
British Empire, 124, 125
British Isles, 90, 94, 121, 162
British Museum, xv, 162
British Rail, 184
Brooklyn, New York, 281
Brooks Art Museum, Memphis, 224
Brownsville, Tennessee, 6, 225
Buckingham Palace, London, xiii
Buckinghamshire, England, 155
Buckner, General Simon Bolivar, Confederate States Army, 238
Buddhism, 24, 27, 40, 42, 64, 280–81, 308
Buell, General Don Carlos, Union Army, 238
Bulgaria, 24, 132
Bullock, Colonel J. Lee, Confederate provost marshal, 232
Burma, 58
Burne-Jones, Edward, 171, 173
Burns, Oregon, 71, 72–73, 76
Burns, Robert, 72
Burren, County Clare, Ireland, 83
Burris, Charlie, 78
Burton, Richard, 196
Butler castle, Kilkenny, Ireland, 4
Butterfield, William, 183
Byhalia, Mississippi, 225
Byron, Lord (George Gordon), 198
Byron, Robert, 32, 33, 34, 62, 186, 196
Byzantine Art, by David Talbot Rice, 186
Byzantine Empire, 104, 105, 123
Byzantion, 108

Cage, John, 134, 135
Cahn, Morris, 77
Cahn's Coulee, Powder River, Montana, 78
Cairo, Egypt, 35, 197
Calcutta, 58
California, 8, 67, 291
Callan, County Kilkenny, Ireland, 4
Callicott, Burton, 220
Calvary Episcopal Church, Memphis, 210, 219, 222
Camden Town, London, 146
Canada, 243
Canaletto, 158
Candia, 109
Capers, Gerald, 207, 208, 222
Carbon County Museum, Rawlins, Wyoming, 79
Caribbean, 14
Carlsmith Building, Hilo, Hawaii, 306
Carlyle, Thomas, 167
Carmichael, Hoagy, 284
Carpaccios, Venice, xvi, 120
Carpenter Gothic, 227
Carrick-on-Suir, County Tipperary, Ireland, 4
Carter Family, 245
Castiglione, Baldassare, 141
Castle Ward, County Down, Northern Ireland, 161
Cathedral of San Marco, Venice, 107, 116, 127
Cavalier, The, Sewanee, Tennessee, 11
Cavendish, Lady Elizabeth, 187
C. C. Kennedy Annex, Hilo, Hawaii, 306–7
Central High School, Memphis, Tennessee, 224
Chamonix, France, 24, 62
Chapel Royal, Hampton Court Palace, London, 143
Charleston, South Carolina, 20
Charleston harbor, 265
Charlie, 278
Charlie Vergos Alley, Memphis, 213
Charterhouse School, England, 180
Chattanooga, Tennessee, 240, 263, 266, 267

County Carlow, Ireland, 151
County Durham, England, 189
County Galway, Ireland, 94, 162
County Kerry, Ireland, 90, 91
County Tipperary, Ireland, 90, 105
County Waterford, Ireland, 163, 164
County Wexford, Ireland, 164
Court Square, Memphis, 222
Covent Garden, London, 163
Cowan, Tennessee, 252, 267, 270
Cowan Road, 267
Crete, Greece, 197
Crivelli, Carlo, xvi
Cromwell, Thomas, 142
Crown of Thorns, 109
Cruinniú na mBád, Kinvara, County
    Galway, Ireland, 86
Crump, E. H., 222–24
Crusaders, 108–10, 112
Crushua, Kinvara, County Galway,
    Ireland, 86
Cuan An Óir, Kinvara, County Galway,
    85, 86
Cumberland Plateau, 251, 263, 267
Cumberland River, 238

Dalmatian Coast, Adriatic Sea,108
Daly, Jackie, 88
Damascus, 121
Dandolo, Doge Enrico, 108, 125
Dandolo, Henricus. See Dandolo, Doge
    Enrico
Dante, 171
Danube River, 197
Darius the First of Persia, 38
Darul Ehsan, Pakistan, 39, 40, 42
Dass, Baba Ram, 60, 62, 65, 67
David, RT's travelling companion in India,
    53, 55, 57, 60, 61, 65, 67
Da Vinci, Leonardo, 119
Davis, Jefferson, 229, 240, 253
Daws, Gavin, 297, 298
"Dead, The," by James Joyce, 9
Decherd, Tennessee, 267
Deep South, 5, 7, 243, 249
Dehradun, India, 42, 65

Delhi, India, 45, 46, 47, 50, 51, 53, 57, 58, 59
Delta, The. See Mississippi Delta
De Morgan, William, 174
Denver, 79
DeSoto County, Mississippi, 205, 231
Diaries, 1984–1997, by James Lees-Milne,
    192
Dickens, Charles, 139, 140, 146, 152, 154
Dickinson, Emily, 16
Dingle Peninsula, County Kerry, Ireland,
    90
Dirmicius, Abbot of Regensburg, Ger-
    many, 90
"Dixie," 254
Dixie Love Oil, 203
Dixon, Harry St. John, 231
Doge's Palace, Venice, 107, 113, 121, 127
Dogtrot, 246
Domain (campus of the University of the
    South, Sewanee), 10
Donovan, 95
"Don't Fence Me In," by Cole Porter, 80
Doorus Peninsula, Kinvara, County
    Galway, Ireland, 84
Double dogtrot, 245, 246
Doughty, Charles Montague, 196
Dragon Preparatory School, 185
"Dream Children," by Charles Lamb, 178
Drury Lane, London, 162
Dublin, Ireland, 15, 20, 90, 105, 125, 309
Du Bois, W. E. B., 205
Duck River, Tennessee, 259
Dugdale, John, 186
Duke of Beaufort, 192
Dulwich Picture Gallery, London, 158
Dundee, Mississippi, 205
Dungaire Castle, Kinvara, County Galway,
    Ireland, 86
Dunton, Theodore Watts, 180
Dupré, Marcel, 130, 131
Dusk Road Games, by Robert Grenier, xvi
Dutch Charlie. See Charlie Burris
Dylan, Bob, 64

Earl of Sandwich, 278, 290
Earl's Court, London, 168

Iraq, 34
Ireland, 12, 18, 58, 84, 87, 89, 90, 104, 105, 106, 107, 110, 115, 120, 121, 124, 125, 126, 149, 162
Irish Churches and Monastic Buildings, by H.C. Leask, 90
Irish Georgian Society, 99
Irish Miles, by Frank O'Connor, 91, 245
Irish Sea, 90, 105
Irish Times, The, 85
Isfahan, Iran, 31
Islam, 24, 27, 30, 34, 41, 42, 59–60, 64–65
Istanbul, 11, 15, 16, 19, 24, 25, 26, 28, 45, 53, 132, 133
Italianate style, 220, 221
Italy, 15, 113, 115, 132

Jackson, Andrew, 207, 250
Jackson, Stonewall, 211, 240, 266, 270
Jackson, Tennessee, 10
Jaffa, 121
Jagger, Mick, 193
Jake, RT's travelling companion in the Middle East, 26, 27, 133, 134
James I of England, 150
Japanese in Hawaii, 278, 279, 280, 281, 282, 285
Japanese White-Eye *(Zosterops japonicas),* 287
Jefferson Davis Park, Memphis, 217
Jefferson, Thomas, 206
Jerusalem, 108, 109, 121
Johnson, Dr. Samuel, 154
Johnson, Robert, 203
Johnston, General Albert Sidney, Confederate States Army, 219
John the Conqueroo, 203
Jones, Inigo, 143–44, 150, 189
Journey Motor Court, Memphis, 206
Judaism, 30, 123
Julius Caesar, 105
Jumpoff, Tennessee, 270

Kabul, Afghanistan, 37, 38, 53
Kadiköy, 25
Kahiko style of Hula, 310, 311

Kahn, Florence, 178
Kaikodo Building. *See* Hilo Masonic Hall
Kalakaua, King David of Hawaii, 293, 299, 303–5, 306
Kalakaua Park, Hilo, 303
Kalaoa Camp Road, Hamakua Coast, Big Island of Hawaii, 287
Kali, 55
Kalua pig, 284
Kapi'olani, Chief, 298
Kashmir, 58
Kathmandu, Nepal, 37
Keane, Seán and Dolores, 87
Keats, John, 150
Keikis, 309
Kelmscott House, Hammersmith, London, 150, 172, 174
Kelmscott Press, 168
Kamehameha I, King of Hawaii, 290–91, 292, 293, 299
Kamehameha III, King of Hawaii, 278
Kamehameha the Great. *See* Kamehameha I
Kennedy, C. C., 306
Kent, England, 172, 173
Kent, William, 189
Kentucky, 9, 215, 236, 253, 258
Kenyon College, 250
Khan, Hazrat Inayat, 23
Khan, Pir Vilayat, 24, 29, 30, 62
Khorasan, 26, 35, 36, 133
Khrishna, 55
Khyber Pass, 37, 38, 46
Kilauea volcano, 298
Kilkenny, Ireland, 4, 121
Kilmacduagh, County Galway, Ireland, 120
Kilmakadar, County Kerry, Ireland, 90, 91
Kimchi, 286
King, B. B., 203
King Cnut, 145
King, Martin Luther, 223
King William Street, London, 146, 147
Kino'ole Street, Hilo, 306, 309
Kinvara Bay, 86–87, 97
Kinvara, 83–87, 89, 90, 120, 162
Kipling, Rudyard, 67, 169, 179

Middle Tennessee, 214, 231, 246, 247, 248, 249, 259, 264, 267, 273
Mid-South, The, 217, 225, 232, 246
Mikanele (Missionaries), 279, 289
Milam, Margaret, 6–7
Milan, Tennessee, 10
Milano, Italy, 113, 123
Miles City, Montana, 78
Milestown, Montana, 77
Mirò, Estaban Roderiguez, 206
Mississippi Delta, 201, 202, 204, 223, 234
Mississippi River, 5, 8, 19, 20, 80, 202, 204, 207, 244
Mississippi, 5, 7, 209, 210, 214, 219, 220, 223, 230, 231, 234
Missouri, 215
Mitchum, Robert, 87
Moir, John Troup, 307
Moncrieffe, Iain, 198
Mongols, 26, 34
Montagu, Lady Mary Wortley, 196
Montaigne, Michel de, 181
Mont Blanc, French Alps, 24
Montana, 77
Monteagle, Tennessee, 245
Monteagle Assembly, 246
Montmartre, Paris, xv
Montreal, Canada, xi, xii
Moore, George, 175
Moore, Marianne, 176
More, Thomas, 140
Morgan, Thomas Hunt, 253
Morgenthau, Henry, 305
Morning after the Deluge, The, by J.M.W. Turner, 156
Morris Room, Victoria and Albert Museum, London, 168
Morris, Janey, 171, 173
Morris, William, 150, 152, 167–74
Morritt, J. B. S., 189
Most Serene Republic (Venice), 122, 123
Moulin Rouge, Paris, xvi
Mount Athos, Greece, 186
Moveable Feast, A, by Ernest Hemingway, xvii

Moyne Park, Tuam, County Galway, Ireland, 91, 94–95, 98, 100–102
Mr. Ed's Bakery, Honomu, Big Island of Hawaii, 283
Mujahadin, 35
Murray's Handbook (to London), 177
Murfreesboro, Tennessee, 252, 253, 259
Museum of Appalachia, Norris, Tennessee, 248
Mustafabad, India, 47
Mustang (Tibet), 134
Myers, E. Lucas, xvi

NAACP, 216
Nainital, India, 62, 63
Naples, Italy, 122
Napoleon, xv, 123
Napoleon (tenant farmer), 6
Nash, John, 151, 162, 165, 189
Nashville, Tennessee, 208, 214, 246, 247, 249, 257, 263
Nashville and Chattanooga Railroad, 256, 263
National Gallery, London, 145, 156, 189
Nashville Pike, Tennessee, 256
National Trust, UK, 190, 191
Native Hawaiians, 278, 280, 291, 294, 299, 308
Navarro, Mr., 287
Nazis, Nazism, xiii, 19, 197
Nebraska, 75, 80
Neely, James Columbus, 221
Negro Mart, Memphis, 215, 234
Nelson, Willie, 75
Neoclassical style, 143, 145, 150, 151, 155, 161
Nepal, 11, 24, 58, 134, 135
Nevada, 8
New Mexico, 15, 61, 73
New Orleans, 18, 20, 208, 220, 221
New Rome (Constantinople), 107–8
News from Nowhere, by William Morris, 173, 174
New York Times, xvii
New York, 3, 219, 302, 309

Nicolson, Harold, 191
Nilolopua (former royal palace), Hilo, 305
Nin, Anaïs, 19
Ninemilehouse, County Tipperary,
    Ireland, 4
"No. 2: The Pines," by Max Beerbohm, 180
Norfolk, England, 141
Normandy Invasion, WWII, 258
Normans, 124
North Carolina, 207
Notre Dame Cathedral, Paris, xiv, 111, 146
North Mississippi, 7, 209, 211, 213, 231,
    235
North, The (United States), 9, 208, 216,
    222, 237, 261, 269
Nutmeg Manikin (Spice Finch, *Lonchura
    punctulata*), 287

O'Connell, Jeff, 84, 85, 86
O'Connor, Frank, 84, 91, 245
Odaishan temple, Honomu, Big Island of
    Hawaii, 280
O'Donovan, Liadain, 84
Oglala Sioux, 12
'Ohana, 310
O'Heyne's Church, Kilmacduagh, Gort,
    County Galway, Ireland, 120–21
Ohio, 222
Okimoto, Tadao, 280, 281, 284–86
Oklahoma, 10
"Old Forest, The," by Peter Taylor, 250
"Old Hundred" (hymn), 263
Old South, 11, 214, 233, 244, 284
Olmstead, Frederick Law, 260
Omaha, Nebraska, 79
One Hundred Years of Solitude, by Gabriel
    García Márquez, 62
Onomea Sugar Company, Big Island of
    Hawaii, 282. 307
Opium, 304
Oranmore, Country Galway, Ireland, 87
Order of Pole Bearers Association, 216
Oregon Trail, 74, 80
Oregon, 72, 73, 75, 76
Orient Express, 24, 25, 28, 45, 132

Orvieto, Italy, 113
Osborne, John Eugene, 79
Otey, Bishop James Hervey, 259, 265
O'Toole, Peter, 87
Ottoman Empire, 123
Overton, John, 207
Overton Park, Memphis, 224, 250
Owl Café, Memphis, 220
Owl Mountain Springs (Peter Taylor's
    fictional name for the Monteagle
    Assembly, Monteagle, Tennessee, 146
Oxford, England, 176, 185, 186
Oxford, Mississippi, 211, 244
Oxfordshire, England, 172, 173
Oxford University, 153

Pacific Ocean, 8, 281, 289
Pakistan, 34, 36, 38, 41, 42, 45, 46, 49, 65,
    281
Pakalolo, 278, 309
Palace Hotel, San Francisco, 303
Palace Theater, Hilo, 310
Pala d'Oro, Venice,109
Palazzo Ducale, Venice, 114
Palestine, 121
Palladio, Andrea, and Palladianism, 144,
    154, 162, 280
Palmer, Samuel, 170
Paniolos, 291, 301
Papaikou, Big Island of Hawaii, 282, 284,
    286, 307
Paris, xiv, xv, xvi, xvii, 11, 16, 19, 24, 76,
    109, 111, 113, 130, 143, 162
Parker's Crossroads, site of Civil War
    battle, 237
Parkhurst, Colonel John G., 240
Parrott, George, 77–79
Parsons, Gram, 75
Parsons, Niamh, 87
Pau hana, 283–84
Pau Hana (book), 304
Peabody, George, 219
Peabody Hotel, 201, Memphis, 203, 213,
    218
Pele, 298

Ukulele, 303

Uncle Tom's Cabin, by Harriet Beecher
Stowe, 171

Unfamiliar Fishes, by Sarah Vowel, 303

Union Army, 209, 210, 238, 252, 255, 257,
269

Union Pacific Museum, Omaha,
Nebraska, 79

Union Pacific Railroad, 74, 77

United Community Church, Hilo, Hawaii,
308

United States of America, 107, 125, 184,
206, 243, 278, 295

University of California, Berkeley, 24

University of Hawaii in Hilo, 311

University of the South, The. *See* Sewanee

University Crossing, Sewanee, 269

University Place, Sewanee, 265, 269

Unukupukupu Halau, Hilo, 311

Upstairs, Downstairs, 154

Urbino, Italy, 123

US Navy, 209

Vancouver, Captain George, 290

Van Dorn, General Earl, Confederate
States Army, 231

Varanasi, India, 54, 55, 57, 59

Vatican II, 163

Vaughan, Henry, 89

Velasquez, Diego, 189

Venetian Empire, 123

Veneto, 118

Venezuela, 282

Venice, xiv, 24, 25, 45, 54, 104, 107, 109,
110, 113, 114, 115, 119, 121, 122, 123,
125–26

Ventry, County Kerry, Ireland, 91

Vicksburg, Mississippi, 202, 269

Victoria and Albert Museum, London,
150, 168

Victorian Gothic, 243

Victorianism, 151, 154, 161, 163, 175

Vienna, 76

Vietnamese in Hawaii, 278, 308

Vietnam, 281

Vikings, 104, 105, 124, 145

Vincent, Tip, 77

Virgin and Child by Niccolò da Pietro ,
115

Virginia, 5, 215, 269

Visigoths, 105

Vita Nuova, by Dante, 171

Vowell, Sarah, 303

Voysey, Charles, 190

Vrindavan, India, 60

Wagonhound Road, Wyoming, 74

Waikea Sugar Mill, Big Island of Hawaii,
306

Wailea, Hamakua Coast, Big Island of
Hawaii, 277–87

Wailuku Female Seminary, Hawaii, 295

Walmart, 301

Walpole, Horace, 150

Walthamstow, London, England, 150

Walud, Baha ud-Din, 26

Warden, George, 77

Warnes, Jennifer, 94

Warshall, Peter, xvii

War of the Roses (Tennessee), 248

Wars of the Roses (England), 140

Washburn, General Cadwallader C.,
Union Army, 213

Washington (state), 69, 73

Washington, Booker T., 205

Waste Land, The, by T.S. Eliot, 140, 144,
146–47

Waterford, Ireland, 121, 151

Watkins, Sam, 255, 270, 272

Waugh, Evelyn, 184, 186, 187

Webb, Philip

Webb, Beatrice, 169

Wedigh, Herman von, 142

Wentworth, Lady, 198

Western Carolinian (newspaper), 207

West Memphis, Arkansas, 8

Westminster Abbey, London, 113, 143

Westminster Bridge, London, 158

West Point Military Academy, 210, 235

West, Rebecca, 178

West Tennessee, 5, 6, 10, 207, 209, 213,
221, 223, 225, 230, 241, 247